Edited by Michèle Aina Barale, Jonathan Goldberg,

Michael Moon, and Eve Kosofsky Sedgwick

My

FOREWORD BY DOROTHY ALLISON

Amber L. Hollibaugh

Dangerous Desires

a queer girl dreaming her way home

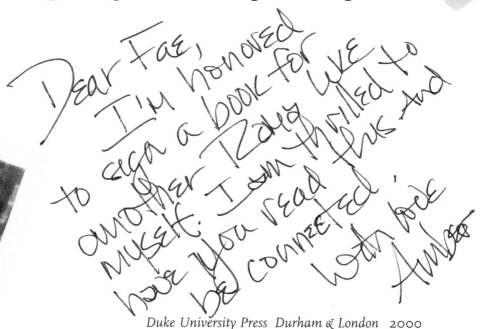

Dear Fae,
I'm honored
to sign a book for
another Reyd like
myself. I am thrilled to
hear you read this. And
be connected.
With love
Amber

Duke University Press Durham & London 2000

2nd printing, 2001

© 2000 Amber Hollibaugh

All rights reserved

Printed in the United States of

America on acid-free paper ∞

Designed by C.H. Westmoreland

Typeset in Scala with Gill Sans Extra

Bold display type by Tseng Information

Systems, Inc.

Library of Congress Cataloging-in-

Publications Data appear on the last

printed page of this book.

to

Jenifer Levin,

who found me in a

dark hospital room and

captured my heart

to

my stepsons, Mak and Van,

who have changed my life forever

and to

Ken Dawson,

sweet friend,

remembered, loved, honored,

missed

We are, I am, you are
by cowardice or courage
the one to find our way
back to the scene
carrying a knife, a camera
a book of myths
in which
our names do not appear.

—Adrienne Rich,
Diving into the Wreck

Contents

Foreword

by Dorothy Allison

How does change happen? What is it that makes a difference in the way people see each other? How do you confront people's assumptions about what they truly do not understand and get them to rethink their prejudices? What, truly, is it that we can do to contribute to greater justice and understanding between people from different backgrounds?

These are the questions Amber Hollibaugh and I have been worrying about for all the years we have known each other. Not intellectually, not dispassionately: neither Amber nor I are dispassionate about hatred or fear or shame. We have been hated. We have been afraid. And, oh yes, we have been ashamed. None of that produces dispassion. It provokes terror, anger, and, eventually, hatred in return. No, when Amber and I talk about changing the world, we are talking about something very specific, very clear, and very simple. We want not to be hated for who we are, where we come from, and what we do. We want what we imagine everyone else wants—the freedom to be ourselves.

The life story that Amber tells in the course of examining desire and race against the backdrop of growing up poor and despised is a deliberate rebellion against shame and fear. The risk she takes is enormous. This is who I am, she says. This is how I was shaped, and this is the work I have done to sort out all that is strong and valiant about growing up working class, femme, and "perverse." This is what *perverse* really means—to be disobedient to the rule of fear and hatred and shame, to seek one's own definitions and ideals regardless of what others insist are the limits to what you may want or have.

The work Amber has managed over decades of political activism and embattled passion—that work is a gift to all of us. It is also the fulfillment of a promise, a bargain she and I made long ago.

"I'll tell you mine if you'll tell me yours," I promised my new friend, Amber, in a coffee shop in Manhattan more than twenty years ago. I had rarely met anyone I so instantly trusted and understood. Amber had just moved to New York and was looking for work. We had friends in common and knew each other by reputation as activists. I had edited half a dozen feminist and gay magazines. She had fought the antigay Briggs Initiative in California and been part of an alternative bookstore collective. We also knew each other's "bad" reputations as dyke flirts and femme provocateurs. "You've got to meet Amber," people had been saying to me for years.

I watched Amber load her coffee with sugar and cream and tuck a couple of extra packets of sugar away in a pocket for each one she used. I sipped my black coffee and watched her eyes, the way she tracked the waiter through the crowd and glanced down every moment or so to the bag tucked between her boot heels. My own bag was clamped between my calves and the legs of the chair, and I had already tucked away a few sugar packets, even though I no longer used it in my coffee. When the waiter came back with our toast, I caught the way Amber looked again at the little change purse by the side of her plate. She was calculating whether she could get something else and still leave a decent tip. I knew that calculation. I knew this woman.

"You want to share something?" I asked Amber, and she smiled at me in such a way that I knew she recognized what I had just acknowledged. We had almost nothing. We would share what we had. Within minutes we were talking about the other things we shared—a passion for old paperback books with steamy covers, high-heeled boots, leather jackets, and hard-eyed women who scared us almost as much as they fascinated us. Finally, after several cups of coffee, more stolen sugar packets, and torn hunks of greasy toast, I said to her what I would say many times over the years.

"I'll tell you mine if you'll tell me yours."

What I offered my friend was the dangerous revelation of desire. I began a sentence with "I want," and we both blushed and looked around. I told Amber: I want to write a great book—I want to make a difference—I want to have adventures and take enormous risks and be everything they say we are and not give a damn what anyone says. Amber told me: I want to live in this scary city and do everything they say we do—date famous gorgeous strong women and wear outrageous clothes and carry it all off with such a sense of style they don't even see me coming—I want to make movies and write articles and speak to academics without fear, or at least not let them see that I'm afraid.

I want to tell secrets, I said.

Yes, Amber said. We looked at each other for a while.

Then we laughed and wiped tears out of our eyes, ordered more coffee, and shifted to safer topics—sexual techniques and butch girls we had dared to use those techniques to enthrall. For us, the topic of lust was less dangerous than those desires we had just addressed. Saying "I want" and meaning it was more dangerous for us than naming our various sexual adventures. Revolutions begin when people look each other in the eyes, say "I want," and mean it. We meant it.

Danger is a loaded word. The term gets thrown around too easily sometimes. "You are in *moral* danger," the bishop of the Mormon Church told me when I was sixteen. He had begun to figure out that I might be a lesbian and sought to save me from the danger he saw in my desire. Half the words he used that day I did not understand, but when he said *danger,* I knew what he meant. In truth I knew more than he, but it was all too clear to me that the danger I was confronting was poverty, not sex. I was my mama's girl, raised a believing Baptist, and the sin I was committing was trying on Mormonism in the hopes of a scholarship to college. The bishop wanted me to join him on my knees in prayer. He wanted to introduce me to a nice young man and lead me toward chastity or motherhood. What I saw in that man's sincere expression was *mortal* danger—a lifetime of babies and self-hatred and fear. I have seen it over and over since in the faces of both men and women, some of whom have genuinely cared about me and my survival.

Why is it that people who consider you as in danger always want to control you so as to make you safe? Why is safety so important? Risk is, after all, an inherent part of human experience. I grew up hearing my uncles tell my nephews, "You want something, boy, you got to take a chance." It did not matter whether they were talking about learning to drive a car or asking a girl to go dancing. Put your foot on the gas, and see what you got. Maybe you'll crash and burn. Maybe you'll discover a talent for gliding on the straightaway. Venture, risk, take a chance, and test your mettle. When you grow up poor, you know that everything you want involves risks, specific and implied dangers. You learn to calculate, and the calculations for girls are always more dire. Is this worth the cost? Can I pay the bill and the tip? Can I manage what is demanded and what is implied?

All my life I have known that everything I wanted had a cost and that I could not always get away without harm. The day I got the notice of the National Merit Scholarship that would pay my way through college, I gave up any notion of ever going back to church and saw my mother's face break in a way I had never seen before. She was happy for me, deeply happy, and terribly afraid. I was going off where she had never been, to face dangers she could only dimly imagine. She had been a waitress for twenty years; she had served iced tea to college graduates. I was moving across the counter, was heading into mortally dangerous territory. I was foot to the metal and gone.

Amber and I knew intrinsically the difference between what people thought was dangerous and what was truly dangerous—more dangerous for working-class femmes than for the kind of women who thought class and possessions could buy them some measure of safety. This is Byzantine territory. Growing up poor *does* inculcate a stance of toughness that is all about protecting the underbelly of desire. It does not necessarily make you stronger or better than those who do not have your experience; it just makes you behave as if you were stronger and, yes, better.

That tough stance is vitally important when you have no other way of protecting your fragile sense of self, particularly when nothing else provides any reassurance of worth. Perhaps the daughters of the upper classes are as fragile as we, but I do not know that. Nor am I able to easily dismiss the protective stance I learned as a girl. In a culture that equates the female with fragile and glorifies the most delicate images of the feminine, I grew up constantly damned with the label *workhorse*. I was supposed to be unbreakable, to work hard and hold in contempt the fragile flowers of true femininity while stewing with jealousy for what they were that I was not. There was no winning that contest. All I could do was be tough and pretend I did not care—did not want. I was told from childhood that I was not entitled to any tenderness and learned on my own that to admit to any tenderness, or, worse, a desire for tenderness, was an invitation to abuse.

Imagine, then, the world Amber and I inhabited. Female and

strong and hungry for love, we were fearful of any tenderness while wanting it all the time. The trick always seemed to me that I had to not *need* tenderness. The trick behind that trick is how hard it is to accept what you have had to resist needing. Yes, wanting makes you vulnerable. Desire is dangerous. "I don't care" is a stance many of us developed to shield ourselves from the world's contempt. Amber and I grew up hearing "Who do you think you are?" and knowing it meant we were not entitled to expect anything but contempt and frustration. We learned bravado and disdain in order to survive contempt and self-doubt. We embraced our most fearful desires simply in order to know who and what we were, to treasure what the world disdained and what we barely allowed ourselves to experience. Femme girls dance on razors every day of their lives, and some days it is only bravado that keeps us upright.

Writing, I used to tell my students, always feels like going naked in public. Everything shows, even those parts of yourself that you never wanted to acknowledge. Develop a stance, I said. Get your feet under you, your metaphorical feet—your sense of purpose. There is a reason for the enterprise, and you need to have it in mind as you do the work. Telling your story always has the possibility of changing the world—particularly if the story you have to tell is not one everyone thinks they know. I thought I was entitled to tell my students to bare their souls. I believed myself a writer who had stripped off all disguise, all protective layers. I had told the worst thing imaginable when I spoke about being raped as a child, about not being protected by those I loved, about growing up poor and terrorized, and, perhaps most dangerously, about growing up the lesbian child of a Southern working-class family. I had said things no one in my family believed should ever be acknowledged, said those things and survived. I had even felt vindication in the work. Sometimes I think I have pretended writing was easy because I wanted so much the books others would write, the secrets they would reveal. These days I try to pay more attention to what I have hidden from myself. I tell my friends and students that, no, writing is not easy. Telling secrets is never easy. Going naked in public is more dangerous for some of us than others, and the fear is always there.

For years I have been talking to Amber the way I talked to my students. "I know you're working on those films," I would say after

I moved to California and she stayed in New York. "But you're writing, too, aren't you? How is your book?" We would meet in Boston or Los Angeles at some conference or reading, and right off I would take her hand. "Are you working on your essays?" I watched her nurture lovers and their books, watched her set hers aside over and over again to help someone else, some person or cause or passionately held political conviction. I knew, of course, that Amber did not think of herself as a writer but as a revolutionary.

After the revolution we will all write our memoirs, a friend once told me. It was a joke, but it was not. For years I have worried that that is what it would take to get Amber to finally put her book together—a sense of the revolution accomplished. I call myself a *Zen feminist,* tell everyone I don't believe in postfeminism. I certainly do not use the phrase *after the revolution.* I know that change is the only permanent condition. Also, I have too many friends who were going to write a book "when things settled down," friends who died before they could write a page. For a few years there I sincerely feared that Amber would be another one. But finally she told me she was making the time to finish her manuscript, that she was stealing time from everything else in her life to do it. I knew how great a change Amber was making. For those of us who grow up in permanent crisis mode, there is always something more important than the writing. There is always something more important than our own lives.

I became a novelist because I felt there were large and important stories going untold as well as too many old stories constantly being retold in a stale and vicious language. My life and the lives of those I love were misrepresented in most of the books, movies, lyrics, and television programs I found as a young woman. Whether we were identified as rednecks or poor white trash, we were always portrayed in the same terms—either with a cloying sentimentality or with a brutal contempt. Worse, as a lesbian, I found myself confronted with a society that seemed to see only one social issue at a time. This meant I could talk about poverty and class but not about sexuality and gender identity. I know that everything I have ever written is only a small part of what needs to be written, that all the stories I have ever told are only a fraction of those that remain untold.

I also became a novelist out of fear. I feared biography, the act of saying, This is what really happened, and this is what it means. The grace of fiction is that you can tell a larger story than the world has yet acknowledged—and pretend, at least in part, that you are not completely present in the story you tell. I wanted and needed that reassurance. The burden of biographical narrative is that talking about your real history takes some of us back to the most painful and destructive of emotions. Too many of us grew up feeling the same overwhelming rage and outrage. We hate having to explain our lives. We hate the response we get—pity or contempt. We hate having to name what we have worked to keep secret—desire or lust, resentment or jealousy, fear, guilt, spiritual hunger, shame, and, yes, moral confusion, that lifelong sense of being wrong, wrong from birth and never going to get right. Those of us born poor and despised sometimes speak in code or shorthand on these subjects. It is easier that way. We can step back from some of the pain inherent in our experience. But stepping back does not achieve what we want most to manage. It does not change anything. We have to step in, fully inhabit the landscape, and then invite others into our world. We have to say, This is me, my desires, my beloved, my mama, my daddy, my sisters and cousins, and my first great heartbreak. This is me covered in snot and misery and still feeling desperate, stubborn pride. This is what it is really like—not what you thought it was like.

Wrong from birth is no reason not to embrace the grace of the full story, but what it takes for some of us to admit the full story—that is heartbreakingly difficult. Never imagine that any of us speak easily of the things we tell you. As an incest survivor I seriously considered killing myself before speaking about it. When Amber is able to say *sex worker,* she does so because she has learned to speak back to that callous voice screaming *whore* when she believed the word meant something about her soul.

As a girl my rage and resentment at all that I and my family were denied got in the way of my ability to see other people as I saw myself. I knew we were despised—for being poor, for being Southerners, for being racist, barely educated, easily provoked to violence, and full of a crippling resentment toward anyone who had more than we had or seemed to be living an easier life. Some of those things I hated in myself and tried to resist. Sorting out what was terrible in our lives and what was strong was a long struggle. I am not sure that I can be all that certain about some of the simplest of my hard-won conclusions. For example, I believe that the rebellious self-reliance my family taught me to prize is an integral part of the lack of entitlement I also felt. Poverty rarely encourages self-examination. Poverty makes strong, angry people with dangerous and hidden cracks in the apparently seamless facade. I ran across a title once that jolted me into a new perspective on how class and experience shapes us. It was one of those wonderful anthologies about working-class women. The phrase I copied out was *strong in the broken places,* and I remember how powerfully that phrase resonated in my life. That is what we are. The strength is scar tissue. It comes from working at the damage until the damage becomes a place of surprising power.

You will find that power in Amber Hollibaugh's essays. You will also be reminded of what I sometimes have pretended is not still true—that too many of us are unknown. Too many of us lead lives that read like fiction to the general public. If we are to hope for a genuine change in the prejudices that continue to dominate our society, we need more books like this one—more occasions in which individuals take the risks to tell the stories we do not know or have not let ourselves acknowledge.

The world is changed through story, each of us giving over what we know for what we do not yet know. Our perspective widens with every landscape brought into view. You were in the civil rights movement? You danced in a cage for ten- and twenty-dollar bills that you hated even as you caught them in your fists? You were a lesbian, and you feared rape had made you who you were? You were part Cherokee, part Romany, dark eyed in a family of blonds, more boy than girl, and more pervert than either? Tell me. Give me your experience in story, and I will embrace it as I have embraced my own. We will see what it means together. When we begin to see the human dimensions of all our stories, the world begins to alter. Bakersfield to Greenville to Wooster to Brownsville to Littleton to Watts—each story enlarges the human imagination, brings us closer to the revolution some of us still pursue.

I welcome you to my friend's essays, to the unique, sharp-eyed glance of a woman who had to fight to be able to say "I want." In Amber's life, desire has been made sacred. Whether she is writing about the female body, the femme psyche, or the fearful need to admit desire itself, Amber has vindicated all our lives.

Acknowledgments

These essays are the products of my dialogues with many people in many communities, a lot of whom are friends who have struggled with me, encouraged me, and engaged with me and with these issues through the years. I have been honored to have them in my life and to have had the joy of living such a rich intellectual, activist journey. I thank you all.

This work has been done over a very long period of time, with people at every point who have helped me. But, because it has been so long in the works, I may have forgotten someone who was important. Please forgive me in advance.

To Jeff Escoffier, who has been my best friend, best reader, and best critic for twenty-odd years, and to Dorothy Allison, who has always known why she is critical to my survival.

To Jenifer Levin, who worked as my editor on the book—both helping decide on its content and reworking many of the new essays—and who believed in the importance of this book when I was afraid to finish. Her work, her support, and her love have made an extraordinary difference.

To my writers group—Allan Bérubé, Jonathan Katz, Judith Levine, and Jeff Escoffier.

To all the friends I have loved, learned from, and lost in the AIDS epidemic. And to all the extraordinary women who have fought to get lesbian HIV issues recognized, especially Risa Denenberg and Sally Cooper, or who have worked at the Lesbian AIDS Project and become my friends, especially Doralisa Goitia, Rochelle Burrough, Iris Maldonado, Linda Ellis, and Jackie Barnes. And to Tony, Helen, and Dorothy Bartholumucci. And to all the HIV-positive lesbians who have died without being acknowledged.

To my best girlfriends: Beck Young, Katy Taylor, Ellen Gurzinsky, and Marcie Gallo.

To the friends who have kept me alive and given so much of themselves to me and to this work, especially Marj Plumb, who helped get this book moving when I had almost given up.

And to Beth Zemsky, Allan Bérubé, Kim Christensen, Daniel Wolfe, Chandan Reddy, Tony Valenzuela, Deke, Carmen Vasquez, Gail Pheterson, E. G. Crichton, John D'Emilio, Alisa Lebow, Nan Cinnater, Jean McGuire, Barbara Herbert, Jade McClockland, Margaret Cerillo, Evelyn Hammond, Louise Rice, Ivy Young, Kris Kliendienst, Alix Layman, Nikhil Pal Singh, Mary Stanford, David Meachum, Nathalie Weeks, Tim Sweeney, Eric Rofes, Colin Robinson, Sally Zierler, Helene Kendler, Phyllis Raskin, JoAnn Wypijewsky, Punkin Stevens, Scot Nagagawa, Andy Spieldenner, Jonathan Katz, Angusuk (Richard La Fortune), JEB (Joan Biran), and Cindy Patton.

To the San Francisco Lesbian and Gay History Project and the Radical History Review Collective.

To my doctor and friend Bobbie Cohen, who remains a model of passionate politics and a vast heart.

To old friends, allies, and editors who helped me at many critical points: Cherríe Moraga, Gayle Rubin, Carole Vance, Lisa Duggan, Ann Snitow, Barbara Smith, Honey Lee Cottrell, Kitty Krupat, Modern Times Bookstore folks, John Gagnon, Jewelle Gomez, Patrick McCreery, Esther Newton, Larry Gross, Scot Tucker, Nan Hunter, Evelyn Hammond, Marcia Paley, Richard Goldstein, Michael Warner, Philip Derbyshire, Jeffrey Weeks, and Leah Lilith Albrecht Samarasinha.

To Heidi Coleman, who worked on the manuscript at the end, formatting, inventing, rescuing, and reassuring.

To my agent and friend, Harvey Klinger.

Finally, to Ken Wissoker at Duke University Press, who has become a friend in the process of our work together on this book, and to the Duke staff whose work with me has meant so much.

Introduction

In 1997, I attended the Prostitutes and Sex Workers International Conference in Los Angeles. Late on that first night of the conference, I wrote to my lover:

> *Ironic that the conference is in L.A., so close to Bakersfield and to the California growing valleys I was fleeing. The smells here, the crickets, the outrageous colors of the flowers, so garish and beautiful, all bring me back to my own younger self, a very defiant, angry, terrified, teenage lesbian stripper. Freeways and motorcycles and men three times my age. Prostitutes are women, like you said, who mark our lives by the scars on our bodies. So I am looking at the bottoms of my feet, at the scars there, remembering.*
>
> *I was dancing in a cage, the go-go stripper kind, dancing to Otis Redding, dancing hard. One man would not stay back, kept reaching into the cage trying to catch my feet and ankles, kept putting twenty-dollar bills into the cage. And I kept kicking them out. A set was fifteen minutes, no stops onstage; then they would open up the back of the cage and you'd come hurtling out and down the steep back stairs into the dressing room. This guy had been out front all night, getting drunker, waiting for each of my sets, then pushing the money through the bars as he grabbed for my feet.*
>
> *I was tired. It was my next to last set, and I'd had it up to here with him, with his money and his fingers. Finally, I took his money and started to build it into my routine—rubbing it on my body, moving it between my legs. He kept putting more twenties onto the stage, money he thought guaranteed him my time, my body, after the music ended. He kept putting twenties there until I had a stack of them in my hands.*
>
> *Slowly I ripped every fucking twenty-dollar bill up into tiny pieces and sprinkled them outside the cage over his head while he screamed about whores, about cock teasers, about me. Then he left. At least that's what I thought.*

When I came out for my last set he was nowhere around. I danced
that fifteen minutes so tired I came off the stage not even looking down to
see the stairs. Too bad. He'd broken glass and spread it on each of the steps
leading to the back room. I hit that glass going a hundred. It split my feet
apart before I could stop, pounded it deep inside the creases. I almost bled
to death.

All day I've been thinking of that time, remembering being that young,
that tired, that angry, that scared, that lonely. Thinking about power and
about lacking it. Too many cities, too many tricks, no woman to love me
back to life then. So. Tomorrow. More stories, more talk with women and
men like myself who remind me how I got here. The remembering is hard.
Hard and good.

This was the trip which brought me home again, back to California, and back to my own history—of sex work and prostitution, of forbidden desires, radical politics, fundamental, life-altering change. The
conference brought me face to face with all the things about my history that remain no matter how far I travel, how different I appear.
It reminded me, too, of how far I had come. And it underscored how
indelible some aspects of my life remain.

Now, from a distance of thirty years, I can look in the mirror and
see both the angry, damaged, bleeding girl, and the woman she would
become. And I know: This is a good place to examine how I got from
there to here—what I left behind, what remained.

When I sat down to write this introduction, I wrote, "Every woman
knows what getting busted for being a whore really means." My editor
started laughing when she read this, saying, "Everyone doesn't know
what this means. Explain that sentence." I thought, Ah, here is why I
wrote the book. To explain how and why all these pieces, like being a
hooker and a Communist, a lesbian femme and an organizer, make
sense to me and to what I believe in. Becoming a writer and later
making films has been my way to re-create a missing reality, a voice
I knew but rarely heard spoken around me, a history I could scarcely
find.

This book also springs from the tensions I have lived with as an
uneasy member of my own movements, facing contradictions which

sprang from my own particular erotic desires and class experiences. These essays have been my method of grappling with what I was endeavoring to understand, what I couldn't or didn't resist, what I was afraid to speak about in the revolutionary groups that I loved, needed, and feared.

I have always been interested in sex, how people did it, made love, came together, expressed desire, fucked—and why. And I have always been fascinated by the results, by the needs that shape the course of human lives and how passions, disappointments, or unsought punishments have altered their direction.

I've lived a great deal of my own life on the run from my desires and the legacy of my own sexual history. Often I was angry and afraid of the feelings and fantasies alive in my body, terrified about the meanings behind my own passions and of where those desires would lead me. Too often I sought to forget my desires while simultaneously acting them out.

So for many years I led a double life: working as a Left political organizer, filmmaker, and writer during the day while supporting myself as a Vegas stripper and, as a young woman, earning a living through prostitution. A dyke in the Left before Stonewall, and a high femme lesbian during the growth of lesbian feminism, my erotic yearnings were often in direct opposition to the very political movements I was committed to creating.

When you sit down to read these essays, you may wonder why, at the beginning of a new millennium, it matters what happened one night in some faggot's hairdressing salon in a small agricultural town in California or some meeting to resist Anita Bryant held in 1979 in the living room of a dyke who would not reveal her name. What reason is there for remembering dusty trailer parks and bad teeth? Or the evening a queer rebellion called the Dan White riots erupted in the streets of San Francisco? Why talk, now, about the first picket lines constructed by feminists against feminists—women who, until that moment, thought they shared an unbreakable sisterhood, a movement, a vision, an anger, a desperately necessary hope of transforming biology and gender, and instead found themselves confronted with divisions we now take for granted in the year 2000? Is it possible that the sex wars brawls between women in the 1980s predated a similar sex battle between gay men in the AIDS-defined 1990s? Most importantly — *why does any of this matter?*

These are the questions which feed the essays in this book. So many of us from those earlier struggles have survived as political players, acting to make a difference throughout the battles and turbulence of the last thirty years. We know firsthand that it is not a static history. These writings collected here are my recounting of these battles, these issues, these transforming crises, these defining heartbeats, these hopes. They are here because I believe that history matters, that it is one of the few tools within our grasp which we can use to reconstitute our understanding of our individual human lives and longings and our larger collective experiences — experiences which shape and situate each of us.

I am passionate about this kind of historical narrative, one which sets out to mark and detail the too-often forgotten, ridiculed lives most people lead. My life as a queer woman, a too-poor girl, a mixed-race hooker, a left-wing activist, was never meant to be remembered or told, never meant to endure or to count. At best, the lives of the people I came from was the stuff of derision, the fodder for mean-spirited humor. This is the juncture between myself and history with a big *H* — and I know it.

To listen now to the common telling of "our" times and "our" lives, you would think that everyone just wants to be rich. This routine mumbo jumbo suggests that no one would collectively struggle against injustice or oppression, fight to build a new labor movement, no one would struggle to reclaim our right to sex, confront a horrific prison system, speak out against anti-Semitism, demand truth and justice for themselves and others, insist on the right of all women to self-determination, name and resist racism, question state power — or dare to be deeply, differently queer. And certainly, in the year 2000, we have become just too damn postmodern for ideas like radical social change or — dare I say it? — revolution.

But I don't think this is true.

What I do think is that we are asked to not know the actual contours of the world around us or even the contours of our personal lives. So, then, how are we to determine the significance of the world around us, a world that is acting on us and through us? How can we make sense of it when all we are fed is a constant stream of bad information or no information at all, given "facts" without context, told endless hypnotic stories of greed and abuse of power as though these stories were somehow glorious or exemplary, representing the best we can hope to bring to human endeavor and social promise? That, together with the manipulative "pity" of a Mother Teresa, is presented constantly as all that is possible for this period of history. If we don't see ourselves or others who resemble our experience, the experience itself becomes suspect.

This is part of how history in our country is sculptured so that it will represent only certain values, ideals, and necessities while hiding, disguising, or burying others. But stories of another kind—stories of human resilience and courage that engage us differently and more deeply—rarely appear in the bulk of our daily media-speak, or in the majority of books in the stores where we shop, or in the films that are readily available to us.

This is how some of us, most of us, disappear from our own worlds. We are left stunned and sightless, faltering and wordless to understand our own chronologies, the beauty of our languages and communities of origin, left mutely searching for the ordinary words which might describe our powerful sexual desires, our hopes, our families, our visions, our stubborn bravery in the face of a desperate, chancy, dead-end world.

We are given no language in which to name the pride we felt growing up among people who survived desperation or poverty, racism or anti-Semitism. There are no idioms to describe the reality of coming from commonplace neighborhoods where people work too many jobs —if they can find them in the first place—going to those jobs every day regardless of how they feel. The lives of people who get paid too little and try to love each other enough to make it all worthwhile anyway, people who never become famous and never expect to.

Today in this country, we cannot truly honor or describe these complex, overlooked lives . . . our lives. There is no language equal to these stories, so it becomes even more impossible to say how these unnamed communities often serve as places of despair and betrayal, of violence and ridicule. At one and the same time, these absences represent our survival and our jeopardy. Often, they were all that we ever had, all that we ever hoped to have.

Because the history of *these* people interests and inspires me, I have used my own lived-within understanding of such a way of life as the basis for this book. It is why I have included pieces spanning such a long period of time. I want you to see how my own thinking, spawned through a lifetime of economic and emotional struggle and extraordinary escapes, lived in complicated worlds and realities, has evolved or changed over the years or how it hasn't.

I was born dirt poor. There were no words in the places I grew up to explain my Gypsy father's burnished rust dark skin or his daughter's blonde-haired whiteness. His Romany people—my people—were invisible then, as they are today, though I can still remember sitting in the caravans of my father's clan hearing the language he spoke only there, watching and listening to my grandmother's stories while she was still alive. Looking at pictures from my childhood, I am stunned at what they reveal and what was never spoken—my father's Gypsy darkness, my mother's Irish whiteness, the eerieness of being a white child in a biracial family. No one knew what to call Romany people—Gypsies—and, in the 1950s, there were no commonly accepted explanations of the complex constructions of mixed-race families. If it were not about crossing the absolutely forbidden, racialized line between black and white, it didn't exist. So we didn't exist.

The same things were true about money and ranking, about who had it and who did not. Neither inside my family nor in the larger world in which we lived were we to ever speak about our poverty, our daily struggle just to get by, what we did to survive, and where that left us when it didn't succeed. Yet, in school and everywhere I went, everyone "knew" about me, knew about my family, and acted on what they knew. Who would sit with me? Who would invite me to their home? Who could I dare ask to the trailer courts and small houses where we lived? Who else wore hand-me-downs resewn by their mother? Who were the other kids, like me, without the small, necessary, common, significant objects—new lunch boxes, adequate school supplies, a pair of dress shoes—which are the currency of class?

Class. It was a word I would only discover as a fifteen-year-old, after being warily handed *The Communist Manifesto* by my senior-year history teacher—in the private school where I had been given a scholarship but had no skills to manage the transition from trailer park to European tutelage. A first-generation son of Lebanese immigrants, he knew exactly why I was having trouble.

My Dangerous Desires is a book of essays written between 1979 and the present. It is an exploration of those memories and hungers—the ones I was forced to survive *and* the ones I have sought out or hidden from. Sexuality and radical politics are the dangerous avenues I traveled to fathom myself, to chart my life and comprehend the lives of others. These essays are a collection of writings by a lesbian sex radical ex-hooker incest survivor rural Gypsy working-class poor white trash high femme dyke. They delineate some of the ways I learned to struggle for power, lie, get a meal, try to change the world. Much of the work gathered here was written so that I could see my own life on paper, see the lines in the faces of the women I have loved, feel again a forbidden butch's hands across my breasts. These writings have been a way for me to remember and endure. They are part of the map I constructed over the years to try and find my way in the world.

I want you to see why issues of sex, class, desire, or race, of being femme and wanting butches, have engaged me from the beginning and continue to engross me today. My hope is that these essays will thread together seemingly disconnected themes like union struggles and erotic needs, prostitution and the feminist sexual nightmare, class or race struggles and sexual passion, with the larger and smaller questions which shape our daily lives and our political battles. Butch or femme, transgender, bisexual, top or bottom, drag queens, drag kings, b-girl (butch girl) tricksters, effeminacy—how do these things fit together with race and class and social change, how do these things meet, affect each other, disappear, or remain? And how does activism inform and affect all these questions, identities, and desires?

I am interested in writing about our actual, messy, passionate, imperfect, desiring lives—lives filled with unresolved issues, difficult love affairs, and breakups which simmer with disappointment and pain. To write about how impossible it is to blindly flee—but never forget—a complicated community of birth or a complex and imperfect radical movement.

For this reason, I have generally kept the essays in the book chronological. So you can trace the steps I've taken, the falls I've had, the ideas I've explored to figure out what was happening around or inside me, the despair and anger which have often served as fuel for my work. So that you could taste my own working-class joy in loving those women I have so passionately desired. So you would know why it's been worth it.

Each of us creates the boundaries of our own myths and legends, our own truths and faulty actualities. Each of us remembers selectively and with ragged difficulty. Even the events that have fundamentally marked us lose their immediate power and detail as we age and change through layers of daily experience. Yet, as faulty or selective as our memories can often be, they are also resilient and insistent, demanding that we not forget the textures, shapes, and meanings of our authentic and indispensable selves.

The memory of our histories is often constructed to work as our conscience as well as to configure our secret desires. We wander through our own minds endlessly, figuring and reconfiguring our stories, our memories, our realities, so that they will line up with the choices we are making, the dreams we are desperately fashioning, the stories we hope will explain us, the lovers we desire, the world as we wish it to be. Yet more often than not the space between what we know and how we understand it remains cloudy, opaque, and disconnected. How the world actually fits together and makes sense, how the way I dress or smell or think aligns with the way I was raised, the colors or languages of my parents, my expectations and experiences of desire, and how these things connect with me and then with HIV and AIDS or with my gendered body, with class and the economy—all this seems to most of us like a puzzle with half the pieces missing.

Yet where our own personal narratives meet with larger historical events often results in a profoundly unique human drama of transformation. What might have happened if the AIDS epidemic had come in the 1950s rather than after the creation of a radical queer liberation movement? What would women's liberation have looked like without the invention of the birth control pill in the 1960s? What would have happened to lesbians coming out in the 1960s or 1970s without the explosion of feminism? What would any of the later 1960s movements have resembled without the earlier power of the civil rights struggle, which birthed us all? And what would that struggle have looked like without the preceding period of radical opposition that created the modern labor movement—a movement built by communists and socialists who struggled for labor representation, tenants' rights, racial justice, and the eight-hour workday through the 1920s, 1930s, and 1940s?

These are not abstract questions. I got pregnant before birth control was easily available. I had an illegal abortion that nearly killed me. I was ashamed and furious at what had been done to me and to countless other women by backroom hacks. I was overwhelmingly ready for the collective explosion of anger and insight which created a liberation movement around gender and female lives. It was thousands of experiences like this which swept so many of us into the various movements we joined, weaving and building our personal histories into a struggle big enough to challenge the culture that had birthed us, damaged us, and given us dreams.

This kind of macrohistory, and the intimate microstories it rests on, is rarely spoken of now. But it is exactly what always fuels the actual foundation of transformative grassroots movements of any kind. It is why I think these stories and essays are broader than my own personal chronicle. These essays fill and document a vacuum, an absence, an invisible narrative which has always existed, running parallel to the narratives which are recognized and retold as though they are the "common" experiences of all of us, even in the radical movements in which I have lived. I was different from many of the women and men I joined in the Left and the subsequent movements in which I functioned, though I was hardly alone in my background or experience. But to look at most of the documents from those movements—the books and pamphlets and films—tales such as my own would hardly tell you that people like myself were there, were players, that we mattered to the outcome. Or we didn't.

So, too, on the surface, it would seem that being born poor would never be an issue in the Left or in the radical parts of the lesbian or feminist movements in which I traveled. These are movements with deep commitments to the exact issues that commonly disappear elsewhere. But they are also movements dominated by women and men from very different class and racial backgrounds and histories—read white or upper class or male or straight—than the people or issues often being advocated. Championing poor and working-class people, people of color, sexually different people, and radical change in the abstract is one thing—sharing or relinquishing power and control to people whose histories and experiences, whose theoretical understandings are based on very different assumptions and needs, is another thing entirely.

Being poor weds itself to your essence, embeds itself in your spirit, your heart, wraps itself around the convictions you carry, around every expectation and dream you harbor. People know it about you, can sense it even if they can't say exactly what they know. When I joined the Left, I had none of the lingo, little of the theory, and none of the assurance to manage a seamless entry. All I had was my stubborn passion to change the world. I was raw, hungry, eager. It all showed—all the confusion and ignorance, all my stories that seemed out of place or inappropriate. Everything about me seemed ragged. Nothing fit, nothing worked together, nothing about who I was could I explain or defend or value—*not yet.*

But I couldn't leave. The Left, the civil rights movement, women's liberation, gay and lesbian liberation, were all I had and all I wanted. I was tired of running from myself and from my own history. I believed passionately in the possibilities presented by radical social change. And I had learned a new kind of resistance from the Left—bigger than the stubborn individual kinds I had mastered growing up and surviving. This time my insurgency was born of an anger and a hope for something beyond personal survival.

I wanted everything—differently. I wanted to take all that I had discovered *home,* take these movements that I was a part of or that I had helped create back to the trailer court and so take all my own selves back to the places and the people who had birthed me and who I had never wanted to leave in order to have a life determined by hope. This is why I wrote the essays in this book. For myself and for the anonymous people I had come from, or desired, or met in my life, so that we could finally be seen—with all our difficult voices—in the radical movements where we belong. I have wanted to find you, to tell you that I am here, to invite you to remember me or add your own unique experiences to our common purpose, our collective tale. To come home with me. To join me in changing the world.

Using memory and experience, and matching that with hindsight and summary—with a progressive politics built of hope, intelligence, and critical understanding—is one of the few things which can transform us, help us bring about new ways of loving and living together in this world, without the despair and the terrible damage most people are forced to suffer and endure. Ultimately, it can save us. But that will happen only if we *know* and use history as a living thing, history which is deeply personal but which also dares to search beyond the individual lives each of us has led, to create and invigorate a passionate, uncompromised, radical, unafraid-to-ask—*and unafraid-to-tell*—kind of history. A history which makes it possible for each of us to tell the truth and then to claim or to change the real lives we have led while moving forward the profound hopes each of us carries for a generous and transformed world.

A Queer Girl
Dreaming Her Way Home

I have lived on the wrong side of sex since birth. This is both who I am and who I was meant to be, though it isn't all there is. I grew up a mixed-race, white-trash girl in a country that considered me dangerous, corrupt, fascinating, exotic. I responded to the challenge by becoming that alarming, hazardous, sexually disruptive woman. Most often this happened without a plan or a design.

My coming out as a high femme lesbian only added to the fears, lies, and misconceptions of those deeper, older experiences: of being born and marked inherently *other* because of the people who birthed me. This deviance, perversion, this otherness is woven into the fabric of my earliest experiences and memories, piercing the very sides of the dresser drawer my parents used for a crib.

We were motorcycle-riding poor-white (Irish) and dark-skinned (Romany) Gypsy trash. I was given birth by these particular men and women, people with their own complicated histories and deeply compromised choices. They are who I grew up loving. And this life, my life, has led me back to them again and again in order to confront and ultimately accept myself. I have needed to remember them, see them before me, in order to comprehend the world. They were not my choice, but they were my survival, what I required to endure, and to create a worldview layered with my fusion of sex and color and class.

When I look at the essays in this book, it seems to me that I have been building their very sentences for a long time, placing them like marks on the ground to utilize again some day for myself, so that I could travel back to the place I fled in fierce, hopeless love, dread, and nameless grief so many years before . . . back to my earlier self, to the towns and fields I grew up in, the memories and the nightmares I could tell no one, back to the smell of the places I hid to survive the violence in my family, back to the child, staring at the skeleton of a future with no eyes in its sockets. No matter how rough, the terrain of my history is what I have always used to invent and understand my dreams, my sexuality, and my need to go home.

Going back isn't what started me writing, though; anger was— anger and loneliness. I was homesick for a place and a people I'd thought I hated—and angry at how my own uneven teeth, exhausted body, and physical scars still betrayed my origins. I was increasingly tired and furious at being in a middle-class world peopled with none of the bitter brilliance, powerful resilience, and savage survivors' humor I had grown up knowing and which I still relied upon in myself to keep my own life recognizable. I was tired of whiny movement women who seemed to want only what they thought the men of their class already possessed—rather than being amazed at the very privilege of their assumption and their "wanting" in the first place. *Tired* doesn't really capture it. I was sick at heart over a feminism and a Left driven by a deeply ungenerous disregard for difference. People in both movements had few skills to manage working with anyone whose life history fell outside a certain, very particular kind of whiteness, an imperious class confidence.

I was also scared. All the stories I could gather and spin at this rally or that conference seemed to be sending me further and further away from the person I knew myself to be. Where was I going in this new world, in the attempt to run away from the one I had fought so hard to escape? What exactly was I piloting myself into? This was a world that I had hungered for with such desperation, a world of books and language and bodies that didn't ache at the end of the day and certainly not at the beginning. I dreamed of a world away from the fear and desperation that had governed my own childhood. But where was this new life taking me? What kind of person was I becoming? I had trouble, sometimes, even recognizing myself. Whose language was now moving through my lips, whose images, whose truths and lies? Even the stories that had once seemed my own, as I repeated them in meetings and consciousness-raising groups, now seemed overdone in my ears, exaggerated in untruthful ways. The people I drew didn't smell like the people I knew—those human beings who were really the spine and flesh of my history. They were too perfectly tragic, too comically downtrodden, too pathetic. I knew my mother would be disgusted. She would also be ashamed.

There was some terrible lying going on here. I existed in a circumstance where the only language for my own life was one of grave silence and profound omission. My own shame and confusion about who I was and where I'd come from kept me from thinking I could ever write or speak in public, could ever create a life of integrity for myself—one of the mind and the spirit, a life I could respect. I had never met another me in any of the movements I was a part of. This was, looking back, not because there weren't many of us there but because our experiences and histories were assumed to be nonexistent in those rooms and lecture halls and at those demonstrations. They weren't called for, weren't valued, weren't understood. Because of that I was alone in any room I entered, and I had no way to find others with corresponding lives full of the stories and laughter, the heat and undercurrents that propelled my own class, sex, and race history forward.

I don't mean this literally. I didn't need to meet up with another woman whose life was a cookie-cutter version of my own. Her language didn't have to roll from her mouth with the same phrases as my aunts and cousins and nieces, her poverty or pleasure need not trace precisely the same shapes as my own. What I longed to hear again was a *culture* of similar expectations and longings, of lives rooted in familiar desires and in the regular stories of simply desperate needs, understated and quite ordinary. I wanted a commonality of the skin and flesh in other women and men who had survived these commonplace terrors of existence and who still had a fierce desire to never forget. Who really understood that this *not forgetting* was a necessity, the core of their own survival, rather than just the bitter price paid.

I longed for a movement of other women who would still smell of sex captured in the back of a '56 Chevy or a Harley and a field. Who had an uncompromising taste for lovers with the power to map and navigate their own ferocious desires for going under in a female erotic context. I wanted a narrative with the texture of its sex drawn through the hands and mouth of a woman who would take your body under water with your arms held back at your sides until you gasped for breath, and still she wouldn't let you go. I wanted somebody here to howl with the pleasure and the terror of the whole damned thing. I began to realize that I was hungry for *sound* in a class- and color-silent world. I operated alone here, hiding and remembering, and I had become afraid in a new way now about my own geography of desire and the curves and edges of my own sexual, racial, and economic history.

But the delinquencies of my upbringing and my desires only confirmed a deeper chronology of disturbing questions in which the ache for another woman's mouth was simply the most obvious crime I committed. My history didn't seem to fit together with the dreams I harbored and the movements I had joined. No one had to say it out loud. I knew it more clearly than anyone around me. Popular culture, casual remarks about "poor white trash" or about being "gypped," television humor and the empty bookshelves of the trailers and little houses I grew up in, all spoke it more expressively than any single assertion.

It's hard for me to remember those days before I had the hope of the Left—and then of women, of sisters, and beyond that of differently gendered women, a kind of third sex, who desired their own kind. My hope was for a revolution so complete that no one would ever have to face my life choices again. That was the context for my early activism, though I really didn't understand it as clearly then. It was the civil rights movement, the Left, and then women's liberation that broke the repetitive pattern of sameness, of small worlds and smaller hopes, in which I grew up and to which I seemed destined. How to tell people who have never felt that desperation what it meant to discover the world of ideas and imagination that is the basis of revolution. To rip yourself, literally, from the flat, minute range of alternatives poverty presents you with from birth and explode into revolution— grand, total, world transformation for yourself and for all the people you love, people you have had to leave behind in that trailer park in order to escape their fate.

Before the movement, I could only try to slip my dreams inside a wedding gown or onto a Harley Davidson. By the time I was eleven, I was nearly six feet tall, and my body suggested a sexuality I had yet to embrace. I had become a trophy girl at the Saturday night motorcycle track we went to each week. My father raced his bike or worked on the pit crews of his other male friends. At the end of a series of races the winners would be called onto the field for their prize. I would pull my dress tightly around my hips and ride that big Hog out onto the center field. Leaving the bike, I would pick up every winner's trophy as his name was called, bringing each man his prize. As they accepted, each man in turn would pull my body into his across the tank of his bike, moving his mouth over mine. I dismissed their kisses. But I loved the feel of surrender in a public space and the crowd's approval. To be publicly claimed and taken—this was a perilous sexual energy which I could play with in that ridiculous spotlight. I would never be a prom queen or a good girl, but this offered me a kind of irresistible female claim to a distinguishing, edgy charisma and ironic magnetism, gave me an identity in the world. It was what I had. And I would learn, quickly, that every identity has its price.

By the time I was twelve, I was considered a whore and treated as one. Each boy who went out with me bragged about the ease of his sexual conquest on our first date—in order to match the lies of whatever boy had gone before him. In response, I began to date older men. Before my thirteenth birthday I began to see a thirty-three-year-old motorcycle mechanic, Hack Hackley, who raced bikes and was one of my father's best friends. I had my first full-time summer job, getting a pair of roller skates as part of my official uniform so I could start waitressing at the nearby drive-in hamburger stand.

Most everything I craved then was fiction and excitement. I hungered for men with the same indiscriminate longing for escape and improbable meaning I attached to all my fantasies. The endless romance I sought, the life I wanted, was epic and filmy, not what it really was: a few strung-together drive-in movie moments in the back seat of some guy's car. I had measureless Technicolor illusions, gaudy and without focus, dreams of ecstasy, of seamless joy and perfect escape, of having a beauty I didn't possess and a power I couldn't command.

I read Harlequin romances and *Love* comics in piles, devoured all I found. I wouldn't have known a "good" book if it had materialized next to my bed—and I probably wouldn't have been interested. Those novels fit my urgency and my terror of the real world perfectly. Even when it began to dawn on me that I wanted women, these books stayed central to my imagination. I merely adjusted their gender. Or I didn't notice. It wasn't the sex of the men in these books which compelled me; it was the man's total power to define and control the world around him. It didn't seem remotely possible for a woman like myself to play that role, to determine or control the world. These were gendered fables of class and power, and I was completely willing to believe in love as my answer. I also accepted the feminine angles of romance, the stance of ultimate receptivity. At this, I imagined myself a master.

The Harlequin books always featured mousy, unnoticed women (beautiful underneath the frump), women with a limp or a withered arm, secretaries who could take shorthand at 120 words a minute. Women who were otherwise rudderless or without skills, women in pain and grief over an unrecognized life or an impossible love. Whatever else they were, these books were closer to a literal description of myself and my lack of options than most other books or magazines around, from *Reader's Digest* to *Family Circle*. Those narratives abounded with stories of women who were upbeat, heroic, optimistic, talented. The babes in my Harlequin books had nothing going for them except the secret of their inner ability to express love and faithfulness to a male partner who was disillusioned by the world. Even today when I'm sad or hopeless, I find myself yearning to sink into one of those books.

The only other thing I believed in was acceleration. On the back of any too-fast-moving motorcycle, or sitting next to any driver with a foot pressed flat on the gas pedal of a furious car, I felt released inside, free in a suspended span of pleasure. It was only that physical force which proved itself equal to the task of sublimating my fantasies.

In the middle of this dream-laden life, I was filled with directionless longings. I dreamed without any differentiation in my aspirations, my possibilities, or my needs; I would become a nurse, or win a million dollars in Vegas, or be sought out by a classy girls' college in Connecticut. I would be discovered and become a famous movie star. I would marry Elvis. I would move to Placerville, move to Europe. My father would stop touching me. I would get married before I got pregnant. I would wake up happy.

Each vision I conjured seemed urgent, yet I lived my daily life without any of the knowledge or tools necessary to make a real escape. I lacked both the ambition and the strategy to elude the creeping reality that hardened around me like cement with each passing season. Even more crucially, I lacked an interior world that might have helped me

My Gypsy grandmother

(above) My dad and granddad; (right) my dad and grandmother

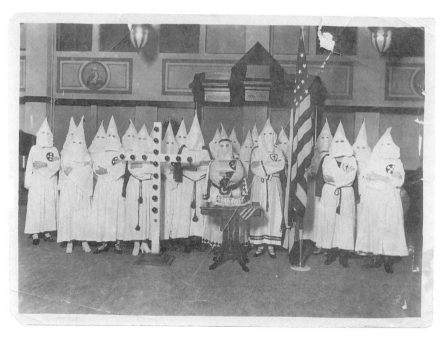

Klan women who were in the group that branded my father and grandmother—both photos were taken secretly by my great-grandmother

My mother and father with my dad's parents. Also shown (in the cowboy hat) is my grandmother's lover, "Uncle" Pike

My mother standing behind my father

My mom and dad with her parents, her oldest sister, Mary, her sister's husband, Jack, and one of my cousins.

My mom and her mother

My father and mother; (below) my father and mother at
a motorcycle race he'd just won

*My father and my grandmother (my mom's mother)
on the bike in Bakersfield*

One of our trailers

create or develop an authentic way out. I lived daily with a deepening recognition of the hopelessness of my prospects, filled with an increasing hysteria as I watched the door squeaking shut on my chance to do anything different than the generations of women who had gone before me. Mostly, I slept.

I had always used sleep as an answer. No one in my family could find me in the rural fields surrounding our trailers or houses, and I would lie sleep-cyed by the hour, the day. I knew early on that imagination and daydreams were the most expressive reality I had. The magical power of my storytelling father, the laughter and intelligence of my mother, could not offset the equal doses of family violence and despair that settled into a pattern I was helpless to alter. My mother was full of an inarticulate rage that seemed to be calmed only by the whippings she performed on me daily. My father's, brother's, and uncles' endless sexual desire for any female in the family, neighborhood, and county were commonplace. Our overall poverty could not be escaped. There was no place to hide from the rigid anger of my mother's mute disappointments, her body of female bitterness, or the sexual vapor which emanated from all the men. No room had locked doors. No child would have been allowed to use a lock if there had been one. And I was the only young girl of the brood who survived.

Throughout my childhood, both my parents struggled to provide a kind of imaginary sorcery which they hoped I might use to rescue myself from our existence as throwaway people. Their aspirations for me were of an existence not decimated by despair or bitterness, and they worked each day to provide, with their willpower, what they could not provide with their capital. They were each totally committed to this project in their own ways, attempting to wrest for me a different kind of childhood than they had known, to fabricate from their own resistance something better for their daughter. But that could not obscure all the other forces arising, not simply from economics but from within each of their individual personalities. Each of my parents was both my ally and my betrayer—strange fusions of shelter and hazard. My father remained the only faulty protection I had against my mother's daily violence; my mother was the hoped-for, utterly failed hope against my father's sexual violations. I was the child both of their potential and their tragedy, the product of their dangerous pathologies and of their intense allegiance. My only way to escape their fate was with their help. It was a help they had no idea how to provide. Still, it was a help they were desperate to furnish me.

Poverty is a terrible educator and a worse psychologist. The pathologies each of my parents struggled to subdue in themselves are mute testimony to the power of the human spirit and to its vulnerability. Willpower alone could never conquer the rivers of anger and grief each had sustained in their own paths to adulthood. No love of me, or of each other, could erase the marks of that historical stream; its waters eventually overlapped everything else in our universe.

That's partly why I can barely remember the literal and commonplace events of my childhood. It is what makes the bulk of each memory so conflicted, bordered with shadowy menace and a violent edge. This first became obvious to me when the women's movement began and I entered my first consciousness-raising group. The anger in those groups as we remembered arrogant or abusive fathers, brothers, and male cousins was palpable. But the collective reconstruction of our mothers was only allowed to be tragic. I didn't know what to do with those few memories I could pull forward—not of my father's hand striking me, but of my mother's. Of her face brutally set in the daily anger she shared with the only other female in her galaxy: her daughter. Her terrible sadness and fury, a sadness and fury I increasingly understood as I got older and faced the same choiceless expanse she could never escape. She had given birth to her first child at the age of fourteen, had seen that child die and its father desert her before her sixteenth birthday. This scarred her life with a traumatic, savage sorrow that no one and nothing could ever alter. I loved her desperately, even though I feared her far more than I feared my father. I have never known how to write this part of the story: of my loving and fearing her all rolled up in a package whose pieces are not distinct. What can I make of these recollections clouded with childhood loneliness and female-driven violence? It was my mother who hid in bushes watching me as I played. My mother who could not cry.

Yet she was also the dazzling female icon of my childhood, gunning the engine of her motorcycle in our front yard, her bleached blonde hair wild as she pushed that motorcycle faster to match and challenge my father, who was furiously racing his own bike down the back roads of California. I sat behind him on those trips, laughing at the speed and joy of it all, alive with her beauty racing alongside. I loved it when she rode that motorcycle up to the front of my school to pick me up, on those days she wasn't driving a school bus through our county to gather up or drop off other kids. She was as wild as my father but more relentless. She would take a dare farther, ride faster, lay her bike almost parallel to the road when rounding a corner, wear the highest fuck-me pumps with the tightest leather jacket I ever saw—it curved seamlessly around her body.

The first time they put me on Dad's bike I was a year old. They laid me over a pillow tied to the gas tank, and I rode between my father's arms. People thought we were crazy. Throughout the 1950s we rode as a family, belonged to a motorcycle club all the years I was growing up. My father rebuilt bikes, raced dirt bikes, speed bikes. The family did long-distance runs. We piled children into old beat-up pickup trucks and onto the back of every bike in our club. We built a special box for the dog, which we attached to the front of Mom's motorcycle when we went camping. Even in California in the 1950s, even among other poor families, we stood out.

But none of this could detract from the dominant cycles of unhappiness and unanswerable need which perpetually surrounded our family. Sometimes there were five children, sometimes only me. Children in the brood moved between households and adult family members like fish in a pool, living first in this wild pocket, sometimes beneath that rock. I tended to stay put because my parents stayed together, but for most of the children living with us it was a sometimes thing. I would come home from school, and there would be four where, in the morning, there had been only me. They would stay for months or years; then they would be gone abruptly. New cousins emerged, left, returned.

In our home there was only one other consistency besides poverty, and that was racism. The slash of it rode against my father's copper skin and Romany heritage, and it functioned like a poison river through the construction trades in which he struggled to make a living. His beauty was different, red-brown, distinct. This was a person born by the side of a river, who had traveled in Gypsy caravans until he left high school to work full-time. His mother, my grandmother, had also lived in those caravans as she had worked as a hooker in the small towns along the West Coast. And it was in one of those small Oregon towns that he and she were attacked by the Klan, beaten and branded, the letters KKK burned into their bodies.

His hands were long, slender, strangely disproportionate to his six-foot, four-inch frame. His nose was Roman. He knew how to build an entire house without using any nails. He could fix any car, ride any motorcycle, race any jalopy and win. He could repair anything, was a superb grease monkey, could build with leftover scraps of lumber. His world did not end at the physical. He would spin magical stories for me, filled with flying people and talking frogs, around the campfires we built. He taught me to make a mattress of pine needles and how to track. He taught me wonder. But all those multiple skills of his, combined with my mother's whiteness and her hard work as a seamstress, basting and mending other people's clothes, doing other people's laundry, driving buses, and erratically selling Avon door to door, were not enough to sustain us. There were better years and worse ones, but you could never count on a thing. Each of them worked long, relentless hours. It was never, never enough.

In their need for each other, in their marriage, each longed for things the other could not give or receive. She hated sex; he loved it. He was expansive, joyful, optimistic, magical, obsessed, overwhelming, controlling, sexually off the deep edge, male. She was tougher, smarter, craftier, much more bitter, sexually frozen. She could never forgive the way poverty had shrunk her life; he lived outside it in his mind. The glass half full, the glass half empty — they could not concur. But they had known each other since childhood, and they were wed in an experience of survival deeper than any of their differences. They were a unit against everyone and everything — even me.

Only through my father's unwanted sexual attention did I ever challenge my mother's power in that marriage. She could not hold out for me, could not even afford to acknowledge the forbidden desires my father had for me, for other women in the family, for other women always. She stubbornly refused to see or believe or comprehend it. This left me, his only daughter, vulnerable to his obsessional sexual aggression and acts I was too young, too powerless, to refuse. Like nearly all women literal and imagined, I was on his list of personal lusts. I felt his heat and his need, and I feared saying no—as if I could have—risking the loss of both father and mother if I resisted.

I did what I could. I hid from each of them whenever possible. There was a crawlspace beneath our home that became the closest shelter I could find from his pursuit and her turbulent hand. It was just under the window in my bedroom, and I could slip out there in seconds to lay silent until the house was still again. I spent too many hours of my childhood huddled there next to my dog, crying and dreaming of a different life, a safe life, with the same father and mother I loved, imagining them transformed this time, fixed, repaired. I would finally be safe . . . safe.

So it is no wonder to me that I crave both safety and peril in equal amounts and that these two qualities are wedded in my psyche like twin sides of the same desire. That *is* desire for me. I know that all women try to construct a shell of safety for their desires, a shape for their sexuality which allows it to flourish even in the midst of this mess. It is necessary for any woman who wants to survive her own capacity for heat and surrender to find a way to play with power in its many manifestations. I would discover it slowly through the construction of my own high femme identity—and the butch corollary. It was there, in butch gender-fuck, that I could see my own femme drag queen self. Bigger than life, turning gendered bodies inside out, shooting them through with the ironies that have always contradicted biology, the dreamed-about spheres of the possible.

Before this, though, there was no sexual focus in my world—certainly not in my teenage world—that actually seemed my own: neither my mother's frozen refusal nor my father's thoughtless pursuits. I knew only that traditionally gendered bodies failed to excite me. There was the lingering, unanswered question of the kiss I could never find, the kiss I had never known. To be embraced by a different kind of being, an unimaginable and unnamed female gender trickster, someone physically skillful, masculine but fluid, sexually confident, her mouth pulling my own body across the tank of a motorcycle, center field, after the race—longing without words to give it breath.

An extraordinary world for me, butch/femme. But my route to this hidden erotic system was in no way direct. It came later. How to

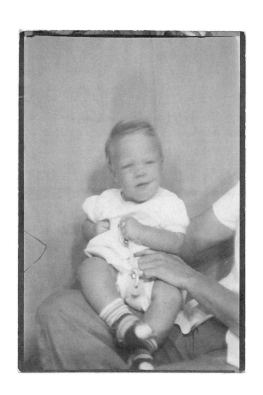

*Pictures of me
as a baby*

Me at three

(below)
My mother and I "do" femme

Me at four or five

Me and my dog when I was about eight

Me at eleven

Me at twelve

Me and my brother

(below)
Me at thirteen or
fourteen

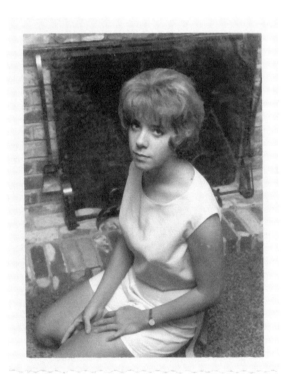

Me as a trophy girl at the races

have my mother's wild beauty and my father's ferocious sexual power and intensity? A woman's relentless mouth and a cock deep inside my body. How? The desire which finally began to correspond to my interior imagination was first spoken to me by butch women who were quiet, hurt, twisted up in their hearts, deeply fearful, razor sharp, tender gender foreigners. Those women seemed to spring from the same deeply troubled, captivating pool that had given me birth. From the first time I saw butch women, they were the only satisfying complement to and corresponding reflection of my own image, my own eros. In their bodies, their complex genders, their eyes, the power of their hands and mouths, the wonder of their hands and their cocks, I could ride through and sink inside my history with all its humiliations, force, and beauty. I could find refuge. They could take me under. Through the sheer power of their desire for another woman they could take me home.

The world is only as vast as our comprehension of it. The circumstances and possibilities of our desires remain impossible when they are unimaginable. In my life, now, I am struck by the fact that the universe in which I currently reside is one which I could never have imagined as a lonely preteen trophy girl, barely avoiding pregnancy, skimming the surface of her own death. I didn't even know what I didn't know. There is no map for an invisible world, no path out of a closed system, no name for undefinable hope or longing.

As I grew, so did my wildness and increasingly mean-spirited rebellions. At twelve, I finally told my mother about my father's sexual attacks on me throughout childhood. She called me a liar; she refused to question him. She believed, I think, that her own survival was intrinsically tied to her economic and emotional relationship with him—and nothing would ever alter that terrible, necessary perception. As I grew into a ferocious teenager, my mother became desperate. We fought relentlessly. I no longer bothered ducking her hand or avoiding her voice, and I didn't hesitate to retaliate, either, whenever I could. I began searching out ways to hurt her. I could no longer afford to remember that I loved her. She had made her choices clear: we were not allies against my father's uncontrolled sexuality. So my mother and I fought, enemies as only survivors on the edge can become.

The turning point came when I fought back physically. She had slapped me across the face; I stepped right into it and struck her, hard, as she stood before me. (I can still feel her skin on my hand.) It had been building for months—all our arguments about my staying out with men or women, coming home irregularly, nearly flunking out of high school. I was riding a downward cycle my mother knew only too well. Whatever else was true, however bitter things were between us, she did not want this to happen to me.

I was fifteen when she found a list of ads for private boarding schools in the back of a *Vogue* magazine she'd read in some doctor's waiting room. She knew nothing about these schools, but she was desperate enough to surreptitiously tear the page out and bring it home. Then she wrote to each school, requesting information about scholarship programs. And she filed applications for me to each one that replied. Six months later I was accepted into a newly created "low-achiever/high-IQ" scholarship program at the American School in Lugano, Switzerland. I left California for the first time in my life and boarded the first airplane I had ever been on, flying to Europe. For the trip, I tinted my bleached-blonde hair with a vaguely pink rinse to match the magenta suit I would travel in. I was ready, all right: a poor white-trash girl with impossible fantasies. It seemed to me, then, that all my endless daydreams were about to come true, that the effortless life and release I'd longed for were about to be mine. I imagined that I was about to be freed somehow from the poverty and insignificance of one world and released magically into another—a new world that, I imagined, would welcome and discover me, desire me, treasure me completely, without violence or violation.

The reality was more brutal than I could have anticipated. Touching down in Lugano, I found myself at a school for slightly rebellious ruling-class children on their way to Harvard or Vassar. The school itself was a castle, a set of imposing, sculptured gray stone buildings on the palatial grounds of an estate. The rooms were enormous, harsh, stately, cold. I had escaped my old world, but I was completely alone there, without any idea about how to survive the vast psychological distance left to travel. Nor did I have the slightest idea of how to go about visiting the opera in Milano, reading Chaucer in Middle English, or traveling to Paris for the weekend.

Humiliations began early: no one wanted to share a room with this smelly new girl whose clothes, they said, were "like trash." Despite their mild attempts at rebellion, these kids knew exactly how crucial it was to bunk with the son or daughter of Costa Rica's president instead. I was saved from complete isolation and ridicule only because the most affluent girl in school—another misfit, but a very sophisticated one, a pipe-smoking, gender-bending child of the American South, whose father owned the largest blanket-manufacturing company in the world—befriended me.

I lasted there less than a year. In that time I was forced to realize the dimensions of a world I would never possess, never be invited to join. Paradoxically, it was at that school where I was first introduced to the Left, to the ideas of Marx, to the notion of civil rights and of protest movements. My favorite teacher, himself a first-generation son of Lebanese immigrants and a graduate of Dartmouth, was—unbeknownst to the school—also a member of the Communist Party of America. I approached him in tears one day, ashamed and desperate because my grades were so terrible. He told me that I was never meant to be at that school in the first place. Then he handed me *The Communist Manifesto* to read. I did. It was the first thing I'd ever come across that talked about material possessions and the lack thereof, about something called *the working class,* and it began to finally make sense, for me, of my family's poverty, of the circumstances that had controlled our lives and which—especially at that school—seemed to disgrace me so. It enabled me to stay, and to struggle through, and barely—just barely—to graduate. I became the first person in my family with a high school diploma.

I returned to California an awkward and self-conscious sixteen-year-old, bitter toward both parents. I had seen all they couldn't give me—things my schoolmates had effortlessly with a month's allowance or a well-placed phone call. Humiliating as the past year had been, it had also made it impossible for me to stay in my hometown for good, impossible for me to forget the tantalizing taste of possibility, of different ways to be in the world. *I had been away.* A learner. A student of great ideas. Having taken the trip outside, I was forever changed by it. Now I had to leave. It was just a matter of when.

In that first strange month of my being back home, my parents built me a desk and shelves for all my books. They framed a map I had brought back of the Parthenon, bought me bookends and a study light. None of us knew what I was supposed to do with these things; they just seemed required somehow, now that I was a high school graduate and the owner of such large, impressive-looking tomes. Those books were my trophies, the stuffed heads on my wall; they were proof that the sacrifice had somehow been worth it. My parents were awed by them, held them in a kind of reverence and dread. And—without admitting it—so did I.

We circled those bookshelves like wary hounds after large and frightening prey. I would shut the door to my little room and open their pages, leafing through them again and again. They reminded me that I had been somewhere else. And, to my parents, they were a sign of how I had become different, how I had traveled without them to places they could not imagine. We had grown irrevocably apart. I was no longer duplicating the motions of women in my family. Now, it was clear, I was becoming a different kind of survivor.

A week after the shelves were up and the books in place, I returned home in the middle of the day to find my mother in my room. She had taken all the books out and spread them around her, some half open, some with crumpled pages as if they'd been thrown there, and she was surrounded. And she was crying—my mother, who had never cried in front of me. I stood on the threshold, too stunned to speak. We stared at the books and at each other. Finally, she said, through all the tears, "I don't understand any of these books, nothing that's in them, nothing they say. How can you read them if I can't? Who do you think you are?" Then, still crying, she left.

A short time later, I left, too.

For many years I was a nomad. By 1965, I'd hitchhiked often, routinely, across the United States. A stripper, prostitute, drifter, dreamer, revolutionary. And, for many years, revolution and the dream of it were enough. The civil rights movement that exploded in America with the Freedom Summer of 1964 gave many of my own longings voice, and I was honored to be a part of it, working for a short time as a member of SNCC (Student Non-Violent Coordinating Committee) in Mississippi. No power I have ever encountered is as comprehensive as the human dream of changing the world. It was a dream as big as my needs and my vision and as radical. I knew instinctively that it was merely the bottom line before real possibilities could emerge. And, at sixteen, I was ferocious in my love of possibilities. It's a fierceness I've never lost.

After participating in the Mississippi Freedom Summer, I lived in New York City for a while. I lived in Berkeley, California, in its heyday during the 1960s. I was a United Farm Workers organizer. I belonged to two communes, snuck desperate men trying to escape the U.S. Army across the Canadian border, marched in protest against the Vietnam War in cities all over the country, laid in front of Black Panther offices late at night to keep police from firing inside, and got my first tear gas mask at eighteen to use in the street riots I regularly joined. Then, late at night, I did sex work. Prostitution made it possible for me to afford an existence most middle-class and upper-middle-class radicals I knew assumed as inherently theirs by right.

The 1960s was an amazing time in this country, an explosion of previously unstated yearnings, hope, and fury. It was a historical unearthing of the truer principles that built and organized our lives, not the rhetoric of jingles, mantras, all the banal shortcuts we'd been forced to learn to stay alive: "land of the free," "bring me your cold, your tired, your poor," "pull yourself up by your own bootstraps," etc. This is a land with a powerful language of choices and freedom, yet it offers only the wealthy liberation from fear and need and silence. It is a nation constructed upon a complicated history of theft and slavery, of racism and hatred for women. And it is layered with a deep tradition of betrayal toward far too many woman, children, and men. Poverty is this country's dirty little secret, profit its foundation. It took me too many years to find this out.

Some things in your background never go away; they are both a burden and a tool of survival. Sex as labor—as earned income—was one of them for me. Throughout the 1960s and 1970s, when I didn't have paid movement jobs, I worked in the sex trades. I told no one, not my commune members, nor my best friends, and no one ever asked; they just assumed that I got my money like they did—that I, too, was a graduate student who taught huge classes, received a monthly check written by well-to-do parents, maybe drew income from a family trust fund or some other long-standing inheritance. It didn't matter. I lived my movement life with all those impossible movement hours but never attended college. I remained alone with this sense of myself as an outsider (even though I was secretly very proud to be the first member of my family to ever actually graduate from high school).

I worked sucking men off or stripping in old vaudeville houses in San Francisco, Chicago, New York, Boston, Vancouver, Montreal, Toronto. I worked in roadhouses if I was desperate enough or in classier burlesque houses when I'd decided to stay put for a while. The trade adapted well to my radical life. Every city has a strip joint, and I was young and white and had a great body for the work. I was also profoundly angry at men, which only enhanced and embellished my shows.

I had learned to do Hawaiian dance, along with all the half-Hawaiian children growing up alongside me in the farm valleys of California. Hawaiian women who had married white GIs during World War II and moved to the mainland wanted to teach their children their traditions and language. The participation of mongrels like myself made it "American," and all the kids in my area did it. Dance school wasn't how my family could enhance childhood; Hawaiian dancing was.

Early on I used that skill to become a showgirl in Vegas, making real money for the first time in my life and gaining my first sense of personal power over men. It was revealing for me. The women in my family were survivors who had no real authority since they could never determine the bottom line and live it. They couldn't afford to. Men were the bottom line—until I started dancing in Vegas, Stateline, and Reno. Onstage for that hour or more, I could move men's bodies back and forth as I wanted, could make them ask, beg, sweat. I could create something they wanted to touch and taste and hold. I gained a power I had never before possessed. I could hold their wanting in my hands. And I could refuse them. Heady stuff.

Dancing, stripping, hooking were all pieces of that logic. I had pleasure; I had work; I could tell the difference. It was hard work, but it wasn't as bad as picking tobacco leaves in the fields of Connecticut, where the edges of the leaves cut your hands and nicotine sap soaked into the cuts so they never healed. It was a lot better than harvesting hops in Bakersfield or ironing clothes in the backrooms of a dry-cleaning plant in Houston, better than working the night counter at the Donut Shoppe in Folsom, packing ice-cream cones into boxes as they came off the line in Chico, or ending up pregnant at fifteen. I understood early, and with unclouded eyes, about options.

But what did my escape into the Left mean, in practical terms? I had no tools to truly access this new world, no language or experience to use which would afford me entry. I was inarticulate. And humiliated at my own ignorance. So I slept with men in the Left just to overhear their conversations about Marx and the foundation of capital. I fucked them without hope of ever being good enough for them to love. But still I learned. I wrote down the titles of the books that lay around their beds, spilled out of their bookshelves. Then I went home and read. I gave those men what I knew how to give, and they took it without ever seeing me. They were a different kind of customer, though I didn't see it that way then. Of course I wanted them to think me brilliant, worthy, valuable enough to be remembered for more than a night. But I didn't expect that. Sex was my tuition, and I paid it willingly.

Sexuality and the State

The Defeat of the Briggs Initiative and Beyond

In 1978, my political organizing work led me to become involved in working against the Briggs Initiative in California. The birth of Briggs signaled the first terrifying beginning that rightist groups made in this country to force statewide referendums aimed at diminishing or taking away the civil and human rights of gays. I found that grassroots organizing around gay identity and sexuality was a powerful experience. We were brought into coalitions with unlikely groups—labor unions, for instance. And, for me, this was a re-markable experience because, in a literal sense, I actually went home for the first time since my teen years—to Folsom, Placerville, Turlock, Bakersfield, all the dried-out, impoverished little California towns I'd known as a child. There, I argued politics, sex, and morality with fundamentalist preachers in front of their rural ministries, had to use martial arts to ward off a bunch of punks from breaking into my van one night and killing me, met closeted and openly gay men and women in the most unexpected of places—and learned to be a real public speaker, debater, leader. To this day, I consider it one of the single most important things I've ever done. Traveling around Cali-fornia organizing against Briggs, I began to realize that, under the guise of talking about "homosexuality," American heterosexuals were really talk-ing about their own desires, their own sexuality. I began to realize that, in an essentially puritanical culture, homophobia created a convenient cloak for dealing with otherwise veiled or forbidden erotic themes, which everyone grappled with.

INTERVIEW WITH AMBER HOLLIBAUGH
by Diane Ehrensaft and Ruth Milkman

"One of the most fundamental interests of the State is the establish-ment and preservation of the family unit. Consistent with this interest is the State's duty to protect its impressionable youth from influences which are antithetical to this vital interest. This duty is particularly compelling when the state undertakes to educate its youth, and, by law, requires them to be exposed to the state's chosen educational environment throughout their formative years.

"For these reasons, the State finds a compelling interest in refusing to employ and in terminating the employment of a schoolteacher, a teacher's aide, a school administrator, or a counselor . . . who engages in public homosexual activity and/or public homosexual conduct directed at, or likely to come to the attention of, school children or other school employees. This proscription is essential since such activity and conduct undermines the state's interest in preserving and perpetuating the conjugal family unit."

So begins Proposition 6, the antigay initiative sponsored by State Senator John Briggs which Californians voted down in November 1978. Unlike most other antigay initiatives on the ballot in recent years (in Miami, Eugene, St. Paul, and elsewhere), the Briggs Initiative was defeated, by a vote of 58 to 42 percent. Although clearly calculated to appeal to the same anti–"big government" constituencies that approved Proposition 13 (the Jarvis-Gann Initiative) in June 1978 — not to mention the pro-family, anti-feminist sentiments on which the New Right has tried to build itself — Proposition 6 was unsuccessful.

Part of the explanation is that Proposition 6 was quite different in content from earlier antigay ballot initiatives. It was directed not only against gay people, but it also would have mandated the investigation and dismissal of any school employee who engaged in advocating, soliciting, imposing, encouraging, or promoting private or public homosexual activity "directed at, or likely to come to the attention of, school children or other school employees." That is how "public homosexual conduct" is defined in the text of the initiative. A school employee who indicates in a private conversation in her or his own home that she or he agrees with the existing California law providing that, as consenting adults, gay people are free to do whatever they want in the privacy of their homes, might be fired under the terms of the initiative, regardless her or his own sexual preference.

In this way, the initiative threatened heterosexuals quite directly, although it was directed primarily against gay people. Moreover, had

Proposition 6 passed, its provisions regarding the hiring and firing of schoolteachers would have held "notwithstanding any other provision of the law"—superseding union contracts. Familiar with Senator Briggs's long antilabor record in the state legislature, the California Labor Federation (AFL-CIO) went on record against Proposition 6 very early in the campaign, and many city and county central labor councils followed suit. It is not likely that they would have come out so strongly against the more usual sort of antigay measure.

There was one other important difference between Proposition 6 and the antigay initiatives that were passed elsewhere. While previous initiatives had called for the repeal of existing statutes prohibiting discrimination on the basis of sexual preference, the Briggs Initiative would have introduced positive discrimination against gay people and supporters of gay rights. In this era of concern about "reverse discrimination" (catalyzed by the Bakke case, which also originated in California), it is not surprising that many Californians were suspicious of a proposed law which mandated special treatment for a particular group of people. As the *San Francisco Chronicle* (10 October 1978) commented, "It would appear that while the public may not be willing to endorse any special enhancement of homosexual rights, neither is the public willing to specifically deny homosexuals any of their civil rights because they speak out about their sexual preferences."

Nevertheless, polls taken several months prior to the November 1978 elections showed that the initiative had majority support, and gay activists were pessimistic. In August, 53 percent of those people polled by the *Los Angeles Times* said that they would vote yes on Proposition 6, with 41 percent against it and the other 6 percent undecided. By October, the polls had completely turned around, with the *Times* finding only 40 percent favoring the measure, 56 percent against it, and 4 percent undecided.

Some striking variations in pro– and anti–Proposition 6 attitudes along sex, race, regional, and education lines were revealed by a poll reported by Mervyn Field in the *Chronicle*. Opposition to Proposition 6 was greatest in the two major metropolitan areas of the state, the Los Angeles–Orange County area and the San Francisco Bay area. More generally, the northern part of the state registered stronger opposition to the bill than the south, which parallels voting patterns in the Jarvis-

Gann Initiative of the preceding spring. This reflects the consistently more conservative flavor of southern California.

More women than men were opposed to 6. Those with education beyond high school were much more anti-6 from early on in the campaign than people with high school or less educational attainment. Ethnic variations are particularly striking. While blacks were strongly and consistently opposed to the initiative (by late September they represented the strongest oppositional group, with 63 percent indicating a "no" vote in the polls), Chicanos tended to favor the bill. The same black-Chicano voting differences had appeared in response to the Jarvis-Gann bill. These figures are hard to interpret, however, because the ethnic differences coincide with regional and religious variations. More blacks than Chicanos live in urban areas of California, and the heavier distribution of Chicanos in rural areas may help to explain their voting behavior. Religion may also have been a factor. Catholics, among whom there are many more Chicanos than blacks, were more strongly in favor of the bill than other religious groups. Also, many blacks, but few Chicanos, are employed in the state sector, and therefore blacks could more easily recognize the threat posed to them by the antilabor thrust of the Briggs Initiative. Finally, the merging of the homosexuality issue with a housing issue may have affected the situation in San Francisco, where Chicanos have for the last few years been facing competition from gay people from surrounding neighborhoods for scarce housing.

Ironically, the group trend that was most expected did not materialize. As part of a New Right strategy riding on the crest of successful antihomosexual campaigns, the Briggs Initiative was expected to rally avid conservative support, which would be reflected in a large rift between Democratic and Republican voting patterns. And, in fact, as late as August the gap was there, with Republicans far more supportive of the bill than Democrats (August polls: Republicans, 70 percent yes, 22 percent no; Democrats, 54 percent yes, 38 percent no). But by the November election the political winds had shifted, the gap had narrowed, and both Republicans and Democrats took an anti-6 stance.

Two additional reasons for the success of the campaign against Proposition 6 stand out. One is that leading politicians in both the Republican and Democratic Parties publicly opposed the initiative. While neither party made any real effort to mobilize people against Proposition 6, their stated positions surely had some impact on the outcome of the referendum.

Ronald Reagan's public opposition to Briggs should be seen in this context. It was the most surprising and perhaps the most significant sign of a genuine united front among mainstream politicians in opposition to Senator Briggs. Reagan had much to lose since Briggs, as everyone knew, was interested in running for governor and was partly aiming to build an independent power base. Briggs's appeal to homophobic sentiments was directed at the same right-wing forces that Reagan had been working on consolidating within the Republican Party. Consequently, Reagan took a staunch anti–Proposition 6 position while simultaneously appealing to the same conservative base Briggs himself sought to win over. Reagan pointed out that the proposed law would be "very costly to implement" and that it "has the potential for real mischief." He offered a direct counter to Senator Briggs's appeal to voters' concerns about children, saying, "What if an overwrought youngster disappointed by bad grades imagined that it was the teacher's fault and struck out by accusing the teacher of advocating homosexuality. . . . Proposition 6 is not needed to protect our children. We have that legal protection now" (*Los Angeles Times*, 23 September 1978).

The second key factor in the defeat of the initiative was the outstanding educational work done by the "No on 6" organizations. Ironically, Briggs's antigay measure initiated what is probably the fullest public debate over homosexuality and homophobia ever to take place in the United States. The outcome was that unprecedented numbers of people—including the very schoolchildren Briggs said he wanted to protect—were exposed to progay arguments. It was a tremendous opportunity to defend sexual freedom and to talk about sexuality in an explicitly political way, and the gay Left and its supporters took full advantage of the opportunity.

There was a great deal of debate among anti-6 organizers in the course of the campaign as to whether to employ a strategy emphasizing the ways in which the initiative violated civil liberties and human rights or a strategy that directly confronted homophobia in all its cultural and political manifestations. Advocates of the "human rights" approach argued that the risk of alienating people who might otherwise vote against the initiative was too great to justify dealing directly with all the hard questions surrounding the issue of homosexuality. Those who argued for a direct approach to homophobia countered that the real issue was homosexuality and the only way to win was to face it and convince people that their fears and preconceptions about homosexuality were unfounded.

In the following interview, Amber Hollibaugh, who was a full-time "No on 6" organizer with the San Francisco–based California Outreach Group, explains why she favored the second, antihomophobia approach. In addition to working in many aspects of the campaign in San Francisco, she traveled all over California speaking against Proposition 6, especially in small towns and rural areas. Out of this experience, she has developed some useful ideas about how to address sexual issues effectively as a lesbian, a socialist, and a feminist.

DIANE EHRENSAFT: In this interview we want to analyze why Proposition 6 was defeated. Let's start by talking about what forces worked against Proposition 6 and what forces supported it.

AMBER HOLLIBAUGH: The forces that were for Senator Briggs's initiative were interesting because of their ultimate narrowness. When the campaign started, we—the gay and lesbian Left—assumed that almost all of the Right and much of the center would be for Proposition 6 and against homosexuals. And that wasn't a paranoid fear. Defeats had happened in Wichita, Eugene, St. Paul, Dallas, and Miami, and we faced a wave of antigay sentiment in the nation. Homosexuality is an incredibly new and controversial topic. It wasn't even an acknowledged part of American life until the last decade. In California we felt that we were facing an overwhelming majority of unsympathetic people, especially because Proposition 6 was drafted in a way that made it possible to mobilize support in sensitive areas: sexuality, homosexuality, and children, particularly in the schools. I don't think there's been much of a tradition of dealing with sexual forces in the schools in this country.

The forces that we figured would be against Proposition 6 were the gay movement and sections of the women's movement, period. We did not assume support from anywhere else because no other groups had shown support. Neither the Left in general, nor the labor movement, churches. Never, especially when it has not been phrased as a human rights issue, has there been direct and active approval of homosexuality and homosexual teachers and homosexual workers in school systems. If an ordinance couldn't be oked that banned sexual discrimination in housing and employment, if we lost every time on something like that, then an issue posed around advocacy of homosexuality in public schools seemed like a definite loser. I felt that they had found our weakest points because the issue was posed, first, in terms of parents' right to control their children's education and, second, in terms of homosexuals as child molesters, the sexual abusers of young children. Not only were we advocating homosexuality and jeopardizing children's sexual lives, but we would be sexual aggressors. We were the people who caught young girls and boys in the bathroom.

Most of us assumed that the best that could be done was an enormously intricate educational campaign against the assault we expected. There were members of the Left gay community who did think we had a chance to defeat the proposition, but they were a tiny voice in the wind, and most of us thought they were off the wall.

RUTH MILKMAN: But in the end the anti-6 campaign did get support from people that you originally didn't expect to get it from? How important was that support?

AH: I don't think there was nearly as much movement as there should have been. But I was surprised that we got support from organizations that I thought of as traditionally heterosexual, even though there are gay people in them: the trade union movement, the teachers' associations and unions, child-care workers, health-care workers, and churches, at least certain denominations. They were not waving the red and purple banner in front of marches, but they were there.

RM: Don't you think those groups mobilized because they felt directly threatened by the Briggs Initiative? Had it passed, heterosexual teachers perceived as deviant in any way could easily be accused of "advocating" homosexuality and fired. Because union contracts would not protect teachers from being fired under the initiative, the labor movement, in particular, recognized the bill as an attack on workers' rights.

AH: I can speak to that by telling you about my experiences speaking to Teamsters' locals about Proposition 6. We did a lot of speaking in places like that as out dykes, and lesbians don't walk into Teamsters' unions and speak about lesbianism too frequently. We selected places we thought were crucial because we never get into them.

RM: When you spoke in situations like that, did you mostly talk about the antilabor aspects of Proposition 6?

AH: I would start out talking about the general antilabor implications and then talk about being homosexual. Usually I would say something like, "It's very interesting that part of how this bill is antiunion, or antilabor, is the submergence of homosexuality in your workplace. There are gay people in this room, in your union, that you will never know are gay. You have to deal with the homosexual issue whether you know it or not because people you work with are homosexuals whether they're out to you or not. I have to come and speak because the people who are actually gay in your union can't be here, can't be acknowledged as gay people. What does that mean, not to be able to acknowledge the primary things in your life? What would it mean to you not to be able to acknowledge your children, your primary relationships, your parents?" I would talk about what it means to hide an enormous amount of your life. And people were blown out because they didn't think that they knew homosexuals. It was a shock—for people who consider themselves heterosexual to be confronted with the notion that they had worked and lived with and loved gay people in their own communities even though they hadn't known that they were gay. You know that quote that Judy Grahn [in *The Work of a Common Woman*] has that gay people, lesbians, are exotic in Paris and deviant if they live next door. Most people don't think they've even known somebody gay and will cling to that in the face of great evidence. Even if you can point out that their sister never got married and has always been suspected of being gay, they'll insist that they've never known a homosexual. Also, people sometimes genuinely don't know that they know gay people and they were confronted with having to meet one for the first time. People would say things to me like, "I'm very glad that you're here tonight. I have to admit, though, that I'm very surprised that you're a lesbian. I mean, you're attractive."

Actually, most of the areas that I worked in were not in major cities but in rural areas. Trade unions in rural communities play a very different role and are absolutely not central to how communities get mobilized around issues even if big unions exist there. Central meeting places were much more churches, PTAS, and more social areas of the community, rather than trade unions. For example, I debated this man named Reverend Royal Blue who's a top fundamentalist preacher in northern California. The week before I was there he had a fundamentalist rally that had twenty-five hundred people at it. He has these Statues of Liberty that roll out on the stage with blinking green lights in their eyes, and fifty children come out waving American flags. It was tense, very tense. But he ended up blowing it because he assumed an agreement with his audience that he was wrong about. He ended up having questions from the floor. Somebody said, "Do you think homosexuals should be imprisoned if it's that unsafe?" He was feeling cocky and said, "Well, let me put it this way. I think Hitler was right about the homosexuals." He went into this whole rap about killing homosexuals. He was serious, out there, saying, "I think we should find a humane way to kill these people." Smiling the whole time.

And so I looked out at the audience, a big audience, with a lot of his congregation. The audience's age was my parents' age, in their fifties. Which meant they were in World War II and would define themselves as antifascist. I said, "Well, you know, Reverend Blue, my guess would be that most of the people in this audience fought against someone that had this kind of position in World War II, and my guess is that this audience does not support genocide. I may be wrong, but I suspect that most people don't feel that mass murder is an answer to a sexual question." The audience started applauding, and then I said, "Since you've raised it, let me talk about this as an important issue because I think fascism is something that concerns all of us." People came up to me afterward and apologized for him. People wouldn't talk to him. He blew it by thinking that he had that common agreement with the audience. I think a lot of people in the Right will do that if you don't panic and isolate yourself from the audience. Many of the Right's spokespeople really are that bad. And if you can push them to put that out, not just accuse them of it but make them expose what they really think, most people will be shocked. Most people really don't believe in murder.

DE: Can we look more closely at the strategies used by anti-6 forces in the campaign that account for the unexpected shift in public sympathies from a pro- to an anti-6 stance? The polls that were taken early in the campaign showed that most people did support Briggs's initiative, probably because they didn't know much about it. It sounded like another antigay initiative, and people, for whatever reasons, most likely homophobia, were sympathetic. But that really changed in the course of the campaign. Why?

AH: It's complex. If the issue had not been posed the way it was, we wouldn't have had the support that we did. The way Briggs wrote the initiative meant that it forced people to examine it who otherwise might not have been sympathetic. I don't think we could assume the massive anti-6 wave that emerged if the issue were "Do you like homosexuals?" People were exposed to the issue and saw in a variety of ways how dangerous it was. Because there's so much more work to be done even to begin to broach the depth of people's fears about many sexual issues, I certainly wouldn't think homophobia has been wiped out. But it's been brought up, it's been challenged. One of the most profound things about the Briggs Initiative is that it forced people to have to deal with sexual issues in a society that actively represses nonoppressive forms of sexual searching. This society encourages things like sexual "liberation" for a minority of the population but by and large does not encourage sexual debate on controversial issues. It doesn't do that around sexuality for women, and it certainly doesn't do that around same-sex issues. The campaign transformed that.

DE: It also educated children. Children know more about homosexuals now than they ever would have known.

RM: Which is ironic in view of Briggs's intention.

AH: It certainly is since the man wanted to suppress any homosexual questioning in anybody. I don't like the "thank you Briggs in spite of yourself" school of thought because I'd just as soon not have somebody else define my issues for me. But I do think it critical to understand how important it is that in a statewide election a sexual issue was confronted and not swept under the covers. It was right out there as an antigay issue, an antilabor issue. That's how it was talked about in every single newspaper, and that's what people had to counter in order to be credible.

In that context, there was one part of the gay movement that I wanted to isolate in anti-6 work—that part of the gay movement that didn't want to be gay. I'm referring to David Goodstein and that part of the "gay" movement whose strategy, right there in the pages of the *Advocate,* was that the campaign should be funded by the gay community but organized and directed by straight public-relations firms. Further, no gay people should have anything to do with the campaign because, as they said, "We are our own worst enemies." People who saw us would hate us as much as we expected, so we should go back in the closet and let concerned, good heterosexual PR firms conduct the campaign. They could educate the voters without making them tense, basically by not being gay. That kind of idea is as dangerous as anything Briggs could say. It *is* the end result of something like a Briggs campaign, which neutralizes sexuality as an important part of people's lives. It forces people right back into the closet, it makes you dead, and it makes you crazy. If you can't be gay when you're attacked as a gay person but everybody knows you're gay, you don't have anywhere to go, you can't do anything. I did not want to work with that section of the gay movement. Letters to newspapers illustrate the centrality of sexual issues in the 6 campaign. The letters that went to the editor when a paper would take a position, saying, "I want to know about homosexuality, I want to know if these homosexuals want to rape my children, I also want to know if I have to support the school system that pays these kind of people." That was how the issue was articulated by proponents, so people against 6 had to deal with those issues, too. Any organization that tried to play down those things was not very successful in its organizing. It's the difference between a human rights approach and directly confronting homophobia. We didn't decide abstractly that it was important to raise sexual issues—we had no choice.

Yet there was at least a partial convergence of the conservative Right and the progressive Left in their concern about the infringement of the state on people's lives. Some of our support was very conservative, like from the libertarians. Their line was that the state has no right to legislate sexuality—that you have to keep the state out of the bedroom.

DE: Proposition 6 played up concern for children. Reagan's position was: We need to protect our innocent children, but this law puts too much power in the children's hands. This is quite a dangerous thing you're proposing, Mr. Briggs, to give children so much power, because they will use it against adults. Although Briggs claimed to be protecting these same children, the campaign resulted in exposing these "innocent little minds" to the issues of homosexuality. So the "protection" got translated into sex education.

RM: Another irony is that the issue was seen in terms of gay men in the classroom even though most teachers are women.

AH: Exactly. Briggs always assumed that he was talking about gay men, not lesbians. He had to attack lesbians in a very different way. Consequently, when you were a dyke and went out to talk in places, people looked at you and didn't know what to do. Women are not assumed to be child molesters, you know. So a lot of the implied threat of homosexuals being in the schools didn't hold up when you said, "Hey, I'm a gay woman. I'm a lesbian, and are you accusing me of child molesting? I don't think it's true, period. As homosexuals, we don't do that, but confront me. Are you saying that women molest children?" Most people know it is not women that molest children. They may not want to confront the fact that it's *straight men* who do. One of the most successful arguments that I used during public speaking was to say, "The majority of child molesters are heterosexual men. Do you think that you want to deal with that issue by legislating heterosexual men out of the school system? Because that's who you would have to keep away from children in order to stop molesting."

Sexual Formation

DE: Did people ever respond, "Well, I hear what you're saying about child molesting, but that's not my concern. My major concern is the influence of a teacher on my child's sexual formation. I don't want gay people telling my child what's good for him or setting an example for him to follow. I don't want that kind of shaping of my child going on in school, and I have rights as a taxpayer."

AH: That was a sticky one. I don't know that we dealt with it successfully, and the campaign reflected that. It was a painful question. You didn't want to say that children aren't influenced by the sexual choices that they see available to them because one of the things that you most wanted to talk about was the right for children to know. I felt, for instance, it was critical to talk, not just about heterosexual children being frightfully overwhelmed by sexuality, but about homosexual children. That is *never* discussed. There are gay people that knew that we were homosexuals from very early ages and had nowhere to go. We were part of the frightening rates of suicide of young adolescent children. What does it mean to go through puberty and not be able to describe your primary sexual fantasy? Sometimes I tried to talk about that, to force people to deal with the fact that gay people aren't always over the age of twenty-one, that that's not the only time you know you're gay. And that shocked people. It was good for a rousing ten- or fifteen-minute screaming fight in a debate. And it did help people see that sexuality is not something that suddenly bursts upon you at the age of consent but is something that you live with and shape through a long process. Also, I would try to talk about the real issue, which is, "Do we want *any* kind of sexual discussion and sexual consciousness among children?" That didn't work in the sense that everybody agreed that, yes, we do want sexual consciousness. But at least it focused the issue where the fear is. People are really terrified of having sexuality, especially children's sexuality, discussed as a primary issue, in the same way that they're terrified of having women's sexuality being discussed and known. If you can refocus it like that, it also avoids making us, homosexuals, the enemy but points to the whole question of sexuality. People are terrified, not just of gay people, but of sexuality and sexual forces that they cannot easily understand. Women's fear of child molestation can be manipulated but is also a genuine fear because women know very intimately about sexual coercion. So their fear is based partly on the reality of male violence in this culture and partly on irrational fears about who's going to hurt their kids. If you don't address it as a complex issue, you can't even begin to have a good discussion. That's what some of us discovered through the campaign, though we never came up with a complete answer. Even inside the gay movement there's controversy about how somebody becomes gay. For instance, during the first third of the campaign, we stressed that child psychologists suggest that children's sexuality is formed by the age of three or four. So we would say, "You can't claim that we're going to take these young people at fourteen and form them." Then, we got some interesting criticism from lesbians who felt that their sexual choices had been made differently than that line supposed. Additional criticism came from other gay people who said, "What if we're child-care workers who work with children under those ages? Should we not be allowed to? Is it only after a predetermined age, when kids are 'formed,' that gay people can be around them?" When we realized that we were isolating gay preschool, child-care, and health workers and realized the implications, we had to rethink that line. It forced a level of discussion in the gay movement that we have only begun to have. We don't know why we're gay; we do not know that. Each one of us has our own concepts of how we became gay, depending on how soon we knew it, whether we're male or female, what class or race we are, all those things. We had pretty much agreed to live and let live in the gay movement around that issue, but this exploded it. There were big fights about how people become gay, particularly between gay men and gay women, because they have very different definitions of their sexual formation. More gay men, for instance, felt comfortable saying they were gay from a very early age. I think gay men and gay women differ in this way because men see themselves as sexual and women do not. Women see themselves as the object of sexuality but not the active one, sexually. So women didn't think they were straight or gay when they were six. They didn't think about being straight or gay when they were sixteen necessarily. They thought, Could I be a wife and a mother? Women are not encouraged to see themselves as erotic, to see their erotic capacity, so they don't think of a partner in sexual terms but more in emotional, social, or economic terms. Men are encouraged to seek out sexual partners at six and eight and ten and twelve. They experiment sexually. It's not that little girls don't, but they do it in a very different social context. You draw very different conclusions about your options depending on whether you see yourself as passive or aggressive.

DE: Girls are allowed a lot more emotional interplay, which is very physical in early ages. Any number of heterosexual women have had a lesbian relationship in childhood. Often they're playing out a heterosexual fantasy, but it's their way of having sexual control without having to do it heterosexually. So you'll have one playing boy and one playing girl in an explicitly lesbian, preadolescent or early adolescent relationship with a lot of physical intimacy, love, and caring. Childhood lesbianism is an experience shared by adult lesbian and heterosexual women, making it very hard to define the early formation of female homosexuality. Related to that, you said earlier that women know what sexual molestation is because they know what sexual coercion is in their own lives. It's interesting that more women than men were against 6.

AH: To me that was terribly exciting. It was significant because women also sensed the danger in the sexual description of the bill, that it could be used against them as women. Women were more open to understanding how sexual issues can be a direct threat in your life and were the ones who posed the question of child molestation but knew the true answer to that question. If in speaking you spoke very honestly to women about the nature of the sexual question and had a feminist analysis of sexuality and sexism, you were much more able to attract women who were in the middle of the road. Men have fixed notions of sexuality, and, by God, they ain't movin'. Women are caught in a sexual turmoil around sexual issues, including the discovery of their own sexual potential. And their children's. They, much more than their husbands, are the ones that deal with questions like masturbation and Johnnie sleeping with Joey and little Suzy making it with her girlfriend in the dollhouse. They directly confront a spectrum of sexual issues in their own lives and in their children's lives. If you're willing to acknowledge that women have deep and significant perceptions, sexually, and you're willing to tap into that as a resource when you go to the community, then you understand better the dynamics of Proposition 6 and where we were finally accepted and acknowledged. One time I was speaking in a church, saying that we (gay people) had children, too, that we love each other, just like anyone else. A woman in the audience looked at me and said, "What you're saying really makes me angry because you make it sound like there's nothing different in homosexuality and heterosexuality except the sex of the person you are lovers with. I don't know a lot about it, but I suspect that's not true. I think there is something different about it." And I sat there and realized of course there's something different. She hit it right on the head. Was I going to be safe if I pretended to be just like her only married to a woman? Is that the image I wanted to present of homosexuality? So I said, "No, you really are right and have called me out correctly. I'm scared to talk about what I think is unique in a homosexual experience. I don't know how to talk about that because I don't know what you'll think. It's hard for me to explore that because it's my life and something I protect carefully because of people like Briggs and how they describe what it means to be a homosexual. I want you to understand that there are things that are common in our lives. I keep thinking if I talk about my life in ways that are common to yours, you'll see me not as an enemy. But, be that as it may, let me say I do think homosexuality is different."

I talked about what it means to be a sexual outlaw. I used that visual image to talk about what it meant to be female and try to discover my own sexuality in a society that refused to acknowledge me as having rights of my own as a sexual person. I would link that to childhood sexuality and end up having very moving discussions with women in the audience. The men were still raising their hands, going, "But Ronald Reagan says that da-da-da," and these women would just be turning around saying, "Shut up, Hank. . . . Now the real question is, I have a daughter who's just begun to discover orgasms, and I don't know what to say to her about what that means in her life." I would talk about what it meant for me to be a dyke, what it meant to define my own sexuality in relation to another woman, to acknowledge it, to want it, to want myself. That has a lot to do with what lesbianism is and why it's such a moving and threatening sexual possibility to experience something very intimate and special in loving, feeling, and knowing someone of the same sex. At one place I was talking, a woman said, "How can I talk to my daughter about sexual potential when *I've* never experienced sexual potential? I don't know anything about sexual potential." I think she exposed something very painful about women's lives. For most women, sexual potential is not even an option or a question. It's not something that women walk around thinking about in a way they can resolve. Not that women don't think about it; it's just that it's a luxury and you cannot use it to make the choices you need to make for survival. So there I would be talking about what it meant to be a lesbian facing women, many of whose entire sexual lives were bare.

I talked about what it meant to fantasize and act on your sexual desire, that it is a frightening thing to know and deal with. If you're a dyke, you have to think through passion because passion between women is very different than what you see happen between Joanne Woodward and Paul Newman on a movie screen. Passion just doesn't come out like that. You don't have models in the same way in a homosexual relationship as you do in a heterosexual one, even if there's role playing. It does not have the same believability. One important part of the campaign was being able to expose the fact that heterosexuality isn't primarily a sexual definition and neither is homosexuality. This cut across preconceived notions that people had that, if you're gay, what that is is sexual and that, if you're straight, what that is is everything. You could force people to look at what that dichotomy meant and how much there wasn't challenging sexual discussion in people's lives to help them resolve sexual issues, particularly for women. Women were not to talk about it, not to know it. Women finally got the chance to say they had the right to be concerned about their own and their children's sexuality and needed an arena to discuss it. What's happening in women's lives is incredible bitterness and refusal to accept silence, and the nerve of that was touched in this campaign.

DE: There's a psychological issue related to the fact that women were against 6 more than men. Mothers of young children are generally less concerned about sex typing of their children than fathers of those young children. Therefore, it would make sense that, in thinking about the issue brought up around Proposition 6, it wouldn't be so unsettling for women that their children be exposed to a spectrum of behaviors as it would be to men, who are more concerned that Johnny be a boy and Janey be a girl.

AH: That makes sense. Still, I would often say, "I think you have a legitimate right to be frightened of your child being a homosexual, but probably my reasons are different from yours. I don't think homosexuality is frightening, but I think to be a homosexual in a heterosexual society where people want to ignore and degrade your sexual love is terrifying. You have a legitimate right to be frightened that your son or your daughter will be in opposition to the sexual majority. But to me what that means is that you need to be both educating yourself and your community and changing that concept of homosexuality as immoral or abnormal. Then the question of a child's sexuality becomes a real choice matter. You're right. It's hard to be a homosexual. It's terrifying. There is more alcoholism. There is an enormous amount of suicide. Not because there's something intrinsic in homosexuality but because there's something intrinsic in oppression that causes certain things to happen in the same way those things happen with women, things unseen and untalked about, but still known to be true. It doesn't mean that you want to wipe out women. It means that you want to make women equal." That changed the nature of the debate because it both validated people's real knowledge and fear of why their children would be destroyed for being sexually different while not playing into homophobia. It took balancing like that to be able to confront the issues, but it was worth it because in the end people were really changed. Their real questions began to be answered. In those situations you don't claim that you have the answers but that you have a lot of the same questions and a lot of the same needs to find a common answer. When you do that, people see themselves in an ongoing process and don't end the debate. They start it.

RM: One last question: How does the work done in this campaign help the Left learn how to talk about sexuality? What lessons can we extract from this experience?

AH: The first lesson that can be gleaned is that we have something to offer if we use our own tools around sexual questions. I think Marxism does enable us to look at sexual questions differently than other approaches do. We're not dependent on weird kinds of behavioralism. The analysis that is starting to come from our work as Marxists and feminists and gay people allowed us to explore the issues with the depth that we did, even though we didn't know much at all. Second, the

Left has got to stop denying the primacy of what are considered sexual issues. We can't think that they're secondary any longer. We can't afford to think that because they're not secondary in people's lives. If we don't think who you partner with and who you choose to or do not choose to raise children with and who you marry and who you care for are absolutely critical to the way that people make every other decision in their lives, we're really way behind other people's perception of the world. That means it's even more critical for us to use the tools and the analysis, including the economic analysis, that we have to tie those issues together and begin to help people analyze their own lives. That's the role the Left should be playing. Our responsibility as leftists is to begin to arm people with the concepts and information they need to take control of their own lives. The campaign started to do that. Wherever we demanded of ourselves and our audience a confrontation around sexual and economic issues, ultimately we won, even if that didn't show up in the vote, because we laid the groundwork for the kind of connecting that we need to do to build a movement. Where we didn't do that, we didn't have answers for people, and where we didn't have answers, we lost. People asked hard questions, and if we weren't open to the questions that they had, they didn't listen to us, and rightfully so. That's an enormous lesson for us that goes far beyond electoral politics; while the "No on 6" campaign was fought out in the electoral arena, the issue was perceived as a sexual and labor issue right down to the line; that's how the vote came out. We need to study this and not any longer support homophobia in our own organizations while we explore and expose sexual dynamics as central in this society. We have got to do it, and if we don't do it, we'll lose because people are discussing and need an analysis and the New Right analysis is there already. Now we have to confront these issues, and that's what the 6 campaign started to do. Where we did, by and large we were successful and were respected for the quality of the campaign that we chose to lead. We did not back away from the hard questions, and I think that that will serve us well in the future.

What We're
Rollin' around in Bed With

By 1978 I'd been out of the sex trades for several years and had settled in San Francisco. There I worked at Modern Times Bookstore and did a lot of Left and prison organizing around women's issues, primarily lesbian issues. This article grew out of a series of conversations that took place between my good friend Cherríe Moraga and me over a two-year span of time. Cherríe's lover was "old gay" and solidly butch identified; Cherríe was trying to figure out just where she herself stood in the butch/femme spectrum of lesbian life. I was trying to sort out just where a high femme–identified ex-hooker girl like me stood in the radical feminist spectrum of lesbian life. We started to talk about all this in depth and eventually decided to do an essay together—the only problem being that, at the time, I was afraid to write anything at all. Finally, we taped many of our conversations, and Cherríe transcribed them. The result, "What We're Rollin' around in Bed With", has become one of the best-known pieces ever written on butch/femme. It was first published in the Heresies, *the Sex Issue (1981), then in a book,* Powers of Desire *(Monthly Review Press), then in Joan Nestle's top-selling anthology* The Persistent Desire: A Femme-Butch Reader. *It remains one of the most evocative internal conversations ever put in writing on firsthand butch/femme lesbian experience (rather than just theory)—which is why, I think, it still seems to resonate so strongly with people today.*

SEXUAL SILENCES IN FEMINISM
A Conversation Toward Ending Them

This article was derived from a series of conversations we entertained for many months. Through it, we wish to illuminate both our common and our different relationships to a feminist movement to which we are both committed.

The Critique

In terms of sexual issues, it seems feminism has fallen short of its original intent. The whole notion of "the personal is political" which surfaced in the early part of the movement (and which many of us have used to an extreme) is suddenly and ironically dismissed when we begin to discuss sexuality. We have become a relatively sophisticated movement, so many women think they now have to have the theory before they expose the experience. It seems we simply did not take our feminism to heart enough. This most privatized aspect of ourselves, our sex lives, has dead-ended into silence within the feminist movement.

Feminism has never directly addressed women's sexuality except in its most oppressive aspects in relation to men (e.g., marriage, the nuclear family, wife battering, rape, etc.). Heterosexuality is both an actual sexual interaction and a system. No matter how we play ourselves out sexually, we are all affected by the system inasmuch as our sexual values are filtered through a society where heterosexuality is considered the norm. It is difficult to believe that there is anyone in the world who hasn't spent some time in great pain over the choices and limitations which that system has forced on all of us. We all suffer from heterosexism every single day (whether we're conscious of it or not). And, as long as that's true, men and women, women and women, men and men—all different kinds of sexual combinations— must fight against this system if we are ever going to perceive ourselves as sexually profitable and loving human beings.

By analyzing the institution of heterosexuality through feminism, we learned what's oppressive about it and why people cooperate with it or don't, but we didn't learn what's *sexual*. We don't really know, for instance, why men and women are still attracted to each other, even through all that oppression, which we know to be true. There is something genuine that happens between heterosexuals but which gets perverted in a thousand different ways. There is heterosexuality outside of heterosexism.

What grew out of this kind of "nonsexual" theory was a "transcendent" definition of sexuality wherein lesbianism (since it exists outside the institution of heterosexuality) came to be seen as the practice of

*(left) My first
butch lover on
her Harley;
(below) and in
the tuxedo
I bought her in
1971*

(above) Me at the Modern Times Bookstore, where I was part of the collective in San Francisco; (below) early 1970s picture of me

Honey Lee Cottrell

Another San Francisco shot of me, photograph by Honey Lee Cottrell

Me at a march against the Briggs Initiative in San Francisco, photograph by Honey Lee Cottrell

Me at a May Day demonstration in
San Francisco in the 1970s, photograph by Jeff Escoffier

*All from the early 1970s in
San Francisco: (above) me with some
of the San Francisco Lesbian and Gay
History Project at a gay pride march;
from left to right, JoAnn Castillo, Roberta
Yusba, Allan Bërubé, Estelle Freedman,
Eric Garber, and me;
(left, top) me and Gayle Rubin at a
gay pride march; (left, below) me
with a Lavendar Left button at
a demonstration, photographs by
Honey Lee Cottrell*

feminism. It set up a "perfect" vision of egalitarian sexuality, where we could magically leap over our heterosexist conditioning into mutually orgasmic, struggle-free, trouble-free sex. We feel this vision has become both misleading and damaging to many feminists, but in particular to lesbians. Who created this sexual model as a goal in the first place? Who can really live up to such an ideal? There is little language, little literature that reflects the actual sexual struggles of most lesbians, feminist or not.

The failure of feminism to answer all the questions regarding women, in particular women's sexuality, is the same failure the homosexual movement suffers from around gender. It's a confusing of those two things—that some of us are both female and homosexual—that may be the source of some of the tension between the two movements and of the inadequacies of each. When we walk down the street, we are both female and lesbian. We are working-class white and working-class Chicana. We are all these things rolled into one, and there is no way to eliminate even one aspect of ourselves.

The Conversation:
Cherríe Moraga and Amber Hollibaugh

CHERRÍE MORAGA: In trying to develop sexual theory, I think we should start by talking about what we're rollin' around in bed with. We both agree that the way feminism has dealt with sexuality has been entirely inadequate.

AMBER HOLLIBAUGH: Right. Sexual theory has traditionally been used to say, "People have been forced to be this thing; people could be that thing." And you're left standing in the middle going, "Well, I am here, and I don't know how to get there." It hasn't been able to talk realistically about what people are sexually.

I think by focusing on roles in lesbian relationships we can begin to unravel who we really are in bed. When you hide how profoundly roles can shape your sexuality, you can use that as an example of other things that get hidden. There's a lot of different things that shape the way that people respond, some not so easy to see, some more forbidden, as I perceive s/m to be. Like with s/m, when I think of it, I'm frightened. Why? Is it because I might be sexually fascinated with it and I don't know how to accept that? Who am I there? The point is that when you deny that roles, s/m, fantasy, or any sexual differences exist in the first place, you can only come up with neutered sexuality, where everybody's got to be basically the same because anything different puts the element of power and deviation in there and threatens the whole picture.

CM: Exactly. Remember how I told you that growing up what turned me on sexually, at a very early age, had to do with the fantasy of capture, taking a woman, and my identification was with the man, taking? Well, something like that would be so frightening to bring up in a feminist context—fearing people would put it in some sicko sexual box. And yet, the truth is, I do have some real gut-level misgivings about my sexual connection with capture. It might feel very sexy to imagine "taking" a woman, but it has sometimes occurred at the expense of my feeling, sexually, like I can surrender myself, to a woman that is, always needing to be the one in control, calling the shots. It's a very butch trip, and I feel like this can keep me private and protected and can prevent me from fully being able to express myself.

AH: But it's not wrong, in and of itself, to have a capture fantasy. The real question is, Does it actually limit you? For instance, does it allow you to eroticize someone else but never see yourself as erotic? Does it keep you always in control? Does the fantasy force you into a dimension of sexuality that feels very narrow to you? If it causes you to look at your lover in only one light, then you may want to check it out. But if you can't even dream about wanting a woman in this way in the first place, then you can't figure out what is narrow and heterosexist in it and what's just play. After all, it's only one fantasy.

CM: Well, what I think is very dangerous about keeping down such fantasies is that they are forced to stay unconscious. Then, next thing you know, in the actual sexual relationship, you become the capturer; that is, you try to have power over your lover, psychologically or whatever. If the desire for power is so hidden and unacknowledged, it will inevitably surface through manipulation or what have you. If you couldn't play captured, you'd be it.

AH: Part of the problem in talking about sexuality is it's so enormous in our culture that people don't have any genuine sense of dimension. So that when you say *capture,* every fantasy you have ever heard of from Robin Hood to colonialism comes racing into your mind, and all you really maybe wanted to do was have your girlfriend lay you down. But, in feminism, we can't even explore these questions because what they say is, in gender, there is a masculine oppressor and a female oppressee. So whether you might fantasize yourself in a role a man might perform or a woman in reaction to a man, this makes you sick, fucked-up, and you had better go and change it.

If you don't speak of fantasies, they become a kind of amorphous thing that envelops you and hangs over your relationship, and you get terrified by the silence. If you have no way to describe what your desire is and what your fear is, you have no way to negotiate with your lover. And I guarantee you, six months or six years later, the relationship has paid. Things that are kept private and hidden become painful and deformed.

When you say that part of your sexuality has been hooked up with capture, I want to say that absolutely there's a heterosexist part of that, but what part of that is just plain dealing with power, sexually? I don't want to live outside of power in my sexuality, but I don't want to be trapped into a heterosexist concept of power either. But what I feel feminism asks of me is to throw the baby out with the bathwater.

For example, I think the reason butch/femme stuff got hidden within lesbian feminism is because people are profoundly afraid of questions of power in bed. And, though everybody doesn't play out power the way I do, the question of power affects who and how you eroticize your sexual need. And it is absolutely at the bottom of all sexual inquiry. I can't say to you, for instance, I am trying to work through being a femme so I won't have to be one any more.

CM: But what is femme to you? I told you once that what I thought of femme was passive, unassertive, etc. and you didn't fit that image. And you said to me, "Well, change your definition of *femme.*"

AH: My fantasy life is deeply involved in a butch/femme exchange. I never come together with a woman, sexually, outside of those roles. Femme is active, not passive. It's saying to my partner, "Love me enough to let me go where I need to go, and take me there. Don't make me think it through. Give me a way to be so in my body that I don' t have to think, that you can fantasize for the both of us. You map it out. You are in control."

It's hard to talk about things like giving up power without it sounding passive. I am willing to give myself over to a woman equal to her amount of wanting. I expose myself for her to appreciate. I open myself out for her to see what's possible for her to love in me that's female. I want her to respond to it. I may not be doing something active with my body, but more eroticizing her need that I feel in her hands as she touches me.

In the same way, as a butch, you want and conceive of a woman in a certain way. You dress a certain way to attract her, and you put your sexual need within these certain boundaries to communicate that desire. And yet there's a part of me that feels maybe all this is not even a question of roles. Maybe it's much richer territory than that.

CM: Yes, I feel the way I want a woman can be a very profound experience. Remember I told you how when I looked up at my lover's face when I was making love to her (I was actually just kissing her breast at the moment), but when I looked up at her face, I could feel and see how deeply every part of her was present? That every pore in her body was entrusting me to handle her, to take care of her sexual desire. This look on her face is like nothing else. It fills me up. She entrusts me to determine where she'll go sexually. And I honestly feel a power inside me strong enough to heal the deepest wound.

AH: Well, I can't actually see what I look like, but I can feel it in my lover's hands when I look the way you described. When I open myself up more and more to her sensation of wanting a woman, when I eroticize that in her, I feel a kind of ache in my body, but it's not an ache to do something. I can feel a hurt spot and a need, and it's there, and it's just the tip of it, the tip of that desire, and that is what first gets played with, made erotic. It's light and playful. It doesn't commit you to exposing a deeper part of yourself sexually. Then I begin to pick up passion. And the passion isn't butch or femme. It's just passion.

But from this place, if it's working, I begin to imagine myself being the woman that a woman always wanted. That's when I begin to eroticize. That's what I begin to feel from my lover's hands. I begin to fantasize myself becoming more and more female in order to comprehend and meet what I feel happening in her body. I don't want her not to be female to me. Her need is female, but it's *butch* because I am asking her to expose her desire through the movement of her hands on my body, and I'll respond. I want to give up power in response to her need. This can feel profoundly powerful and very unpassive.

A lot of times how I feel it in my body is I feel like I have this fantasy of pulling a woman's hips into my cunt. I can feel the need painfully in another woman's body. I can feel the impact, and I begin to play and respond to that hunger and desire. And I begin to eroticize the fantasy that she can't get enough of me. It makes me want to enflame my body. What it feels like is that I'm in my own veins and I'm sending heat up into my thighs. It's very hot.

CM: Oh, honey, she feels the heat, too.

AH: Yes, and I am making every part of my body accessible to that woman. I completely trust her. There's no place she cannot touch me. My body is literally open to any way she interprets her sexual need. My power is that I know how to read her inside of her own passion. I can hear her. It's like a sexual language; it's a rhythmic language that she uses her hands for. My body is completely in sync with a lover, but I'm not deciding where she's gonna touch me.

CM: But don't you ever fantasize yourself being on the opposite end of that experience?

AH: Well, not exactly in the same way because with butches you can't insist on them giving up their sexual identity. You have to go through that identity to that other place. That's why roles are so significant and you can't throw them out. You have to find a way to use them so you can eventually release your sexuality into other domains that you may feel the role traps you in. But you don't have to throw out the role to explore the sexuality. There are femme ways to orchestrate sexuality. I'm not asking a woman not to be butch. I am asking her to let me express the other part of my own character, where I am actively orchestrating what's happening. I never give up my right to say that I can insist on what happens sexually. Quite often what will happen is I'll simply seduce her. Now, that's very active. The seduction can be very profound, but it's a seduction as a femme.

CM: What comes to my mind is something as simple as you coming over and sitting on her lap. Where a butch, well, she might just go for your throat if she wants you.

AH: Oh yes, different areas for different roles! What's essential is that your attitude doesn't threaten the other person's sexual identity but plays with it. That's what good seduction is all about. I play a lot in that. It's not that I have to have spike heels on in order to fantasize who I am. Now that's just a lot of classist shit, conceiving of femme in such a narrow way.

CM: Well, I would venture to say that some of these dynamics that you're describing happen between most lesbians, only they may both be in the same drag of flannel shirts and jeans. My feeling, however, is—and this is very hard for me—what I described earlier about seeing my lover's face entrusting me like she did, well, I want her to take me to that place, too.

AH: Yes, but you don't want to have to deny your butchness to get there. Right?

CM: Well, that's what's hard. To be butch, to me, is not to be a woman. The classic extreme-butch stereotype is the woman who sexually refuses to allow another woman to touch her. It goes something like this: She doesn't want to feel her femaleness because she thinks of you as the "real" woman and, if she makes love to you, she doesn't have to feel her own body as the object of desire. She can be a kind of "bodiless lover." So when you turn over and want to make love to her and make her feel physically like a woman, then what she is up against is queer. You are a woman making love to her. She feels queerer than anything in that. Get it?

AH: Got it. Whew!

CM: I believe that probably from a very early age the way you conceived of yourself as female has been very different from me. We both have pain, but I think that there is a particular pain attached if you identified yourself as a butch queer from an early age, as I did. I didn't really think of myself as female or male. I thought of myself as this hybrid or something. I just kinda thought of myself as this free agent until I got tits. Then I thought, Oh oh, some problem has occurred here.

For me, the way you conceive of yourself as a woman and the way I am attracted to women sexually reflect that butch/femme exchange where a woman believes herself so woman that it really makes me want her.

But, for me, I feel a lot of pain around the fact that it has been difficult for me to conceive of myself as thoroughly female in that sexual way. So retaining my "butchness" is not exactly my desired goal. Now that, in itself, is probably all heterosexist bullshit about what a woman is supposed to be in the first place, but we are talking about the differences between the way you and I conceive of ourselves as sexual beings.

AH: I think it does make a difference. I would argue that a good femme does not play to the part of you that hates yourself for feeling like a man, but to the part of you that knows you're a woman. Because it's absolutely critical to understand that femmes are *women* to women and *dykes* to men in the straight world. You and I are talkin' girl to girl. We're not talking what I was in straight life.

I was ruthless with men, sexually, around what I felt. It was only with women I couldn't avoid opening up my need to have something more than an orgasm. With a woman, I can't refuse to know that the possibility is just there that she'll reach me some place very deeply each time we make love. That's part of my fear of being a lesbian. I can't refuse that possibility with a woman.

You see, I want you as a woman, not as a man; but I want you in the way you need to be, which may not be traditionally female but which is the area that you express as butch. Here is where in the other world you have suffered the most damage. My feeling is, part of the reason I love to be with butches is because I feel I repair that damage. I make it right to want me that hard. Butches have not been allowed to feel their own desire because that part of butch can be perceived by the straight world as male. I feel I get back my femaleness and give a different definition of femaleness to a butch as a femme. That's what I mean about one of those unexplored territories that goes beyond roles, but goes through roles to get there.

CM: How I fantasize sex roles has been really different for me with different women. I do usually enter into an erotic encounter with a woman from the kind of butch place you described, but I have also felt very ripped off there, finding myself taking all the sexual responsibility. I am seriously attracted to butches sometimes. It's a different dynamic, where the sexuality may not seem as fluid or comprehensible, but I know there's a huge part of me that wants to be handled in the way I described I can handle another woman. I am very compelled toward that "lover" posture. I have never totally reckoned with being the "beloved," and, frankly, I don't know if it takes a butch or a femme or what to get me there. I know that it's a struggle within me and it scares the shit out of me to look at it so directly. I've done this kind of searching emotionally, but to combine sex with it seems like very dangerous stuff.

AH: Well, I think everybody has aspects of roles in their relationships, but I feel pretty out there on the extreme end. I think what feminism did, in its fear of heterosexual control of fantasy, was to say that there was almost no fantasy safe to have where you weren't going to have to give up power or take it. There's no sexual fantasy I can think of that doesn't include some aspect of that. But I feel like I have been forced to give up some of my richest potential sexually in the way feminism has defined what is, and what's not, "politically correct" in the sexual sphere.

CM: Oh, of course, when most feminists talk about sexuality, including lesbianism, they're not talking about *desire*. It is significant to me that I came out only when I met a good feminist, although I knew I was queer since eight or nine. That's only when I'd risk it because I wouldn't have to say it's because I want her. I didn't have to say that when she travels by me, my whole body starts throbbing.

AH: Yes, it's just correct.

CM: It was OK to be with her because we all knew men were really fuckers and there were a lot of "OK" women acknowledging that. Read: white and educated. But that's not why I "came out." How could I say that I wanted women so bad I was gonna die if I didn't get me one soon! You know, I just felt the pull in the hips, right?

AH: Yes, really. Well, the first discussion I ever heard of lesbianism among feminists was: "We've been sex objects to men, and where did it get us? And here when we're just learning how to be friends with other women, you got to go and sexualize it." That's what they said! "Fuck you. Now I have to worry about you looking down my blouse." That's exactly what they meant. It horrified me. "No, no, no," I wanted to say, "that's not me. I promise I'll only look at the sky. Please let me come to a meeting. I'm really OK. I just go to the bars and fuck like a rabbit with women who want me. You know?"

Now, from the onset, how come feminism was so invested in that? They would not examine sexual need with each other except as oppressor-oppressee. Whatever your experience was, you were always the victim. Even if you were the aggressor. So how do dykes fit into that? Dykes who wanted tits, you know?

Now a lot of women have been sexually terrorized, and this makes sense, their needing not to have to deal with explicit sexuality, but they made men out of every sexual dyke. "Oh my God, she wants me, too!"

So it became this really repressive movement where you didn't talk dirty and you didn't want dirty. It really became a bore. So, after meetings, we ran to the bars. You couldn't talk about wanting a woman except very loftily. You couldn't say it hurt at night wanting a woman to touch you. I remember at one meeting breaking down after everybody was talking about being a lesbian very delicately. I began crying. I remember saying, "I can't help it. I just . . . want her. I want to feel her." And everybody forgiving me. It was this atmosphere of me exorcising this crude sexual need for women.

CM: Shit, Amber. I remember being fourteen years old, and there was this girl, a few years older than me, who I had this crush on. And, on the last day of school, I knew I wasn't going to see her for months! We had hugged good-bye, and I went straight home. Going into my bedroom, I got into my unmade bed, and I remember getting the sheets, winding them into a kind of rope, and pulling them up between my legs, and just holding them there under my chin. I just sobbed and sobbed because I knew I couldn't have her, maybe never have a woman to touch. It's just pure need, and it's whole. It's like using sexuality to describe how deeply you need/want intimacy, passion, love.

Most women are not immune from experiencing pain in relation to their sexuality, but certainly lesbians experience a particular pain and oppression. Let us not forget, although feminism would sometimes like us to, that lesbians are oppressed in this world. Possibly, there are some of us who came out through the movement who feel immune to "queer attack," but not the majority of us (no matter when we came out), particularly if you have no economic buffer in this society. If you have enough money and privilege, you can separate yourself from heterosexist oppression. You can be sapphic or something, but you don't have to be queer. It's easier to clean up your act and avoid feeling like a freak if you have a margin in this society because you've got bucks.

The point I am trying to make is that I believe most of us harbor plenty of demons and old hurts inside ourselves around sexuality. I know, for me, that each time I choose to touch another woman, to make love with her, I feel I risk opening up that secret, harbored, vulnerable place. I think that why feminism has been particularly attractive to many "queer" lesbians is that it kept us in a place where we wouldn't have to look at our pain around sexuality any more. Our sisters would just sweep us up into a movement.

AH: Yes, we're not just accusing feminism of silence, but our own participation in that silence has stemmed from our absolute terror of facing that profound sexual need. Period.

There is no doubt in my mind that the feminist movement has radically changed, in an important way, everybody's concept of lesbianism. Everybody across the board. There's not a dyke in the world today (in or out of the bars) who can have the same conversation that she could have had ten years ago. It seeps through the water system or something, you know? Lesbianism is certainly accepted in feminism, but more as a political or intellectual concept. It seems feminism is the last rock of conservatism. It will not be sexualized. It's prudish in that way.

Well, I won't give my sexuality up, and I won't not be a feminist. So I'll build a different movement, but I won't live without either one.

Sometimes, I don't know how to handle how angry I feel about feminism. We may disagree on this. We have been treated in some similar ways, but our relationship to feminism has been different. Mine is a lot longer. I really have taken a lot more shit than you have, specifically around being femme. I have a personal fury. The more I got in touch with how I felt about women, what made me desire and desirable, the more I felt outside the feminist community, and that was just terrifying because, on the one hand, it had given me so much. I loved it. And then I couldn't be who I was. I felt that about class, too. I could describe my feelings about being a woman, but if I described it from my own class, using that language, my experience wasn't valid. I don't know what to do with my anger, particularly around sexuality.

CM: Well, you've gotta be angry. I mean, what you were gonna do is turn off the tape, so we'd have no record of your being mad. What comes out of anger—if you, one woman, can say I have been a sister all these years and you have not helped me, that speaks more to the failure of all that theory and rhetoric than more theory and rhetoric.

AH: Yeah. Remember that night you and me and M. were at the bar and we were talking about roles? She told you later that the reason she had checked out of the conversation was because she knew how much it was hurting me to talk about it. You know, I can't tell you what it meant to me for her to know that. The desperation we all felt at that table talking about sexuality was so great, wanting to be able to understand why we are the way we are sexually.

CM: I know. I remember how at that forum on s/m that happened last spring how that Samois woman came to the front of the room and spoke very plainly and clearly about feeling that through s/m she was really coping with power struggles in a tangible way with her lover. That this time, for once, she wasn't leaving the relationship. I can't write her off. I believed her. I believed she was a woman in struggle. And as feminists, Amber, you and I are interested in struggle.

The Challenge

We would like to suggest that, in terms of dealing with sexual issues both personally and politically, women go back to consciousness-raising groups. We believe that women must create sexual theory in the same way we created feminist theory. We need to simply get together in places where people agree to suspend their sexual values so that all of us can feel free to say what we do sexually or what we want to do or have done to us. We do have fear of using feelings as theory. We do not mean to imply that feelings are everything. They can, however, be used as the beginning to form a movement which can politically deal with sexuality in a broad-based, cross-cultural way.

We believe our racial and class backgrounds have a huge effect in determining how we perceive ourselves sexually. Since we are not a movement that is working-class-dominated or a movement that is Third World, we both hold serious reservations as to how this new consciousness raising will be conceived. In our involvement in a movement largely controlled by white middle-class women, we feel that the values of their cultures (which may be more closely tied to an American-assimilated puritanism) have been pushed down our throats. The question arises then, Whose feelings and whose values will still be considered normative in these consciousness-raising groups? If there is no room for criticism in sexual discussion around race and class issues, we foresee ourselves being gut-checked from the beginning.

We also believe our class and racial backgrounds have a huge effect in determining how we involve ourselves politically. For instance, why is it that it is largely white middle-class women who form the visible leadership in the antiporn movement? This is particularly true in the Bay Area, where the focus is less on actual violence against women and more on sexist ideology and imagery in the media. Why are women of color not particularly visible in this sex-related single-issue movement? It's certainly not because we are not victims of pornography. More working-class and Third World women can be seen actively engaged in sex-related issues that directly affect the life-and-death concerns of women (abortion, sterilization, abuse, health care, welfare, etc.). It's not like we choose this kind of activism because it's an ideologically correct position but because we are the ones pregnant at sixteen (straight and lesbian), whose daughters get pregnant at sixteen, who get left by men without child care, who are self-supporting lesbian mothers with no child care, and who sign forms to have our tubes tied because we can't read English. But these kinds of distinctions between classes and colors of women are seldom absorbed by the feminist movement as it stands to date.

Essentially, we are challenging other women and ourselves to look where we haven't gone (this includes through and beyond our class and color) in order to arrive at a synthesis of sexual thought that originates and develops from our varied backgrounds and experiences. We refuse to be debilitated one more time around sexuality, race, or class.

Desire for the Future

Radical Hope in Passion and Danger

By late 1980 I'd moved to New York City to be with a lover—and almost immediately found myself embroiled in what came to be known as the sex wars. This article was first given as a talk at the infamous Barnard Conference on Sexuality in 1981, at which radical antiporn feminists picketed against my participation. (Others were picketed, too, notably Gayle Rubin, Joan Nestle, Dorothy Allison, and other butch/femme- and s/m-identified lesbians.) This conference would go down in history as the iconic catalyst for polarization between different elements in the feminist movement—the antiporn versus the anticensorship groups; the sexually androgynous feminists versus those of us who came out of the old-gay butch/femme tradition; the "vanilla sex" advocates versus the practitioners of s/m. This is also the first article I ever really sat down to write.

When I was ten, I found a set of Xeroxed pages showing 236 positions for sexual intercourse. Later that day I met three of my girlfriends in the field behind my house and stared at those pictures. It was a solemn, hysterical occasion. We studied those images, desperately trying to understand how anyone could enjoy doing what those pictures suggested. Looking first at a picture, then down at our adolescent bodies, we asked, "Do you suppose he puts it in there?" We were in that field till late afternoon, and when everyone else left, I got sick. I threw up for fifteen minutes. Sex and penetration were horrifying ideas. I knew that one day some man would expect me to be the woman in those pictures. I swore I wouldn't be.

Every time I see pornography or hear a woman describe something she enjoys sexually that I can't imagine liking, I feel myself slipping back to that field to stare at those Xeroxed pages again, and I am struck by the extraordinary price women must pay to explore their own sexual questions, upbringing, and experiences.

(left) Me leaving San Francisco for New York City in 1979–80,
photograph by Honey Lee Cottrell;
(above) me at an early gay pride march in New York City
with Lucy Lloyd;
(below) me and Dorothy Allison in Brooklyn in her
back yard, in 1984

The Hardwick Supreme Court protests
in Washington, D.C., 1987 and my arrest,
photographs © 2000 JEB
(Joan E. Biren)

Esther Newton and me when we were first together, in a shot taken for the Barnard Sexuality Conference booklet that the university tried to confiscate

Esther and me in Cherry Grove (above), and with our dogs

Me in 1992

Me in 1994, taken for POZ *magazine*

*My lover, Jenifer Levin,
photo by David E. Franck*

*Ken Dawson (Executive
Director of* SAGE—*Senior
Action in a Gay
Environment), Eli Zal and
me at a* SAGE *board retreat*

Women in this culture live with sexual fear like an extra skin. Each of us wears it differently depending on our race, class, sexual preference, and community, but from birth we have all been taught our lessons well.

Sexuality is dangerous. It is frightening, unexplored, and threatening. Women enter a discussion of sexuality in many different ways. Our histories and experiences are different; the ways we express those differences (and define them politically) are extremely varied.

Many of us became feminists because of our feelings about sex: because we were dykes or we weren't, because we wanted to do it or we didn't, because we were afraid we liked sex too much or that we didn't enjoy it enough, because we had never been told that desire was something for ourselves before it was an enticement for a partner, because defining our own sexual direction as women was a radical notion.

But, in all our talking about sex, we have continuously focused on that part of our sexuality where we were victims. Our rage, which had given us the courage to examine the terrible penalties attached to being female in this culture, had now trapped us into a singularly victimized perspective. Our horror of what had happened to us made it impossible to acknowledge any response other than fury at the images and acts of sexuality surrounding us.

It is painful to admit that the main focus of our feminist sexual theory has been aimed primarily at pornography, as easy to justify as it is deeply feminine. Good women have always been incensed at smut. Our reaction went far beyond disgust at pornography, at its misogyny or racism; we were also shocked at the very idea of explicit sexual imagery. At heart, our horror at pornography is often horror at sex itself and reflects a lesson all women carry from their earliest childhoods: sex is filthy.

But looking at the danger and damage done us is only a part of coming to terms with sex. We should also begin to look at sexuality itself and at what we mean by words like *desire, passion, craving,* and *need.* Do we think that sex is socially constructed? Is there any element of biology influencing or defining aspects of desire? If we think of sexuality as a combination of language, consciousness, symbolism, pleasure, and motion, then how does that fit with our real lives as sexual women? What do we share in common; why are we each sexually different from one another? Should we attempt to wipe the sexual slate clean and begin again? Could we if we wished to? Do we desire what is forbidden? If the forbidden is connected to taboo, how can we resist oppression without destroying our means to excitement? What is the connection between the erotic and danger, the erotic and comfort? What creates the need to "fuse" temporarily with a partner during sex? What are the options created by imagining a separation between sex and gender? What are the dangers? Is there feminist sex? Should there be?

It is important to keep in mind that we're not discussing sexual abstraction but creating the atmosphere and opportunities for ourselves in bed. Our theories affect the way we feel sex today and shape what we consider talking about with each other as well as what we will go home and try. This discussion will change the sensation of our orgasms as well as the way that women in the future will experience their own sexual feelings. The way each of us was raised lies close to the surface of sexual desires, and the explanations we explore today will have the same effect on the women who follow us.

We will never open up women's futures if we censor the dangerous material of this debate before we have begun. We are in grave peril if we edit out of our analysis all women whose sexual histories do not correspond to a "correct" notion of feminist sex. At this moment, we have gone further than just removing experiences and people that don't fit comfortably within our picture of the sexual universe; we have also attempted to slander and quiet those women whose intellectual ideas disagree with or challenge the prevailing attitudes in the women's movement about sex. Those of us who have helped create a feminist movement in order to resist not only sexual violence against women but also sexual stigma, censorship, and repression, who fought to expand more sexual options for women, have found ourselves outside feminist standards, political integrity, and moral authority and have grown silent in our meetings, consciousness-raising groups, and feminist journals and papers.

How have we gotten to this point? Do we, as feminists, truly believe that pornography is the major issue facing all women at this time? Do we believe that if we managed to wipe it out, many other aspects of our oppression would crumble as well? In the struggle against pornography, are we creating new definitions of sexual sickness and deviance? Who are all the women who don't come gently and don't want to; don't know yet what they like but intend to find out; are the lovers of butch or femme women; who like fucking with men; practice consensual s/M; feel more like faggots than dykes; love dildos, penetration, costumes; like to sweat, talk dirty, see expressions of need sweep across their lovers' faces; are confused and need to experiment with their own tentative ideas of passion; think gay male porn is hot; are into power? Are we creating a political movement that we can no longer belong to if we don't feel our desires fit a model of proper feminist sex?

Feminism has always had trouble expressing the radically different ways that oppressions bear on women, just as it has a terrible time facing the idea of sexual differences among women, straight or gay, working class, Jewish, Third World, young, old, or physically different. It is one thing, for example, to speak of the double or triple oppression of working-class and/or women of color but another to reckon with the actual realities of working life. It may make much more sense to spend eight hours stripping than working in a dry-cleaning plant or as a licensed practical nurse or an office worker taking home $132 a week. Sex work may offer a woman not only more money but a greater sense of power. Contrary to popular middle-class beliefs, working in a peep show is not the end of the world. The sex industry and its surrounding communities are often more socially and economically desirable than the jobs or groups of people that form the alternative.

I have always been more ashamed of having a been a dancer in nightclubs when I've talked about it in feminist circles than I ever felt in my hometown, working-class community. There are many assumptions at work behind feminist expressions of surprise and horror: I must be stupid, or I could have done something better than that; I must have been forced against my will, or I was just too young to know better; I have prefeminist consciousness; I had a terrible family life; I must have hated it; I was trash, and this proved it; and, finally, wasn't I glad I'd been saved?

I hear the sentiments endlessly in the feminist movement, distinctions that confuse the reasons for making different choices and what they mean in women's lives. Sex is not the same for all of us, and a movement that is primarily white and middle class (or includes women who aspire to middle-class values) cannot afford to decide who or how women are made victims in a sexual system built on class and race mythologies equally as damaging and vicious as sexist ones. The Man has many different faces, some of them female and white, and our alliances are not automatic or clear-cut.

Unfortunately, the idea that sexual variation, that difference, could be the key to analyzing sexuality and desire, a way of untying the stubborn knots of a bitterly heterosexist culture, has yet to appear distinctly enough in our theorizing about sexuality. As simple an action as patting somebody's ass may have widely different meanings depending on family, culture, time, race, and expectations. When a woman looks at a picture of a man and a woman fucking, doesn't it matter if she is straight or gay, likes cocks or thinks they're awful, was raised a Catholic in a small town in Minnesota or was the only Gypsy child in her community? Doesn't that have a deep and radical impact on what a woman considers pornographic and what she considers sexy? Or are we to believe that there is a "natural" reaction that all women have to sexually explicit images, one that warns us immediately if and when those images cross the line to lewd?

People fuck differently, feel differently when they do it (or don't), and want sex differently when they feel passion. We live out our class, race, and sex preferences within our desire and map out our unique passions through our varied histories. These are the differences that move the skin, that explode the need inside a cunt and make sex possible. Women are always made to pay on either side of the sexual dialectic. We live terrified of harassment or attack on the street and in our homes, and we live terrified that other people will discover our secret sexual desires. Much is forbidden even to women's imaginations. We are deprived of the most elementary right to create our images of sex. It is a hard truth that far too many women come up blank when they are asked what their sexual fantasies look like. Sexual fantasies are the rightful property of men, romance the solid female terrain. Yet most of our ability to act on our desires rests in the possibility of imagining the feel and smell of the sex we want.

When I was younger, I tried to control my imagination more strictly than my sex life; my mind scared me much more than the actual things I was doing in bed. No one had ever told me that I could explore fantasy without ever going further than dreaming. I really believed that if an image rested at the corners of my mind, giving it center stage would inevitably lead to doing it. So every time I dreamed of fucking fur, not flesh, I was horrified. I worried I might still dream of fucking a man, that I would betray both lesbianism and feminism by dreams of penetration, power, and of being overwhelmed. And I panicked when I thought of my mother (and of this desire for her as my lover) or of the multilayered worlds full of desert islands, baby bottles, whips, pleading voices singing for the right to seduce me, winds that whistled between my thighs. At heart, I was much less afraid of how men might imagine me in a pornographic picture than I was terrified of how I might paint myself inside a sexual drama. In my mind, at least, I wanted, needed, to try everything I could think up, needed to see where my own sexual imaginings would take me, and needed to read and experiment with images and materials that excited or alarmed me. Instead, my terror of the unconscious in my own sexual fantasy life was unremitting. I spent too many years struggling against what I was afraid would surface if I let myself go. It was a deeper closet than the one I had been in before I had come out as a lesbian.

It is a bitter irony to me that I was in my mid-thirties before someone explained to me that I was not what I dreamed, that fantasies had a reality of their own and did not necessarily lead anywhere but back to themselves. I had never understood that I might be deeply fascinated by an idea but not enjoy it at all if I actually tried it, that fantasy could give me a way to picture different aspects of my own growing sexual consciousness (or explore my lover's) without going any further. It would also allow me a freedom unhindered by the limits of my body or the boundaries of my conscience. In my life I need monogamy, but I am free to experiment with an army of lovers in my fantasy. In a particular sexual sequence I may have only one orgasm, but in my mind I am capable of infinite climaxes and paths to satisfaction.

I am often shocked by my own sexual world. It is much denser and more forbidden than I knew. But it is also richer and has helped me find the beginnings of the words that might make sex of the body as complex and satisfying as my dreams of it. It has begun to give me back the sensation in my body that had been lost for years.

By providing a distinction between love and sex, fantasy also allowed me to begin breaking my addiction to romance. As a child, I often dreamed about sex, about being pushed down a hill beside our house, tied to a tree, captured by deep-voiced lovers. (My lovers, as children, often dreamed another thread of this theme, being the girls who grew penises, who became Errol Flynn, the pirate taking the women he desired.) As I began to fear these fantasies, I also began to work with feverish energy to rearrange my sexual dreams into a romantic scenario, the rightful arena of sex of a woman. I did it well. I was "swept off my feet," not captured; held closely to a devoted lover, not bound to her bed; and properly married to anyone I fucked (or at least you could hear their begging for my hand in the background). I filled my dreams with men, trying desperately to organize my fantasies correctly.

I was on the run from my own desires. I was angry and afraid of the feelings that were alive in my body. I felt driven between my wish to be a decent, reasonable woman and an equally powerful wish to throw all my beliefs and upbringing away and explode into my own sexual raving. I thought I would go mad with it. Like women in centuries before me, I feared sexual insanity, feeling that my lusts would lead me further and further from the communities I wished would accept me—middle-class intellectuals, Marxists, and, later, feminists—and into the underworld of passion which would envelop me.

By the time I was seventeen, I had begun to seek out these un-named cravings. Against all precaution, I drove myself into crazier and crazier sexual situations, the more forbidden the better. I was burning up. There has never been a time when I was in more sexual danger than then, a time when I sought to forget my desire and act on it at the same moment. But it is always dangerous to refuse the knowledge of your own acts and wishes, to create a sexual amnesia, to deny how and who you desire, allowing others the power to name it, be its engine or its brake. As long as I lived afraid of what I would discover about my own sexuality and my fantasies, I had always to wait for another person to discover and "give" me the material of my own desires.

Each time we have been afraid of our own desires, we have robbed ourselves of the ability to act. Our collective fear of the dangers of sexuality has forced us into a position where we have created a theory from the body of damage done us. We have marked out a smaller and smaller arena for feminists to be sexual in and fewer actual ways for physical feelings to be considered "correct." By recognizing the dangers of our circumstances, we have said, "There is no way to be a woman in this culture and be sexual, too. I will live first with the anger and then hope we can change enough about the world that the women after me may be safe enough to fuck. For now, it will have to be enough." But this isn't enough, and we know it. We have settled for an easy way out of the terrible problem we face. We have accepted a diminished set of alternatives and become paralyzed by the fear.

But there is another way, a way that's more difficult and demands that we take a riskier stance to define and act on our desires. We can begin to reclaim our rights to fight, to experiment, to demand knowledge and education about sex. We can begin in another spot, saying that there is too much we don't know yet to close any doors that a woman enters to try and capture her sexual feelings. We can say that our sexuality is more complex than the things that have been done to us and that we gain power through our refusal to accept less than we deserve. We can dare to create outrageous visions.

The borders are shrinking, and fewer women feel that they can reconcile their sexual desires with their political beliefs. We must live with the danger of our real desires, give them credit and airing. We must demand better contraception, self-defense classes; decent, non-judgmental sex education; the right to control our bodies and set new boundaries of female experimentation and self-knowledge. Feminism should be seen as a critical edge in the struggle to allow women more room to confront the dangers of desire, not less. By selecting our truths, we have censored the hearts of our own future as sexual people. Every history of desire that we have refused to acknowledge has removed us a step in an attempt to unravel and reclaim the daring of our sexual selves. Each judgment has scaled down our own ability to fuck and our desperate need to explore why we feel the desires we each call our own.

The truth is that our current state of feminist affairs has demanded that women live outside power in sex. We seem to have decided that power in sex is male because it leads to dominance and submission, which are in turn defined as exclusively masculine. Much of our theorizing has suggested that any arousal from power felt by women is simply false consciousness. In real life this forces many feminists to give up sex as they enjoy it and forces an even larger group to go underground with their dreams. For the many women who have no idea what they might eventually want, it means silencing and fearing the unknown aspects of their passions as they begin surfacing. Silence, hiding, fear, shame—these have always been imposed on women so that we would have no knowledge, let alone control, of what we want. Will we now impose these on ourselves?

The assumption that women don't need fantasy is just as devastating to a woman's sense of power and pleasure in sex as assumptions that we don't "need" sex really, only men do. And the idea that the fantasies of women are the same as, or merely derivative or in the service of, male values only serves to belittle our already shaky beliefs about our own sexual importance. No matter how sex is played out or with what gender, power is the heart, not just the beast, of all sexual inquiry.

It is the undertow of desire between my lover and myself that propels me through all the "good" reasons I can invent to stop myself from wanting sex. It is erotic tension that ignites the wildness of my imagination and the daring to figure out how to make my desires feel against the skin as I imagined them beforehand. With these, I let go, finally, to another woman's direction and sexual need for me and find ways to crack through my lover's defenses and push her further. I want to be unafraid to be the erotic person I created in my own fantasies as a twelve-year-old girl, dreaming that someone would at last make me scream because it felt so fine. I want to let go, to compel my desires into an experience of my body that awakens me, satisfies me, finally, and doesn't leave me angry and bitter that yet another woman was too afraid of her own passion to push against mine and see how far we could have gone.

Sometimes I want to play, resist, fight against another woman sexually; sometimes I want to surrender. I can't imagine sex without this. In the end, I don't want to do away with power in sex, like a part of the feminist movement; I want to redistribute that power and knowledge so I can use it (and use it better) for myself and my partner. I think that there is a way to confront sexism and racism within sex without erasing the sources and intensity of our pleasures. Doing it side by side doesn't guarantee that sex is free of any fantasy of power, and refusing to experiment with elements of our desires leaves us all the more terrified of our right to sex and satisfaction.

We must say we want sex and set our own terms. We must build a movement that validates the right of a woman to say yes instead of no, a movement that thinks we haven't heard enough about sex rather than too much and which reclaims an eroticism not defined by a simple political perspective or narrow vision which insists on excluding women to sustain its standards. We are searching for ways to examine sexuality, consent, and power. We want to expand what we understand about sexuality so that more of us can live the desires we envision. We must start from where we are right now, from the real bodies we live in, the real desires we feel.

There are four prerequisites for that possibility: (1) the right to discuss openly the shapes and images of our own desires, recognizing how class, race, and sexual preference influence the scope of the discussion and our conclusions; (2) the right to take sexual risks without also risking our right to a secure place within the feminist community; (3) the need to educate ourselves with the best available information about all aspects of human sexuality and have that material available in our own institutions, bookstores, and community centers; (4) the obligation to use, then go beyond, personal insights and histories to create a body of sexual theories as complex as each one of us.

Feminists must enter the fight again, angrily, passionately. Feminism cannot be the new voice of morality and virtue, leaving behind everyone whose class, race, and desires never fit comfortably into a straight, white, male (or female) world. We cannot afford to build a political movement that engraves the sexual reactions of nineteenth-century bourgeois women onto a twentieth-century struggle.

Instead of pushing our movement further to the right, we should be attempting to create a viable sexual future and a movement powerful enough to defend us simultaneously against sexual abuse. We must demand that our pleasure and need for sexual exploration not be pitted against our need for safety. Feminism is a liberation movement; it needs to fight with that recognition at its center. We cannot build a movement that silences women or attempts to fight sexual abuse isolated from every other aspect of our oppression. And we can never afford to build a movement in which a woman can lose her reputation. Feminism must be an angry, uncompromising movement that is just as insistent about our right to fuck, our right to the beauty of our individual female desires, as it is concerned with the images and structures that distort it. This goal is not an end in itself but a means which will ultimately determine the future and direction of our desires. As feminists, we should seek to create a society limited only by those desires themselves.

The Right to Rebel

This interview was one I did in 1979 for a London journal, The Gay Left, *which at the time was the most important and most widely read gay/radical paper in the world. The editorial staff functioned as a collective that included Jeffrey Weeks, Simon Watney, Philip Derbyshire, and others. Reading it today, I am struck by how young I was when I was doing the interview and how, even then, I was trying to work out what I thought about certain key issues. Whatever it says about my earlier days as a leftist organizer, I remember it now as the first article that brought me out around having been a sex worker. Just before publication I panicked, called Philip, and tried to recant that part of the interview—but it was too late; the thing had already gone to press. I include it here as an early representation of some of my thoughts around how sex and radical politics fit together thematically in my own life.*

PART ONE

I came from a small town in California (Carmichael). I hated it and wanted out, but not into marriage. I heard about the civil rights movement, was exhilarated by it, and wanted to get involved. This was 1964. I was naive in my outrage at the Southern community's reaction to civil rights, but that naive anger is as good a way into struggle as any. I felt that we all had to do something; otherwise nothing would change.

I discovered a real sense of community through that involvement: people were trying to kill us, which brings you together! The black community in the South had already built networks of care and concern, and, by being involved on the margins of that, we whites learned that survival was a matter of taking responsibility for each other.

We worked hard and organized, but there were problems, especially for a white woman in a black community. So many racial myths center on that, and I began to feel that we put the black community in even more danger because of that heterosexual racism. We brought down the wrath of God: we were staying with black families, frequently lovers of black men, and certainly their friends, which was horrific in the eyes of the surrounding white community. The violence was incredible—people trying to shoot you all the time, houses you were staying in getting firebombed. The last straw for me was that the man who was head of the family I was staying with refused to sit down to supper if I was there; he said that he couldn't sit at the same table as white folks, it wasn't done. I freaked; this man would come in from working fourteen hours on some white man's plantation, and he couldn't eat his meal in peace. My being there was doing him no good at all.

So I left Mississippi, went up to New York, and worked with the Student Non-Violent Coordinating Committee (SNCC) there, until whites were expelled as the black movement grew into a consciousness of its own need for autonomy and the idea of black power began to grow. That was extremely painful, a traumatic experience where I was forced to confront the face of being white. Up until then I'd sort of thought that if we could just come to love each other it would be OK. But now people that I loved were telling me to fuck off, that it was no good me spending six months in the South—they had to be there all the time. I was white and could pull out of the struggle at any time.

Most blacks had started out as naive as me, but the toll of the struggle was a growing cynicism, a defensiveness that chimed with the growth of a new black nationalism. I didn't understand that; many of us failed to understand it at all and grew embittered. Those who survived that experience remained politicized, and I was hooked. In the society I'd come from I'd been taught that nothing mattered, nothing was worth fighting for, but through that struggle I'd come to know people who believed in something and who were prepared to act on that belief, the right of people to be equal—which was an extraordinary thought in a racist society. The struggle gave me so much, and, even though I didn't know where to go, I couldn't give up political involvement.

Then, for the first time, whites rebelled in the 1960s. In Berkeley, California, sparked by the struggle for SNCC to have the right to raise money on the university campus, the free speech movement was born. It escalated rapidly, involving students from all backgrounds, and was fueled by the resentments of being in an alienating university. The ideas of the beat movement fed into it, too, and soon the antiwar movement spun out of that explosion.

Again, my first involvement in the free speech and antiwar movements was from a naive perspective. I thought killing was wrong but was horrified when people tried to stop troop trains. But within the movement, politics was serious: people had theories, could articulate strategies and tactics, and were often explicitly Marxist. I started to learn about class, found out what imperialism was, and felt a real commitment to building a movement that would control our government, which lied to us, killed people in our name without taking the trouble to ask us what we thought. It was an exciting time, in which I began for the first time to understand what was happening.

But I was also working class; I wasn't a college dropout, and my parents weren't supporting me. I had to work but kept losing jobs because I was a Red, a Commie, and McCarthyism hadn't run its course. So I began to work as a hooker and led this weird double life—over here I was political, over there I sold my body. Slowly I began to understand the power of men over women, too.

Someone in the Communist Party had explained to me that you didn't have to get married—a shocking idea to me because I thought you didn't get married only if no one asked you. The idea slowly dawned, though, that I could be an independent woman. But then there was the whole deal about how women were supposed to relate to men in the Left. I was a hooker for a living, but I was also prostituting myself to the men in the Left for power and for education. The way you got both in the Left then, if you were like me, not so articulate, a poor farm kid, was by sleeping with the men who had them. You fucked for a book. They didn't even go with me; I wasn't some guy's girlfriend, just some guy's fuck. And there was a push in the Left then on all women to sleep around. Those straight men got a lot! Part of the "new world" we were building was men and women together; you were free with your body unrepressed—basically you had to sleep with anyone who asked you. Otherwise you were called frigid, peculiar, or got kicked out of the movement.

Then there was the division of labor within the movement. Men argued and debated with each other, theorized, and women went out and organized. We went door-to-door and asked housewives what they thought of the war: "Hi, you don't know me, but I'd like to talk to you about the war in Vietnam." The reason women were so good later at organizing our own communities was because we'd learned the skills in the 1960s, while the men were arguing with each other. Slowly I grew to hate men, even while I had to sleep with them, all of them, communally, etc. I didn't want any part of it, but I didn't know how to get out of it. So I went through with it, and it's a dull, meaningless memory now. I was lucky. Some women got destroyed.

Eventually I got pregnant by a draft dodger. I got an abortion but got so sick that I had to leave with him and go up to Canada, where we got married so that we could stay together and he could look after me. That was one of the bitterest times. I became all the things I never wanted to be. I'd lost my connection with the Left, and I was trying to be married. I managed it for nine months and was miserable. But you couldn't talk about it with anyone. I had no sexual knowledge. I kept asking myself, "What's wrong with me?" I couldn't make it with men. I could fuck them for money, but I could have no emotional life with men. I didn't know myself to be a dyke. I was just barren.

So I left my husband, organized a strike at McGill University in Montreal, and began to reclaim my political self. This was about the time (1966) that women's caucuses first began in the Left. I didn't want to know. I'd made a decision that I would never sleep with a man again: I was going for power, for leadership; *I was* going to be a heavy. While I was married I'd read Marx, Engels, Lenin, the lot. I came out of that at least a thinker, if not an intellectual: I was as smart as any man on the Left, and, by God, I was going for the big time. And then these women started caucuses! I didn't want to go to them, but I was persuaded, even though I was not impressed. I hated being a woman, which was a lot of what stopped me from seeing I was a lesbian. I hated what women did: I hated their dependence, their tears. The biggest compliment to me was that I thought like a man. Talking with women made me feel bad, and I didn't want to identify with them. I wanted to identify around men's appreciation of my "masculine" part.

Through the caucuses I began to think about my own contradictions: outside organizations I was a nice person, but inside I was a killer. Then at a conference I was one of eight women who gave a paper on Juliet Mitchell's "Women: The Longest Revolution." At the end of an eight-hour conversation with one of the other women—pow! I left the room with her, and we were together for five years. I fell in love and moved in with her. I came out then, and before the women's movement that's how a lot of women came out. We didn't say we were gay; we said we were in love. We said that women were forming new relationships and that we were a part of that. Women came first.

Slowly many women, leftists and socialists, came to the realization that we had to leave the Left to create a women's movement. It was painful for me. I'd fallen in love with a woman, but I had to leave the Left. It was my revolution, but here I was organizing women, with no relation to Marxism seemingly or to any other struggles (the antiwar movement was at its height). I felt alone, and only being with this woman made it possible. During that period I had to face my own self-hatred, my own oppression of women, but through that I could open up to the possibility of women in my life. Only the strength of the beginning of feminism was enough to confront women as tough as me with how misshapen we'd become: we were committed to the Left, but we were cold. The brand of socialism we had was not enough. It didn't change anyone.

We had to face what women had become. I'd fought for power, and now I realized that it was useless. I was torn. Did we have a right to organize separately? Mitchell's article was crucial; it gave us a theory. And the love of a woman was crucial, too, a love not based on power. Lesbianism is about that.

This woman didn't want me for the power I had, for my status, but for who I was. And she didn't lie about the rotten qualities I had either. There was a quality of honesty which I'd never known before and which women had in their gift. Heterosexuality was all about lies; if you were honest in a relationship, you lost the relationship. Both of us could be honest, not have to play games. She'd been wounded, had been tolerated in the Left by men only because she was brilliant. Tolerated, never liked, and I loved her. Neither of us had had someone love us who'd seen us as we were. I began to open up to being soft in a relationship; she didn't hold it against me. Being caring, nurturing, sensual, was not something I finished up having to pay for. We made a commitment to each other for life.

But, but. Our relationship was in the closet. The women's movement had begun by now (1967), but it hated lesbians. We were suspected, and we had to keep the illusion of separate bedrooms. Despite its militancy, the women's movement was terrified of sexuality. Everyone was being dyke-baited.

We weren't gay, not even to each other. We talked about being in love, what it meant for women to love each other, and we talked about celibacy—we were real big on that! Our relationship was classically closet. An enormous emotional intensity, a primary commitment, and very little sexuality. You can't have it in isolation. But what we needed from another woman was not primarily sexual; ultimately it was a validation of our femaleness, only secondarily sexual, primarily emotional.

It was a rich time, discovering what it was to be women, in our relationship and as part of a wider movement. We wrote papers, organized conferences, and went through the rage that resulted from what men had done to us. It wasn't hard to be without men, for example, SDS leaders who spread clap through the women's community. We were exploring an internal women's life that had been invalidated before. Sometimes we discovered how damaged we'd been, and there was a sadness for parts of yourself that couldn't be brought back to life. We feared that men were so damaged that relations with them were impossible. Radical feminism had emerged by now, but in Canada we maintained an unapologetic Marxism that, however, was not protective of the male Left. We kept race and class consciousness while developing our feminism.

But as dykes—we couldn't be out. The first glimmers of understanding what it was to be in the closet came through the very success of creating a women's culture. We were women together, but I couldn't be with the woman I loved in the way I wanted to be. We'd be invited to parties, but most of the women were straight, and you were meant to dance with men. I wouldn't and stayed in the kitchen and got nasty. Any man could walk up to my lover her and say, "Hey, honey, you wanna fuck?" and walk off with her, but, if I looked at her with any emotion, people treated me as though I was an animal. So we stopped going to parties! We didn't have what you might call a political consciousness of the situation!

Our relationship got more neurotic: we couldn't talk to anyone about it. I finally began to realize that I was gay. I read (surreptitiously) *The Ladder,* from the Daughters of Bilitis. Finally, I said, "We're lesbians, we live together, it's obscene that we should have to hide." Her reply was that, no, never, she was not a lesbian, being a lesbian destroys you. If you have to come out, you do it alone. This was heavy. To be out as gay meant I lost the woman I loved. To keep her I couldn't be who I was. It was intolerable. The few lesbians in the Toronto movement had discovered each other, quietly, "I won't tell on you if you don't tell on me" style, and in 1970 we decided to do a forum on lesbianism and feminism. In it we were all going to come out. I was to come out first since I was part of the leadership, with the hope that it would somehow calm people down enough for the rest. (My girlfriend, of course, was freaking out; if I came out, then who was she?) So we did it. I came out, but nobody else did. Oh, they admitted to fantasizing about women and so on. These were stone dykes! Freak out. Within three weeks, my girlfriend and I had split, and I had left Canada, the women's movement. For what? To be a lesbian, and I knew nothing from lesbian.

It was the pits. I'd left the Left for the women's movement; now I was leaving that for a lesbian movement I wasn't sure existed. I was back in the States, with the craziness of the early 1970s, Weathermen and so on. And I'd lost the woman I still loved. Our relationship had been so important even if it wasn't gay. To be gay you have to be able to look at your partner, know what you're doing, and be glad. We couldn't do that. We weren't proud enough to call ourselves *lesbian.* I was confused; I had a political commitment before I had a real understanding. I had to go through all the vulnerability of discovering lesbianism while still being a politico. And I'd lost the woman who'd been my political partner as well as my lover. It was like being deaf and dumb.

I'd maintained some involvement with mainstream Left politics, working with the Black Panther Party and doing draft counseling, but it wasn't an easy glide back into the United States. I was a lesbian, and I didn't want to face it: lesbianism was harder for me to accept than anything in my life. There's something very lonely about gay self-acceptance—or leastwise there was in that period. Coming out—we were defiant, proud, angry—we wore a lot of lavender, but the self-hate is so deep that it takes you years to work through it, and there's no social movement that removes you from that pain. You love the same sex, which is horrible in heterosexual society. No one can make that easier. For me it's taken years. I hated being gay: I knew I couldn't change it. I knew I wasn't straight, I was gay, but I didn't like it. Hell, I don't like being oppressed. Being gay is not something that you learn. At least if you're black you're raised in a community that explains to you what racism is and how to deal with it. If you're gay, first they try to tell you that it's really not true, then they spend years trying to change you. You just have to hate yourself more than straight folks do. Everything that comes at you tells you it's sick, wrong, perverted, demented. You never get reinforced. And what's this puny little movement? Circle dancing deals with all this? That every straight man wants to kill me because I'm a dyke? Nothing deals with that.

I wasn't happy. I felt outside the lesbian movement: I was working class. I wasn't comfortable with middle-class assumptions that gay was good. I felt that gay was right, I was defiant, but I had an enormous amount of self-hate. I was socially conscious, I felt I had a right to be gay, but in bed, alone at night, I did not like being a lesbian. I kept saying, "I can't help it," and felt that I was going to be alone, without a stable relationship. Even being a Communist you feel normal. Being a lesbian, though—through and through you're abnormal, or that's what they tell you and what you believe.

I left Boston, came to San Francisco. I knew that if I was going to find an answer, it was going to be here. San Francisco has a diversity: there are working-class lesbian bars, something I'd not known. There are so many different ways to work out who you are within the definition of *gay*. There are all races, ages, types of lesbians, and there's a strong women's movement here, too. I was also coming home. And I've been here seven years. San Francisco allows you to be a whole lot of things without hating yourself. I feel that I've worked through that self-hatred. I've accepted my lesbianism and also feel that I have some control: my lesbianism isn't some alien thing apart from me. I feel I've reconnected to who I am as a Marxist, a lesbian, and a feminist.

Ultimately, "the revolution will come when I go to a party and be all the things I am" [Pat Parker]. Contradictions are there, but I feel I am more whole. San Francisco gives that to many gay people. It gives you a community to work through who you are and who you want to be.

PART TWO

When I came to San Francisco in 1972, the lesbian community was pretty submerged. It thrived in the space between the gay male community and the black community. But there was a space; San Francisco had always had large communities of black, Chinese, and Latino peoples, a thriving women's movement, and a large Left focused more around working-class struggles than around the war.

The gay male community centered on Polk Street was seedy, flashy, and almost a parody. The Castro was a quiet, residential district. I was removed from it, having a more or less separatist position, although feminism in that form was beginning to fall apart from class contradictions, and I was beginning to feel uncomfortable with that brand of feminism. My lovers were coming out of the bars, not from the movement. There was a contradiction in that I hadn't come to lesbianism as a political alternative. I feel my own history as somewhere between old and new dyke lifestyles. Old dykes were lesbians in isolation—they figured out that they loved women, and that was that. New dykes came out on the upsurge of feminism. A third group, to which I belong, connects to both parts; we were dykes before the lesbian movement but were political as well.

My political confusions began to resolve themselves when I began to work in the gay caucus in the organizing committee for the July 4th anti-bicentennial in 1975–76. I chose to work in the gay caucus as opposed to the women's caucus, a moderately scandalous choice. I was the only woman with eleven gay men, mostly political white gay men. My experience with them was good. It gave me a sense that there were men committed to struggles against sexism, men who were as moved by feminism, in their own way, as I had been. Not men who were guilty about being men, about being oppressors, but men who were moved by the idea of a new way to be men. I hadn't met men like them before; I'd met gentle straight men but wasn't convinced. I hadn't met men before who passionately identified with parts of feminism as their own. I got a real sense of feminism reaching out beyond women, and touching and changing men and how they wanted to be, and impelling them to work against sexism. Feminism was bridging gaps between lesbians and gay men, and I began to spend more time in the Castro, and, though the faggot lifestyle there was alien, it wasn't threatening.

Then the attacks started, and lesbians and gay men started to come together. First, Richard Hillsboro was murdered, and the Anita Bryant thing started. There was a changing wind in the country. Harvey Milk was elected, but he was virtually the only out gay official, proud to be a faggot and a progressive. As the repression increased there was an explosion of gay life that was more positive. People fled to San Francisco trying to figure out what being gay was all about, but with a consciousness that homosexuality was being threatened. The city wasn't a Mecca, and we had consciously to see that we were being attacked and that unless we fought back we weren't going to survive. Lesbians knew that before gay men, and Lesbian School Workers formed as an organization knowing where the attacks would come. The lesbian community by now was the biggest in the United States, and it was a deeply politically conscious community.

And Bay Area Gay Liberation existed, which was a socialist, primarily faggot organization that set the tone of the struggle, maintaining links between the gay male community and the Third World communities. There was a model for coming together and taking up sexism and racism. The Castro area exploded and is now the gay capital of the United States. It reflects a new way of being out, proud, defiant, very sexual and cruisy for gay men. For men it's very butch and raises a finger at all the straight stereotypes. As the street evolved, lesbians were often unsure about how they fitted in, but at least we were not hassled: it was OK to be gay and hence OK to be dykes. It isn't enough, but it's not tiny.

The change was the Briggs Initiative. It was an explicitly political struggle. The gay Left gave a lead, didn't trail behind. The liberal strategy was exposed for what it was — a cop-out. Conservative gay men argued that gay people should go back in the closet and straight people should do the advertising and so on, that being gay wasn't really different, only a matter of sexual choice.

The whole strategy was overturned, and issues of homophobia were debated. Before that, every campaign that had been fought in the United States had adopted that liberal strategy, and we'd lost every time—in Eugene, in Dade County, in Minneapolis. Everyone knows that being gay is different. If we were afraid to confront our own fears, we couldn't face others'. And we had no answer. If someone asked, "Don't you want to recruit children?" we'd say "*No*, we don't want anyone to be gay"; but of course we did. We wanted other people to be gay because we were glad to be gay. We had to confront the repressive notion of recruitment, but we couldn't dodge the real issue. Bryant and Briggs said that if we can take them on in California and win, we can win anywhere. We knew then that if we lost, we lost everywhere. It was frightening, a statewide confrontation. California is huge, a rural farm state. Farmers vote here; agribusiness controls things here. Doing publicity meant going to small farm towns, facing very conservative working people. We figured that, even if we lost, if we told the truth, we'd convince enough people that we could fight back some time and win.

In the face of the repression we became very gay to each other: we didn't know if we'd make it, and the only people you could trust were other gay people. It changed the Castro; we were being filmed, photographed, interviewed, asked questions all the time, and we had to think, to come to see each other and the street, the community, as survival. You couldn't trust straights, no movie stars flocked to our banner, no active liberal support would run the risk of being called *dyke* or *faggot*. All the other campaigns had lost because they'd relied on getting the liberal vote out and it hadn't come through; they hadn't gone into working-class communities and tried to change people's minds. We went to the farmers, to the union locals, to the schools, to the hospitals, to the child-care units, all the places we hadn't been before, and we came out and forced people to think.

Gay people who'd never been political before took amazing risks — everybody took three steps further out. If you weren't out, you came out; if you were out to three people, you came out to three more; and so on. It changed our community because we began to respect each other; we were militant, fought and defended each other. The specific people whom Briggs named—his accusations blew up in his face. For example, Larry Brenner, a schoolteacher in Healsburg, a tiny town in California. Larry's fifty, a schoolteacher of thirty years' standing, a Communist, and also a well-known and respected member of the town. When Briggs attacked him, Larry was well grounded in the community, very out, was proud of being gay and got a lot of support, and Briggs was discredited there. And it was the same everywhere. Gay people started taking care of their own people, their own community, saying, "We've had enough. We're gay, we have a right be gay, and if you can't take it, that's your problem."

And we won, won in every single area of the state where we went and did work. We won because we came out and the community was politicized. A huge number of gay organizations sprang up, it was a real flowering of the movement. Lesbians and gay men worked together and created a renaissance of gay life in San Francisco. Two thousand people stood in line for a film benefit for the "No on 6" campaign. Everyone took literature and used it. If you used traditional political methods, you didn't understand the significance of what was happening. People went out where they had to confront homophobia in their own lives—not going to meetings. Telling your mother, talking to the bus driver on the way to work. No one knows how many people did things and told no one, took no credit, just acted in their own lives. We won, and we created a self-conscious community in San Francisco, lesbians and gay men with a different level of respect for each other.

Then Harvey Milk was killed.

He was important, a faggot, proud, and a socialist. For Harvey to be killed by a man who was the epitome of a homophobe—white working class, ex-cop, family man, and a Christian—was too much. In San Francisco, where it was wonderful to be gay, where you came because you couldn't be gay anywhere else, what did they do? They murdered one of us. We were none of us safe. The murder forced people to confront the ugliness of homophobia. Under our noses Harvey was killed by someone who felt he was safe to do that in San Francisco. And ultimately he was proved correct—he got six and a half years.

That action, on top of the sense of community that we'd built during Briggs, galvanized the community. It was dramatic, if unstated. If they could get Harvey, then we were next. Forty thousand people marched on the night of his murder; two hours after his death, they marched to City Hall to mourn him. Everyone knew it could be them. When Dan White was found guilty and given such a light sentence, it was intolerable. That night we rioted.

The day after the riot was amazing. If you catch a bus, normally you're nervous if you look gay, wondering who's going to jump you, who's going to sneer. The first thing next day I got on the bus, went to the back, and there's these two black kids, sitting there. One said, "Are you a dyke?" I said, "Yeah, so what?" and this kid said, "Hey, you people are ok; you know how to kick ass. I didn't know dykes and faggots could do that." For a couple of weeks gay people knew each other and just grinned at each other. And other people responded. Even people who felt unsure about that kind of violence, somewhere they thought we were right, were proud we hadn't taken it one more time. We had the right to be that angry, we felt we had the right, and feeling that makes being gay a whole different thing. We don't have to die to be gay; they don't have the right to kill us. The gay community too often doesn't resist; and doesn't respect the gay people who do. Sometimes we are our own worst censors. But not this time. Fifteen thousand rioting queers at City Hall: we didn't burn down our own ghetto; we went to where the power was, and we burned that. Which was why they were terrified and why we weren't murdered. If we'd stayed in the Castro, they'd have machine-gunned us. But they didn't want a massacre on their property; it's a different thing from killing people in their own ghetto, separate, where no one sees it and it can be forgotten. Gay people moved from the Castro and said, "You can't keep us home, just let us be gay there; we're coming here because you're here, straight San Francisco."

The violent reaction we had to that violence also changed the community. People said, "Fuck that! They can't do this. We're gay, but we're not going back. We're going to be gayer than ever before, we're going to be queerer, more militant; we're going to take self-defense lessons. We're gonna kick ass! You can't push us any more." "We're going to be gay everywhere; we're not going back." It was the first riot by white folks. It was a revolutionary act by fifteen thousand gay people. It transformed the expectations externally about what the gay community is like, and it has transformed us: we have a different sense of how we're gay in this town. Not only gayer in the Castro, but gayer everywhere. And that's a nice place to start from.

Talking Sex

A Conversation on Sexuality and Feminism

This article — a conversation, really, between a straight woman and two lesbians — was done in 1980 and first published in Socialist Review *in 1981. By that time, the public feminist dialogue on sex in our culture had degenerated — more or less collapsed, I think — into forever being contextualized against the background of "pornography." In this conversation, though, we talked openly about why exploring all sexuality remained important, why it was important to examine all aspects of issues like porn, and why all women on the Left and in the women's movement needed to openly take these issues on.*

THE CONVERSATION
Deirdre English, Amber Hollibaugh, and Gayle Rubin

DEIRDRE ENGLISH: Feminist discussions of sex seem to take place in a vacuum. We often ignore some of the extreme changes going on in society as people react to the ideas of sexual freedom and of equality of the sexes. Those reactions are highly charged, whether positive or negative, and their intensity has often intimidated us. I would go so far as to say that, on the whole, the women's movement is not as far-sighted as some of the more progressive areas in the field of sex research, where psychologists have really come to grips with people's emotions and behavior. They have learned through their practices not to be threatened by the sexual realm; they have developed an acceptance of fantasy, an acceptance of women's sexuality and of diverse forms of sexual expression.

GAYLE RUBIN: You're right. There is certainly a branch of the sex field that is progressive. Many women, even feminists, even dykes, work in that field. Instead of assuming that sex is guilty until proven innocent, these people assume that sex is fundamentally OK until proven bad. And that idea has not penetrated either the women's movement or the Left. Some feminists cannot digest the concept of benign sexual variation. Instead of realizing that human beings are not all the same, that variation is OK, the women's movement has created a new standard. This is like the old psychiatric concept, that dictates a "normal" way to do it. Male/female, heterosexual, married, man on top, reproductive sex was OK. But all other behavior was measured against that standard and found wanting.

DE: The old idea of malignant variation was in the service of a particular kind of social structure, the patriarchal heterosexual structure. But I think that some feminists also have a concept of sexuality in service to society.

AMBER HOLLIBAUGH: The notion that sex has no right to exist for itself, that sex is good or bad only in terms of social relations.

DE: Right. And, at worst, this feminist vision would bar some forms of sexual expression. One of the first things it would probably get rid of is heterosexuality. The man on top, heterosexual, reproductive.

GR: That for sure will not be permitted after the revolution.

AH: No one will want it, you see! These things are all imposed by sexist male domination and patriarchy, which has brainwashed us from childhood into believing that our bodies are driven to this, in spite of the terrifically healthy erotic desires which would bloom in a new, revolutionary society. That's hogwash. My fantasy life has been constructed in a great variety of ways. My sexual desire has been channeled. But what that view takes from me is my right to genuinely feel, in my body, what I want.

What it says is that I have no notion of healthy sexuality and that anything sexual now is unhealthy and contaminated because of the culture I live in. So that the notion of pleasure in sex is now a forbidden one, it's a contradiction in terms. The theory is that lesbianism comes the closest to being a profemale sexuality because it's two women together. However, when you acknowledge power between women, that you would like to be dominated by or dominate another woman in a sexual exchange, that you'll lust after her if you put passion and sexual power into the lesbian description rather than Cinderella, lesbian Cinderellaism, you are told that you have a heterosexual model for your lesbian sexuality, you have leftover penetration fantasies you really should reexamine. There's never been anything in that rap about sex that has much joy, pleasure, power, or lustiness.

GR: I don't think there has been a feminist discussion of sex. And that's not just the fault of the women's movement. People don't utilize the best analysis of progressive sex research because they don't really know about it. I firmly believe that sexuality is not natural, not an unchanging, ahistorical item in the human repertoire of behavior. Which means that, after the revolution, in utopia, it would obviously be different. However, that idea, that sex will change if social reality changes, is confused in a peculiar and perhaps fundamentally Christian way. The idea of sex after the revolution is so removed from anything that we now do that it transcends the flesh itself. It becomes an absence of anything that we do now, all of which is contaminated by this earthly, fleshy existence. So *"sex after the revolution"* becomes a transcendent image of celestial delight.

When we talk about how work will change, we don't say work will disappear. We talk about how what people do will be different, how social relations will be different, but we don't therefore condemn what everybody does now and say that they are bad people for doing it. We treat sex as a special case at almost every point. And we use different standards to judge it.

The late 1960s and early 1970s saw the so-called sexual revolution. Women like me felt that it hadn't worked because it was male dominated, but we still wanted it in a nonsexist way. Other women said, It's male dominated, it hasn't worked for women, and it won't. And we don't want anything to do with it. So basically the people who don't want anything to do with a sexual revolution are now defining the discourse around sex, rather than those of us who want to have some kind of sexual liberation that is not sexist.

Yet this sexual revolution was only a liberalization, so of course it didn't do what we wanted. People's standards for what should have happened are based on the assumption that this was the revolution. It's saying that socialism will never work, look at the Soviet Union.

DE: It's very popular now to say that the sexual revolution of the 1960s was incredibly oppressive to women, that it was just a male-dominated thing. That's too simple. My recollection of it is that it was not an unmitigated disaster. The sexism was there, but women were actually having more sexual experience of different kinds and enjoying it. Women were having more sex that was not procreational and claiming the right to it as well as paying a lower social and emotional cost. There were obstacles, and many women were disappointed. They were often disappointed by the nature of the sexuality that they found with men. That's not too surprising, historically. But the raised sexual expectations created enormous social and sexual gains for women. There was a fresh, post-Victorian discovery of the female orgasm. Many women were actually able to change the way that men made love with them as well as the way they made love with men. Not enough, but there were dramatic changes. Women were fighting for sexual rights and often getting them.

AH: We forget that, ten or twelve years ago, you were a strident ball-buster if you were a woman who was sexually self-defined, who said what she wanted and sought her own partners, who perhaps was not heterosexual. It was not very long ago that the notion of being sexual and being female was outrageous. Part of my attraction to feminism involved that right to be a sexual person. I'm not sure where that history got lost.

DE: We didn't win. We made great gains, but we had enormous losses. Now we're in a period in which a lot of women are looking only at the losses and are saying, Give up, back to square one, better sexual expression. But can't we have a nonsexist sexual liberation? Can't we still go for that?

AH: Marxism hasn't taken sexuality very seriously. It's not only that feminism doesn't take it seriously, but most progressive movements have been very unprogressive about sexuality, and we've inherited that tradition. When we analyzed sexism, we found it hard to separate sex and pleasure from sexism and didn't realize until fairly recently how to use Marxist tools to help look at sexuality in a historical perspective. The Left shares responsibility for the vacuum in sexual theory that the feminist movement has needed to fill. Sexuality has not been thought of as a central part of human life. It has even been thought to be frivolous. Or the Left has been sexually repressive. Lenin said that if women were not monogamous, for the man it was like drinking out of someone else's glass.

GR: I thought all the questions that weren't answered for me in the Left would be answered in the women's movement. In 1968, compared to the Left, the women's movement had everything to say about sex. Not just about gender, but about sex. It's only become clear more recently that feminist theory, although it talks about sex, it mostly talks in terms of gender and gender hierarchy and the relationships between men and women. It doesn't really have a language for sexual desire and wants. Feminist concepts and Marxist concepts are indispensable for dealing with sex. But you have to deal with sex and not assume that if you're talking about class or gender or romance, you're talking about sex.

Lesbianism and Heterosexuality

DE: What you're saying might not be true if the women's movement had not been willing to make women feel guilty about heterosexuality.

GR: What happened around lesbianism is interesting and complicated. Suddenly some of us could go out and be sexual without dealing with sexism and men. And that changed the issues that we faced. Many of us became lesbians in a quest for greater and better sexual experience. And other people became lesbians to get away from sex. Both a seeking of sex and a running from it got involved in early lesbian theory and practice.

AH: Are you thinking about "The Woman-Identified Woman"? [a piece written by a collective called Radicalesbians].

GR: Yes, around 1970, the "Woman-Identified Woman" paper basically argued, in the popular phraseology, that feminism was the theory and lesbianism the practice.

AH: That all women were lesbians or potential lesbians.

GR: And that to be a lesbian was to revolt against patriarchy. All of which made sense.

DE: Therefore, heterosexuals are what? Deviants?

AH: Heterosexuality was an imposed system that women suffered from. But all women—if they only knew it—were woman identified. The lesbian in all of us was closer to the surface in some of us and bubbled forth, while in other people it was silent.

GR: Lesbianism at that time was presented as the oppressed getting together, as if women were the proletariat getting together to relate to each other instead of to the oppressor. At the time it seemed to justify the lesbian experience pretty well, though it didn't account for male homosexuals. Yet it made heterosexual feminists into second-class citizens and created a decade of problems for heterosexual women in the radical women's movement. In retrospect, I think it also abused lesbians. By conflating lesbianism—which I think of as a sexual and erotic experience—with feminism—a political philosophy—the ability to justify lesbianism on grounds other than feminism dropped out of the discourse. If you recognized that it was OK to be a dyke whether or not it was politically correct, that the basic lust itself was legitimate—correct, that the basic lust itself was legitimate—then at some level you had to recognize that other people's basic lust, no matter how it looked in an oppressive time, was also legitimate. And people didn't want to do that. In defining both heterosexuality and lesbianism in terms of one's relationships to patriarchy, the erotic experience dropped out. Definitions of sexual orientation became completely unsexual. And so no one has really had to think explicitly about the erotic components of anybody's sexual orientation for ten years. And this has led to a new hierarchy of what's OK. First, it was that lesbians were better than straight women. And now it turns out that some lesbians are better than other lesbians and some straight women can be permitted to be political lesbians but not others. We now have replaced the old psychiatric view of what's permissible and nonpermissible in sexual behavior with a new hierarchy based on the notion that lesbianism somehow is exempt from the patriarchy. What angers me most about this is the assumption that lesbianism is not a social construct. The fact is that lesbianism is as much a social construct of the current system as anyone else's sexuality. It has a different, specific relationship to the system as a whole. Everything does. But lesbianism relies on aspects of the system as it is. For instance, the sense of lesbianism being a rebellious sexuality is predicated on male supremacy. If men did not oppress women, that valence would presumably be gone from lesbianism.

AH: Parts of the feminist movement basically said that sexuality really wasn't very important and other kinds of relationships had to take priority. Lusting in whatever form was unacceptable. The lesbian was not supposed to be any lustier than the heterosexual woman, and the heterosexual woman was not to be sexual at all. As a lesbian who was a lesbian before the feminist movement, with a lover in the closet, I was told that we couldn't go to women's conferences and stay in the same bedroom, that we were not allowed to show physical desire for each other in public, and that we were not to dance together in any particularly heavy sexual way. We were asked to leave some parts of the women's movement if we were sexual with each other because women had been terrorized by sexuality and were sick of it. Our dirty sex lives were no better than anybody else's, especially since there was no way to keep us out.

DE: Let's talk about heterosexual women and their acceptance of this theory. I find it fascinating and almost funny that so many hetero-sexual feminists, especially in the socialist movement, seemed to ac-cept the idea that heterosexuality meant cooperating in their own op-pression and that there was something wrong with being sexually turned on to men. How many times have I heard this? "Well, unfor-tunately, I'm not a lesbian, but I wish I was, maybe I will be."

AH: "I'm a lesbian in my mind. But I'm still a heterosexual in my body."

GR: The mind is willing, but the flesh is weak.

DE: "And so, for reasons I cannot explain, unfortunately, except for my patriarchal conditioning, I have sex with this man every night."

AH: In the dark, though, in the dark.

DE: "But never mind. I'll never discuss the pleasure I get from it. I'll never raise that; I'll never ask for that to be legitimate. I know it's ille-gitimate and I'm guilty!"

How did it serve heterosexual feminists to adopt a theory that was—on the surface—so self-denying? Partly it was a relief to be able to consider themselves deviant. With heterosexual desire itself, I can see no criticism. But heterosexuality does give you access to privileges that lesbian women or women not associated with men do not have. The feminist understanding of how women are protected by their alliance with men is valid.

I think it was convenient for heterosexuals to be able to feel guilty for this trait, which was advantageous to them and allied them with powerful men, while still being considered a deviant—and not having to change anything. That much is perhaps ironically amusing. But it doesn't advance our thinking, and it doesn't provide honest emotional support to anyone—female, male, straight, or gay. And, for some women, guilt over heterosexual relations sometimes also fed a sad and bitter sexual self-denial.

AH: Maybe some of the confusion about lesbianism and sexuality occurred when lesbianism began to be the model for describing good sex. Everybody, heterosexual or homosexual, used it to describe non-genitally organized sexual experience. That was a way to reject men fucking for a minute and a half and pulling out, a way to talk about non-missionary-position sexuality, foreplay as all-play. The description of lesbian-feminist sexuality actually resembles a feminist description of what good sex is supposed to be more than a description of lesbian sex. And all women in the feminist movement were trying to make love the way dykes were supposed to.

GR: But it's turned the other way now; now sex has to occur in a certain way for it to be good. And the only legitimate sex is very limited. It's not focused on orgasm, it's very gentle, and it takes place in the context of a long-term, caring relationship. It's the missionary position of the women's movement.

Violence against Women

AH: Categories that needed careful exploration—romance, long-term relationships, sex, sexism—a whole variety of things have all got thrown into the same washing machine, and this very odd-colored garment came out. If you combine incorrectly, then you can't do anything within that discussion. That's what I feel about the way questions get raised by the antiporn movement. I don't even want to try and answer those wrong questions, even though the issue is crucial. The issue is taken from us if we question any of the objects of struggle. For instance, if you question pornography's ability to turn out masses of rapists, it is assumed that you are encouraging rape. You have no right to make sexual violence against women your issue. To people like Susan Brownmiller and Andrea Dworkin, pornography and violence against women are seen as absolutely, intimately linked.

DE: I find myself wondering what the purpose of the antiporn movement is in its own terms. Of course, I'm against violence against women. But I don't feel that I can express my politics toward the violence against women because the only form in which a politics opposed to violence against women is being expressed is antisexual. I'd like to take back the night, and I'd like to go on those marches, and if it's a march through dark and dangerous areas of town, I find that easy to do. But if it's a march through the porn district, then I experience it very much as being directed against the women who work in those districts and as an unnecessary attack on a small zone of some sexual freedom. One thing that became clear to me in writing an article on pornography and working on the porn issue at *Mother Jones* magazine is that the issue pushes people's buttons. They polarize and go to their corners very fast. They're scared of each other and scared of what's really being said. If you criticize the feminist antiporn movement, you very quickly get accused of calling those women prudes. Or you get accused of defending pornography or getting off on pornography, and therefore there's something wrong with you. It's difficult even to create a clearing in which we can have a conversation. I think women are almost at a panic point about violence all the time and are in a place where we are willing to make terrible bargains. We will do anything to be rid of that terror.

AH: When I heard Andrea Dworkin speak, she named my relationship, as a feminist, to porn as a form of being raped. I wanted to say, "Do anything to me, but let me still be alive at the end." I had to smash pornography because, if I didn't, it would take my life. It was not one more position I should understand and debate as a feminist but a life-and-death issue. I went to an antiporn conference because I was very confused about my own position. At the workshops I heard some of the most reactionary politics I've ever heard about how we had to smash pornography and save the family. In fact, it was a radical Right critique, much more so than a Left.

GR: We're all terrorized about a range of possible ways that violence is done to us, whether it's rape or being beat up on the streets or whatever. We're all in the state of severe intimidation, and that's a very powerful and strong feeling. The other strong feeling that is involved is disgust and horror at explicit images of sex. Those images can call up disgust and repulsion in people—especially women—who are not familiar with them. What the antiporn movement has done is to take those very powerful feelings around sex and link them to very powerful feelings around violence and sexual abuse and say it's all the same subject.

We all agree about the problem. We don't agree about the solution —would ending porn have an appreciable effect on rape and violence and abuse? But these connections have been foisted on the movement in a really unprecedented way. I have never seen a position become dogma with so little debate, with so little examination of its possible ramifications or of other perspectives. One reason is that anyone who has tried to raise other issues and who has questioned this analysis has been trashed very quickly as antifeminist or personally attacked. This has also affected the better parts of the Left that of course want to be profeminist.

DE: One of the things women have been taught to help repress us sexually is that, if you begin to deal with sexuality at all, if you begin to become explicit, then you will pay the price of unleashing and stimulating male violence. Once you permit yourself to be perceived as a sexual creature, then you become open territory, open prey. Actual sexual violence oppresses us. But the climate of fear we live in also oppresses us horribly and makes us feel that we cannot afford to take any risks to discover our own sexuality and to be experimental in any way.

GR: Let's look back at what we thought that threat was when we were growing up. Part of the problem is that sex itself is seen as dangerous and violent. It is predicated on a Victorian model of the distribution of libido in terms of male and female. There was the good woman who was not sexual. There is the man who is sexual. So, whenever sex happens between a good woman and a man, it's a kind of violation of her. It's something she doesn't want. The good woman, you know, doesn't move. Her husband, of course, is more of an animal, so he gets off. If you were a good woman and had sex, terrible things might happen to you; good women who had sex out of wedlock became bad women. They fell and became prostitutes, and they were excluded from the comforts of family and home.

This model imposes a moral discourse over a class analysis of who is really doing what sexually. Because the women who were by and large hooking in Victorian England were poor women. And the women who were able to maintain their purity were middle-class women or well-to-do women. And this model scares women into being sexually repressed and gives women the idea (especially respectable women) that sex itself is violence.

AH: It was terrifying that there was so little birth control, which added another element of fear to sex.

GR: I'm not denying that there was a semirational basis for these views. But I am saying that the notion that sex itself is violent is very much with us. The woman who raised me was raised by a Victorian. We're not that far away from that system. And you have to remember that, in the nineteenth century, great social resources were expended trying to eliminate masturbation under the theory that masturbation caused insanity, disease, and degeneration.

DE: We live in such a strange, transitional time that we bear the marks —we women—of extreme sexual repression, total lack of images of women being motivated by sexual desire. Even predatory women in the movies are motivated by romance, or romantic pathology. But there are few images of healthy, assertive sexuality or lust. Yet at the same time we no longer want to be sexually repressed.

GR: There's a geography of access to certain kinds of sexual and erotic experience. I wouldn't call them liberated zones because they're not. But there really are zones of more and less freedom. For instance, there is the gay community. There are the porn districts, which provide people with a range of experiences they can't get in a suburban family. Part of what the politics of sex is about is respectable society trying to keep those other sectors at bay, keeping them impoverished, keeping the people in them harassed, not letting people know they are there, and generally making sure that they are marginal. That permits an enormous amount of exploitation of the people in them. One of the reasons why women in the sex industry are exploited is because of the police and social pressure on the industry. It means the people in the industry do not have unions, they don't have police protection, and they can't organize to improve the conditions of their work.

Part of the problem is that we use different standards when we talk about sex than we do for almost any other aspect of life. Whatever your analysis of commodities, people are not upset that we have to go and get food. People are upset at the structure of the organizations that provide and produce the food, but the need for food itself is OK. We don't feel that way about sex. We also feel that it's OK to exchange food for some other service. But, when we think about sex, we think that any social exchange of sex is bad other than a romantic one. I don't think this is either a socialist or a feminist idea. I think it's either a Christian or a Victorian idea.

AH: There's an assumption that pornography is only for men and that there is no female counterpart. But that's not true. A recent article argues that there is a female counterpart, in Harlequin romances. This is my experience. I grew up reading those books; I still read them. These were unacceptable for women—romance books where it took 89 pages for a reluctant first kiss and another 120 to get married and a fade-out. The endless pages of tingling skins and the desire to bruise the mouth have never been described as porn. But that's really what they are.

GR: Well, they are, and they aren't. They're turn-on literature for women, but there's no explicit sex in them. They are not literally pornographic in that sense.

AH: But they are a sexual literature.

GR: Yes, and one of the interesting things about them in terms of the antiporn analysis is that the social relations in the Harlequins and the Gothic novels display a basic sexism unparalleled in the culture. There's always a very strong man who sweeps this woman off her feet, and through romance the gender hierarchy is reproduced. Yet I have seen no one marching in the streets to ban the neo-Gothic novel.

DE: I think that the antiporn movement would say that that's OK because they're harmless, that feminists only oppose materials that provoke violence against women.

AH: I could make a strong argument for the potential violence of Harlequin romances around gender and roles.

GR: I think those novels help teach women a structure of fantasy that enables them to participate in unequal social relationships. One response might then be, Well, those novels have to be exchanged, too. What's interesting is that the question of the social reproduction of the emotional and erotic components of gender hierarchy is reduced to the question of sexual materials. Much of the argument against porn says that what's wrong with it is the bad social relations in it. But since there are equally bad social relations in a whole range of other forms, what distinguishes porn from the other media is mainly that it is the explicitly sexual medium.

AH: Absolutely. In the history of women's sexual experiences from the Victorian era, love has been women's sphere, and men's has been sex. So I don't think it's an accident that Harlequin romances are not sexually explicit but create a romantic fantasy life for women while *Hustler* and *Penthouse* purport to be for men. Women also read them, so I don't want to argue that they are only for men. But the industry at least initially was based on a male market and male fantasies.

GR: The industry of sexual fantasy has been sex segregated. The romances are basically oriented toward women, and porn is basically oriented toward men. Having access to sexually explicit material has by and large been a male privilege. Yet, rather than wanting to get rid of it, since women haven't been able to get it, I want women to be able to get it.

AH: Deirdre said something in her article that I agree with. There's still a long way to go to uncover the feminist or prowomen or equal love life. To get there we need nonsexist sexual images. A lot more of them. In short, maybe what we need even more than Women against Pornography (WAP) are women pornographers, or eroticists, if that sounds better.

DE: But that doesn't mean that women will want to create and consume the same sexual imagery that we currently see in the domain of pornography. They might. But they might create something completely different.

GR: Well, we might. And we probably will. But some of the worst and major victims of the antiporn sentiment have been indigenous feminist eroticists. And it's gotten to the point now where, in the women's movement, if anything is sexual, it's immediately considered to be violent. The porn that's available now is not so wonderful or gratifying. I mean, I go to a porn show now, and there's almost nothing that's about my fantasies. I see very few women in blue jeans, very few women with broad shoulders and muscles, standing next to motorcycles, and a whole range of other things I find a turn-on. The fact is that there's not a lot of porn oriented toward minorities of any sort. Gay men probably have the best-produced porn. And one reason gay male porn is better is that a lot of it is produced by gay men and for gay men.

What Is Pornography?

AH: What is pornography? What do we define as pornography?

GR: I have a three-part definition. One, the legal definition, is that it's sexually explicit material designed to arouse prurient interest. I think that definition, at least for this historical time and place, is the most useful one. We should remember that porn is not legal; by this definition material that has no focus but to arouse is not legal. In other words, a sexual aim is not considered legitimate in this culture. But we also need a historical definition; that is, porn as we now know it is widely available, commercial erotica as opposed to the older erotica that was hand produced and was mostly something that rich people collected. In the middle of the last century, mass production of erotic materials started to take place, resulting in the cheap, printed dirty book. Third, I have a sociological definition: pornography is a particular industry located in certain places, with certain kinds of shops which tend to put out a product with certain conventions. One convention, for example, is that a man's orgasm never happens inside the woman. Pornography has a concrete existence that you can define sociologically. But that's not the current, so-called feminist definition of porn.

AH: What's that—"what we don't like is pornographic"?

GR: The definition used in the antiporn movement is that pornography is violence against women and that violence against women is pornography. There are several problems with this. One is a replacement of the institutional forms of violence with representations of violence. That is to say, there's been a conflating of images with the thing itself. People really don't talk about the institutions; they talk about the images. Images are important, but they're not the whole thing.

Actually, if you walk into an adult bookstore, 90 percent of the material you will see is frontal nudity, intercourse, and oral sex, with no hint of violence or coercion. There are specialty porns. There's gay male porn; that's a big subgenre. There used to be a genre of porn that featured young people, although that's now so illegal that you don't see it anymore. And there is a genre of porn that caters to sadomasochists, which is the porn that they focus on when you see a WAVPM (Women against Violence in Pornography and Media) or a WAP slide show. They show the worst possible porn and claim it's representative of all of it. The two images that they show most are sadomasochistic porn and images of violence that contain sex. For instance, the infamous *Hustler* cover with the woman being shoved through a meat grinder. An awful picture, but by no means a common image in pornography.

DE: It was self-parody. It was gross, but it was actually satirical, a self-critical joke, which a lot of people didn't get.

GR: They include images that are not pornographic that you cannot find in an adult bookstore. For instance, the stuff on billboards, the stuff on record covers, the stuff in *Vogue*. None of it has explicit sexual content. At most, it's covert. And what they do is draw in images they consider to be violent, or coercive, or demeaning, and call that pornography. That definition enables them to avoid the empirical question of how much porn is really violent. Their analysis is that the violent images come out of porn and into the culture at large, that sexism comes from porn into the culture. Whereas it seems to me that pornography only reflects as much sexism as is in the culture.

The existence of S/M porn enabled this whole analysis to proceed. It's very disturbing to most people and contains scenes that most people don't even want to encounter in their lives. They don't realize that s/M porn is about fantasy. What most people do with it is take it home and masturbate. Those people who do s/M are consensually acting out fantasies: the category of people who read and use s/M porn and the category of violent rapists are not the same. We used to talk about how religion and the state and the family create sexism and promote rape. No one talks about any of these institutions anymore. They've become the good guys!

AH: And now pornography creates sexism and violence against women.

DE: One of the things that has amazed me, and I don't know what to make of it, is that many antiporn activists see red if they hear you say that the violent porn is a minority within the whole industry. They would just not agree with you. Now, when I went into those bookstores, I saw basically what you see. And I agree with your description.

GR: When I went on the WAVPM tour, everybody went, and I stood in front of the bondage material. It was like they had on blinders. And I said, Look, there's oral sex over there! Why don't you look at that? And they were glued to the bondage rack. I started pulling out female dominance magazines and saying, "Look, here's a woman dominating a man. What about that? Here's a woman who's tied up a man. What about that?" It was like I wasn't there. People said, "Look at this picture of a woman being tied up!"

AH: Another example in the WAVPM slide show, there will be an image from a porn magazine of a woman tied up, beaten, right? And they'll say, *Hustler* magazine, 1976, and you're struck dumb by it, horrified! The next slide will be a picture of a woman with a police file, badly beaten by her husband. And the rap that connects these two is that the image of the woman tied and bruised in the pornographic magazine caused the beating that she suffered. The talk implies that her husband went and saw that picture, then came home and tried to re-create it in their bedroom. That is the guilt-by-association theory of pornography and violence. And I remember sitting and watching this slide show and being freaked out about both of those images and having nowhere to react to the analysis and say, What the hell is going on? I found it incredibly manipulative.

GR: Some of the antiporn people are looking at material that is used in a particular subculture with a particular meaning and a particular set of conventions and saying, It doesn't mean what it means to the people who are using it. It means what *we* see! They're assuming that they know better than the people who are familiar with it. They're assuming, for example, that s/m is violent, and that analysis leads to the view that s/m people can't be the victims of violence.

AH: It also discourages anyone from making explicit any sexual fantasy which seems risky to them or from exploring a sexual terrain that's not familiar. It ignores the fact that you learn what you like and what you don't like through trying things out. What it says is that these forbidden desires are not yours but imposed on you. You never experiment sexually.

Yet most people know goddamn well that their sex lives are wider than those standard notions let them play in. They may feel guilty about it, but they know it. So they don't need one more movement to tell them that they can't play.

GR: Anal sex is a real good example, I think, of some of the ways that this all works. It can seem like the most appalling thing in the world, so unpleasant that your idea is that no one else would find it pleasant unless they were coerced into it. And therefore all anal sex is a form of coercion or rape. And the truth is that anal sex for some people is pleasurable and it is not always done under duress. That's true of almost all of the sexual variations. What's one person's horror show is another person's delight.

The Politics of Pornography

AH: In fact, some women working in the antiporn movement would agree with us about opening up sexual possibilities for women but still believe that pornography is the link with violence against women.

GR: Sure, there are differences in that movement. I just think that they have to be held accountable for the social impact of the politics they're promulgating. I think that to focus on porn as a solution to the problem of violence is wrong. It won't substantially reduce the amount of violence against women. Porn may not be the most edifying form of sexual material that we can image, but it is the most available sexual material. To attack that is ultimately going to reduce the amount of social space available to talk about sex in an explicit way.

DE: I think we're being too uncritical of porn. Your definition of porn is probably more positive than the way pornography functions for a lot of people. It's important to point out that a great deal of pornography is deeply sexist and that it contains a hideous and misogynistic view of women.

GR: It also contains a hideous view of sexual minorities, including the people who do all the stuff the antiporn movement is so upset by, including s/m.

DE: And the constant repetition of those sexist images of women does validate the sexism of sexist people who buy and consume it.

GR: So does the TV they watch.

DE: Yes.

GR: And the novels they read.

DE: Yes, and everything else. But there may be nothing in their lives that ever says to consumers of pornography, that shows that violence against women is a fantasy, that women don't really want to be raped or brutalized. They may never really get the message that porn depicts behavior that is in fact not acceptable to women. And that is a serious problem.

GR: I disagree. I think there is a serious problem with pornography when it does not challenge sexism, racism, homophobia, or antivariation bigotry. But again, while there is sexism in all porn and there are violent images from a variety of media sources, there is not a whole lot of violent porn per se.

AH: Then let's really talk about sexist porn.

GR: OK. I have no objection to being critical of the content of porn, or creating nonsexist porn, and having better sex education, and talking to men about what women really want sexually. But that has not been the agenda of the antiporn movement.

DE: All right. But I want to stress that we are strongly speaking for an antisexist movement, in every domain of society.

AH: Pornography is not the first thing to worry about in trying to go to the root of the things that destroy, brutalize, and murder women.

DE: Right. I don't think I'd try to change pornography first. What I'm trying to say is that what's very important is that there be a strong anti-sexist movement as a point of reference. For example, women should be able to enjoy, say, masochistic pornography or dominance and submission fantasies in a safe context. But there should also be a source of support, a movement saying that that does not mean that women want to be beaten up.

GR: Absolutely. But the fact that we have a movement against sexism does not mean that the movement is always wise or alert to the real sources of distress that people feel. For two or three years now, ever since Anita Bryant, there has been an enormous increase in police activity and state repression against all these parts of the sexual world that are not mainstream. The cost to the people who've been beaten up and who've gone to jail and lost their livelihoods is immense. There is an insidious moral blindness to this reality in the women's movement, one encouraged by the antiporn line. Two resolutions that were recently passed disturb me. One is a resolution passed by the National Organization for Women (NOW) in 1980 that reaffirms NOW's support for lesbian rights but specifically says that public sex, pederasty, s/M, and pornography are issues of violence, not of sexual preference. These are specifically excluded from the definition of a lesbian or gay group that NOW would work with. The second resolution was passed by the National Lawyers Guild, a resolution against porn based on all the analyses we've been talking about, saying that it is violence against women. It encourages the members of the guild not to defend people who are arrested on porn charges and to defend people who are arrested doing antiporn work. This isolates the victims of repression from support and delivers them up to the state.

AH: These resolutions close off the only areas in which some of these victims of repression could hope to find support. They need to be placed in a context, which is the reification of the nuclear family and a new emphasis on male-dominated, heterosexual marriage as the only sexual model. And when the feminist movement focuses on pornography rather than the violence of institutions like marriage and enforced heterosexuality and a variety of other things, it endangers its own future.

DE: But I think that it's very important for us to have a critique of sexist pornography as well as a critique of the antiporn movement.

GR: But issues that are very important to me have been compromised by bad politics. I would love to go, as you were saying earlier, Deirdre, on a march to take back the night and demonstrate against violence. But I would not like to go on an antiporn march. I would love to talk more about the whole issue of the way that the media are involved in the social reproduction of sexism. There are things being promoted in the name of feminist ideology that are destructive. I don't want a viable and powerful women's movement to create social havoc rather than social good! Many social movements had wonderful intentions but left a dreadful legacy. And we're not magically an exception to that.

AH: What we began talking about and what I hope we end on is that this is an opening up of the discussion that will allow us to figure out what these questions are. We're not really arguing that everything we're saying is correct, but the feminist movement has got to allow a wider discussion of all sorts of sexual issues and what they are and how they combine.

Another Place to Breathe

Throughout my adult life, gay men—especially drag queens—have been important to me. Drag queens mattered to me as a femme. But the sex-positive gay male culture in general had always given me space to deal honestly, nonpejoratively, nonjudgmentally with my own sexuality. This 1996 conversation with good friends Gayle Rubin and Jewelle Gomez grounded our feminist discussion of sex in a context that valued gay male sexuality and linked its realities with our own lesbian erotic worlds.

THE CONVERSATION
Jewelle Gomez, Amber Hollibaugh, and Gayle Rubin

Jewelle Gomez, Amber Hollibaugh, and Gayle Rubin are lesbian activists and writers who have known one another over the last two decades as friends and colleagues. They met again with Sara Miles in San Francisco in early 1996 to talk about the impact of gay men's sex cultures on lesbian culture and of gay male sexuality on their own. This is an edited transcript of the afternoon's discussion.

AMBER HOLLIBAUGH: The mythology has been that boys are sexual and girls are not. It's gay men who are promiscuous and lesbians who are monogamous. Those have been the overarching constructs for a lot of community perception and community identification, whether they're true or not.

So, to me, it also makes me think of why I felt close to gay male sexuality for a long time. It wasn't really about the practices so much as the sexual culture, the right to explicit sexual culture and to sexual identities—as different from homosexual identities. Your sexual orientation wasn't challenged by what your sexual practice was.

In the lesbian community, you had to be the right kind of lesbian, or you were suspected of not being a lesbian. And that was true in everything from butch/femme and s/m to a whole variety of identity-merger sexual practices. So gay male sexuality, for me, was kind of an umbrella, a protectionist umbrella for being gay, for being sexual the way that you needed to be, without having to give up your homosexuality.

GAYLE RUBIN. I think problems arise when people generalize about lesbian sexuality or lesbian sexual culture and gay male sexuality or gay male sexual culture. Both these need to be pluralized. What you're talking about, Amber, in terms of lesbian values regarding sex really has to do with a particular lesbian population that was very influenced by lesbian feminism as a political ideology and tended to organize lesbianism around that ideology. I think you are referring to the political lesbian culture and community and the ideologies of that population, which shouldn't be generalized to the entire lesbian population.

I actually think that if you take the whole population of lesbians and the whole population of gay men, what you will find are overlapping ranges of sexual ideologies that are present in both groups but distributed differently. And you'll find a lot of overlapping ideas as well as distinctive notions of sexual conduct and propriety.

One of the biggest differences is that, at least in recent history, gay men have had a kind of institutionalized and commercial sexual culture that lesbians have lacked, and that's had a big impact on how both populations perceive themselves and are perceived by outsiders.

JEWELLE GOMEZ: I think, for me, gay male sexuality has always had kind of a conflicting impact. Since it was the only visible homosexuality, even when it was invisible, it was implied. I think of reading James Baldwin and reading *Giovanni's Room* and having male sexuality be palpable on the pages and my identification with it as a lesbian because that was the only homosexual reference point I had.

So, in many ways, gay male sexuality historically represented a liberation simply because it was visible. On the other hand, I think, for me, it's always evoked traditional male oppression because gay men exist in their sexuality in the privilege of having sex free of politics—in a way. Even though, of course, there is heterosexism, they're not suffering under a recognizable form of sexism throughout their growing up, through their adolescence and into adulthood, so that their practice of sex is privileged in a way that women have had to work through to get to in our practice of sex.

I feel that the period in which lesbian feminism developed its position on sexuality as oppressive, or male sexuality as oppressive, as exploitive, is an understandable part of a process of coming to sexual power. But women as people who have been the target of male sexuality in this society needed to grow through that, through what has come to be thought of as puritanical lesbian feminism, in order to find a way to that open expression of sexuality that men take for granted. And, unfortunately, some women never found their way through and are still kind of stuck there.

I know when the big fight about closing the baths happened in New York—1985 or 1986, something like that—I was one of three women on the board of the group that was starting GLAAD (Gay and Lesbian Alliance against Defamation). The whole idea that there were baths, number one, that men had the economic freedom to create a place to have sex, was something I had to think about. I knew the baths were there. I knew that men owned all the discos and went to the discos, which were another place for sexual expression. So, until it was raised as something that was about to be taken away, I simply thought of those as places of privilege. And then, working with other women and men to militate against the closing of the baths, I started to see gay men start to realize that their privilege was not as widespread as they thought. Or as absolute.

And that, to me, was interesting because for the first time, I think, men started to see their sexual expression as vulnerable. With AIDS it really began, but with the closing of the baths and establishments like that, the idea that men could see themselves and their sexuality as being demonized and threatened, I think, was significant politically.

I was in a community of lesbians for whom sexuality was always a danger. People still feel so oppressed, and it's because they still see male power as the most dominant power in this culture. And women still see ourselves as victims.

GR: I think we should talk about some of these ideas—for instance, that sexuality, if it's sort of easy, is male. That if it's easy, it's oppressive. That if it's male, it's oppressive. There are a number of words that get linked together very often, and I think we need to deconstruct them.

You brought up, Jewelle, one of the issues that is really central to these discussions, and that is the whole matter of historical reference points and context and how much those dominate one's sense of appropriate desire versus how detached they can be.

I think all desires are historically shaped, so it's not like they ever don't have context. However, in my experience of lesbian feminism and feminist ideas about sexuality, a particular notion of historical context becomes the privileged reference point. Evaluating things in those terms tends to make sexual desire subordinate to these political and moral considerations. This contrasts with an attitude more common in gay male culture, where people are not as concerned with context. There are men who care about that, but they seem fewer. I know a lot of guys who think, "If it gets my dick hard, it's fine. Why do I need to care about all this other stuff?"

They're not talking about "if it gets my dick hard, it's OK to rape someone." They're talking about "if I'm in a bathhouse, or if I'm on a date with someone I like, and something gets my dick hard, why should I care about what else it might have meant in some other context? It's not here. We're having fun, we're on a date, let's do it." A lot of the gay men I know just don't feel the need to evaluate every lust in terms of what historical connections it might have to some bad thing that they actually may, in fact, disapprove of. They're not as obsessed with purifying their desires of potentially evil associations. They don't seem to understand the kind of self-examination or discussion or indecision around lust that a lot of women and lesbians tend to engage in.

JG: That goes back to the position of victimization. I think women still feel victimized in this society around their sexuality, which is why women feel that they have to keep that history the dominant thing. Rape is still a threat shadowing every woman. And men feel less vulnerable, so they can make those separations and not consider history.

GR: Women have, in fact, had to pay, on the whole, much higher prices for being sexually active than men. So, of course, being sexually active is imbued with a lot of fear. But you could argue that this is a product of oppression and that indulging it caters to some of the ways in which women have been systemically mistreated.

AH: I'll argue that. I do argue that. That's part of why it's been so provocative, part of why I think that the fighting over sexual terrain and the kind of gendering of sexual terrain has been such a complicated dialogue.

Some of us were really trying to hold out for a sex-radical perspective in the context of our own histories as women, in lesbian and gay communities where we wanted pleasure to be something that we had a right to, without having to explain it to people all the time, where we had a right to take sexual chances and be a part of sexual danger. And that wasn't something that we expected feminism to remove from our sexual terrain.

That's still a very, very difficult conversation. For me, that's one of the things that's the most tragic about lesbian sexuality: I think, for a lot of women, the price of trying to come out has been so high, on top of just the price of being female and sexual in our culture, that trying to integrate power and danger and marginality as an ongoing part of your sexuality is devastating.

Part of my read on lesbian feminism and its resulting narrowness around sexuality is that women are tired. Tired, tired, tired. Tired of hurting, tired of being scared, tired of everything. And the sexuality that ended up getting articulated from that was a sexuality of safety from sex and a really problematic relationship to pleasure and to being a sexual actor. And some of us, as tired as we might be, have never wanted to give that up. I mean, my own sexuality is fundamentally grounded in danger.

A lot of women I know felt their sexuality that way: always around power and always around danger. It's not like I never had a nice orgasm. But somehow, in my mind, my imagination is fueled by danger. And I need it. I need it to feel things. Some of what I have always taken from gay male sexuality is the play and the danger, the combination of those two things. I've also taken from a lot of other parts of gay male sexuality, long before this current period. Like drag, and bars, mixed bars, and the leather community. I wanted their atmosphere of a kind of sexual—

JG: Intensity.

AH: Intensity. That all marginalized communities live within. And that was very important to me about gay male sexuality. They play; they try things out. They didn't decide that something tasted bad before they tasted it.

One of the things that was most interesting to me about gay male sexuality is that men want to learn it. They assumed that learning was a part of sexual desire. I know this is a generalization, but in some ways, just by going to the bars, by going to clubs and baths, whether or not you turned out to be a gay man who was primarily monogamous, you had an expanded idea of what was sexually visible and possible in the world, and you could try it out on yourself. Part of what I've always felt most sad about is the limitations of what I could see and what I could feel and smell and watch about how other women did it. Because there were so few places where I could watch other women do it and have it be acceptable.

GR: And now you're talking not just about the danger element but a kind of normalization.

AH: Exactly. Both.

GR: One thing you're talking about is a way in which sex becomes a normal human activity—and not just sex as something you talk about in terms of your latest romantic escapade but actually seeing people do it with genitals and fluids and props and lube and towels. That that's part of the normal vision of gay male social life. It's not something that's always cut off in a corner, put behind a curtain, or only discussed in the abstract or as romance.

I always thought it was really interesting that most people feel that if they were out having sex somewhere and they ran into someone they knew, from their bank or their church or their school or their office, they would just shrivel and die from the stigma and shame. Whereas there's a way in which, if a gay guy is out at the baths and he runs into his lawyer or his doctor, it's "Hi." It's like running into this person at the movies or a ball game or a restaurant. It's not a big deal, and that was very refreshing. It wasn't about danger. It was about detoxifying sex as an area of insanity and just making it a kind of part of life, and I always appreciated that.

AH: When I was out doing political organizing, a lot of the only reference points for gay sexuality were clubs, and there was a lot of sex going on in them. Those were moments that were enormously revealing in the early days in clubs when it was prostitutes, drag queens, butch/femme, and faggots. You watched people have all different kinds of sexual moments and be in different sexual cultures. It was a gift.

That was where I first learned that you didn't have to be the person sitting next to you in the bar. You could be fascinated by it, but it wasn't a threat to your own personal sexual desires. That's also a legacy I inherited as a woman that I've had to really resist—the idea that other people's sexual pleasures and sexual engines were not necessarily my own. Just because they were doing it, I didn't somehow take on everything that they were doing with all its meaning. It took me a while to separate out my own imagination from my extraordinary interest and guilt from desire.

GR: I guess I encountered gay male sexual culture later in my career as a lesbian than you did in yours because I first came out in the context of a lesbian-feminist political environment. And I was in a small college town where there really wasn't much of a preexisting gay culture of any sort. I slowly worked my way into contact with larger, historically older gay and lesbian cultures. Then, in the late 1970s, I actually did research on a gay male sexually defined population. At that time that was probably considered a complete leap into the abyss, but that's another story.

So I encountered gay male sexual culture in the late 1970s. For me, there was an enormous delight and wonder in it. It seemed a gift of a whole set of ways of thinking that I simply hadn't encountered before.

But, Jewelle, you were referring to this earlier—the way in which men can think about having sexual pleasure as just something they expect to get in this world. It's like you expect to eat. You can expect to have sex. That doesn't mean that you should steal food to have food or that you should force people to have sex, but this is a human need, and it's OK to fulfill it in some way. And there was an ease around it that I really appreciated.

One of the things that I got from gay male culture was ironic, given that the men I was mostly hanging around didn't much like women's bodies. They didn't like bodies like mine. And yet their ease with their own bodies made me feel better about my body and easier about being in a body. It was OK to have a body with holes and sphincters and fluids and sensations. And it was even OK to have a plump female body. You wouldn't think being involved with a group of men who were really into masculinity, muscle, and dicks would ever make you feel better about a female body. But, in fact, it did because they were just willing to get naked and revel in their bodies as sources of pleasure. And it wasn't like everybody there was a calendar model or a body beautiful. There was this sense that bodies were just these wonderful things. You have a limited time with your body, and you should wring as much joy out of it as possible, and this was a perfectly legitimate pursuit. I found this attitude amazing.

Also, there was a way in which the set of available roles for expressing certain kinds of desires was expanded for me by encountering gay male culture. In lesbian culture, at that point in my life experience, I had run into mostly either butch/femme attitudes—that is, if you were butch, you were supposed to go out with a femme, and you were supposed to run the sex—or else it was the flannel-shirt lesbian-feminist hiking-boots mentality in which we all looked the same, even though we all might have done different things. But this exhausted the available roles.

And none of them quite fit me because, for example, I've always been kind of a soft nerdy butch who just adored stronger and more masculine butches. There wasn't much of a framework for that in lesbian culture. But, in gay male culture, there were all these frameworks for butch/butch sexuality and role models for being butch where you didn't run the sex. You could be a bottom and still be a butch, and you could go out with other butches. You didn't have to put on a dress to get fucked. You could put on a dress and get fucked. But you didn't have to.

My encounter with gay male sexual cultures expanded my notions of the possibilities and semantic arrangements for different kinds of desires and roles. But, in order to assimilate this, I had to put away some of my own prejudices. I had to be ethnographic in my approach and set aside some of my own subjective responses.

JG: Which were?

GR: Well, you know what Amber and Eric [Rofes] have called the "ick" factor. I do think there is a way in which many people who have strong sexual preferences for one gender often have some kind of revulsion for the physical characteristics of the other. And certainly I had my own set of these things.

I remember when I first took the San Francisco Sex Information (SFSI) training. At the beginning they do the Fuck-a-Rama. They show a hundred porn movies, at once, with every conceivable act.

AH: Every sex act in every gender combination.

GR: It's a very interesting tactic to make people realize that sex comes in all these varieties. And of course everyone is disgusted by something they see in the Fuck-a-Rama. This is why they show it. It introduces you to sexual variety so you won't make hasty judgments or assume that everyone has the same sexual tastes.

The hardest thing for me to look at was all the squirting, coming cocks. So what do I do? I go and decide to study a bunch of gay men who think spurting, coming cocks are the best thing on the planet. Their imagery is drenched with semen. And, in fact, the clubs are drenched with semen. I had to take a step back from my immediate reaction.

The work didn't change my basic sexual orientation, but it certainly changed my attitude. My fantasy life is vastly enriched by all the imagery I saw. But, as one person told me when I first started doing my work, fantasies are hungrier than bodies. That was a very liberating thing to hear. In this culture we have the idea that if we think about something and it turns us on, then we're supposed to do it. And if it's something that we really don't want to do, we're in conflict with the fantasy. I realized that people have all kinds of fantasies. You can jerk off to them, but you don't have to go do all of those things.

AH: I feel like I have a lot of sense of debt to gay male sexuality, for myself. And I've thought that for a long time. Some, because it protected me when I felt very different from a lot of lesbians around me. It was where I escaped to that was still gay. And—they just didn't care. They didn't care what I was into. It wasn't a big deal if they didn't get it. It just wasn't judgmental in the same kind of way.

I had to work out my own sense of my sexuality, and I needed a neutral place to do it, and the political part of my own community wasn't a helpful place for me. And, in fact, it's true that the only time I've ever tried to commit suicide was when I had to try to deal with being a femme—not with trying to deal with being a lesbian. That was dangerous in my own mind. Up against what I thought I should be, that desire looked so—it seemed so irreconcilable with my own political beliefs that I was just beside myself. Because I couldn't give up my erotic life, and I couldn't give up my political beliefs, and I couldn't bring the two together. And I couldn't keep living in different worlds for both of them. I don't want to make it sound like it was just lesbian feminism or something that did that; I was still in conflict about desire. And desire for what I wanted.

But the other part that I've recognized because of that femme identity, for which I feel an enormous sense of gratitude, is that my femme identity is profoundly influenced, and has been extraordinarily shaped by, drag. I never saw myself as a "natural" woman. I never, ever believed in naturalness.

I wasn't a femme because I felt like I was a "real" woman. Which was kind of the ideology, right? The butches were "guys," and the femmes were "girls," real girls, which is part of why we were suspected of actually slipping into the heterosexual camp because we were "realer" in that sense. That femmeness was "natural." So it wasn't as equally constructed as the identity of anyone else.

JG: Right. As much based on play as butch was.

AH: So I would look around and think, What women look like me to myself? I have always looked like a drag queen. I had always liked looking like a drag queen. And I've always been actually quite conflicted in how not to compete with drag queens. Like in Cherry Grove, I was very careful, for instance, not to wear boas. Because I felt like I had an advantage that was both a limitation and a privilege in this culture. I had the biological body that was represented by men in drag.

JG: You had tits, you didn't need the boa?

AH: I had tits, and I had cleavage, and, hey—And so it was very delicate to try and figure out how to respect the drag queens and be a femme. How could I put them together? I didn't want to compete with them for being the prettiest girl. I didn't want to be more female than them.

They were who I saw myself as, as a woman. And so, for me, that's the other place for gay male culture that's been unbelievably helpful. Because they also knew the irony of not being "real" girls. They knew that they were not girls like their mothers. And I am not a girl like my mother. I am not a femme like my mother, in all her conflict, has ever been a femme. And I'm always not quite the femme I would like to be.

I always feel like that's true around men in drag when you see them take off their wigs and kind of just walk down the street. Somewhere in that I also felt this part of me. There are places when I'm not that high femme. I don't look like what the expectation of myself is, for that piece; I'm not "real" enough.

And there was then a whole community of men, even if they didn't see me as part of them, which they didn't, but that I related to as also witty and brittle and bitchy and kick-ass. I mean, these were the men that I also saw defend themselves and other gay men in bars. These were not feminine images of passivity. These were women who defended their right to be in heels and defended their right to suck guys off and kicked butt when somebody attacked them. And so, in many class ways, I also felt very connected to drag queens around my own sense of marginalization.

JG: I'm not sure if what I learned from gay male sexuality isn't all intellectual gain. And certainly that's not to dismiss it because intellectual gain is really important.

I mean, I was thinking about your stories about the guys in drag and sort of following their lead, in a way, about how to be a woman. For me, as a femme, the people I was following were prostitutes. As a kid growing up, in the bars where my father and my stepfather worked, pimps and prostitutes were my aunts and uncles. And so, as I became self-aware physically, I know I was patterning myself after these women, Miss Joanne and Miss Billy. You know, the women who were like drag queens, larger than life. And so that's where I saw myself, in terms of attitude, physicality, independence.

AH: The right to desire.

JG: I think I probably have a lot more of an intellectual debt to gay men. Starting with James Baldwin and the idea that desire could be hard-edged, immutable, and, as Gayle said, you should be able to expect to have it fulfilled. And in reading and talking and listening to gay men.

Because I don't think I've had that many experiences in the gay male community. And the ones that I've had have always been tempered by my having to put aside my own feminist concerns in order to enjoy their company. Which I am capable of doing. But you know, whenever I have done organizing projects, if I work with a gay man for any length of time, I almost inevitably have to deal with misogyny, so I have tended to not have many extensive interactions, socially. So I think it's mostly intellectual.

AH: What about gay male porn?

JG: Oh, how much do I own?

AH: That's one of the other places that I was thinking of that has really always been important to me.

JG: Yeah. That's true.

AH: That was a place that was queer. I mean, I like straight porn. And I watch it. But lesbian porn, usually, was pretty—

JG: It didn't exist until—

AH: Didn't exist very much. Then a lot of it wasn't my stuff. It was boring. It was really flat. In fact, it was more like campy. You'd kind of sit there, and you wouldn't jerk off, you'd—

GR: Laugh off.

AH: Exactly. If you wanted a place where you could play with desire and see all kinds of explicit sexualities and things happening, gay male porn was the other place for me of entry that I really, again, appreciated gay men for giving me space around.

Even though—I mean, often I think gay male culture has been for me in some ways like what I had to do around straight culture, when I had to change the gender of the person in the song. You know what I mean? I had to do some rearranging in there, but I was also very glad the song existed. And so a lot of times gay male culture has been like that for me. It's given me a gay place, even though I had to do some work.

GR: That creative spectatorship that doesn't require quite as much creativity as doing it with straight porn. And sometimes not as much conflict.

JG: I don't have a real "ick" factor. I don't have things about men that I find "icky" personally. And I've certainly slept with enough men in my life that I know their bodies fairly well. So, to me, male porn, gay male porn, has always been much more stimulating. Because it's just, it's all out there. And it gives you the chance to project yourself into homoerotic situations.

When I think about it, what were the shows I watched as an adolescent? *Star Trek* and *Route 66*. These were two shows whose homosocial qualities were what attracted me each week.

GR: No shit.

JG: There was this intense subtext that I was projecting myself into. And, with gay male porn, I could see myself—I was John Preston in some parts of my mind.

AH: Thank you very much for the cuffs.

GR: I love male porn and see a lot of it. Because of my work, my house is filled with it. It's a running joke among my friends that I'm the dyke with the dick collection. They bring me penises. Someone even gave me an ocarina that you blow through the piss slit to get a sound out of it.

I wanted to say more about this history of lesbians appreciating gay male culture. It didn't just start recently. There's this idea that lesbians just discovered gay male culture in the last couple of years, and that isn't true. It's been going on a long time. Often, until something is contextualized or written down or made into a movie, people think it doesn't exist.

Several years ago, Susie Bright wrote a piece on lesbians reading gay porn for *On Our Backs*. The very first *Heresies* sex issue, from 1981, had an article about fag-hagging women. I'm sure there has been plenty of interaction and mutual learning for a long time.

I want to say some other things about influences of gay male sexual culture on lesbians. Certainly, in terms of s/m lesbians, gay men have been extremely important in that they had an s/m subculture when lesbians didn't. This doesn't mean that lesbians discovered s/m from gay men or wouldn't have done it without gay men or that they're only imitating gay men. But certainly gay men provided models for how to create an institutionalized subculture. There were also gay men who shared technical information with women. They had places to go buy toys or hold events. So gay men had an enormous impact on the emergence of the lesbian leather community. Without the assistance of gay leather men, it would have taken a lot longer and perhaps assumed different forms.

But I do want to disagree with the analysis that blames gay men for all the lesbian behavior that's considered reprehensible or politically incorrect by certain lesbian-feminist factions. Sheila Jeffreys exemplifies such views. I think that's an unfair, historically oversimplified, and condescending perspective. There's been a lot of influence back and forth. Lesbians have certainly influenced gay men, and gay men have certainly influenced lesbians for a long time. And that's not negative.

It doesn't mean that either culture is inauthentic. Cultures borrow all the time—that's the nature of culture. And it is certainly not unique to lesbians or gay men. People borrow and assimilate and retool ideas and artifacts and institutional formats from other cultures and use them for their own purposes. If there are "natural" parts of social life, that's certainly one of them.

JG: Well, I'll jump in. I just want to put in one little thing about the expectation people have about the separation between lesbians and gays, certainly the separations between our perceptions about sex. And I had two sort of funny experiences. One was that I was on a panel with Samuel Delany, who is certainly erudite, intelligent, and you know—

AH: Queer.

JG: Very queer. So we're on a panel, and at some point we were talking, and I said, "Oh, Chip, I just wanted to tell you, I've been reading *Tides of Lust*, and God—" And Chip's eyes bugged open. It was like his mother had just told him she was reading *Tides of Lust*. And he recovered quite well, and he looked at me, and he stroked his beard and just said, "Oh, really. That's very funny." And so I thought, "Have I just made Samuel Delany blush? Wow. Great." I said, "I'm glad I didn't go into detail about my reading of it."

Then recently, at a memorial reading for Essex Hemphill, at A Different Light bookstore, we all read from Essex's work. And I chose a very funny, explicitly sexual piece. And the store was packed, and I was reading it, and I was loving it, and I would look out and see the mostly male audience look at me. They were stunned.

AH: That's what he would love. It was part of his work. That's part of what you can honor in his work.

JG: It was clear that it was not being dragged out of me, that I had not been forced to read this, and that I was, in fact, enjoying it. And trying as hard as I could to read it with the same exuberance that Essex would. There's one funny line, something about his dick was so hard, he thought it was going to crack to pieces and fall to the floor or something.

Afterward, the guys who came up and spoke to me said, "Well, uh, you certainly read that well." I'm like, "I don't have a reading problem; what do they think?" Even though I don't necessarily spend a lot of time with gay men, certainly our cultures get things from each other. And the presumption that they don't is, I think, a mistake that sometimes both lesbians and gay men perpetuate.

GR: And it's also the case that, although both lesbians and gay men have their separatists, not everybody in either community has always shared those views. Even separatists learn from one another in a more indirect way.

AH: I would be interested to know what gay men thought they have learned, sexually, from us. The majority of gay men that I know, even if they think feminism is important, even if they value that part of the dialogue, they do not think that there's anything that's actually about their own desire represented in lesbian sexuality. I'm sure that's not true in s/m communities, but it is very true in other places. So they just look at me like, "Why would I want to know what you do? Why would that be a conversation that would be interesting and informative about my desire?" Whereas I actually do feel like that, often, about gay male sexuality, even if I don't do it the way they do it. But then I'm interested in how people do it, anyway.

JG: They have a much higher "ick" factor than you do, I think.

AH: I just think that a lot of men that I know, gay men that I know, regardless of their passionate relationships with lesbians, their incredible friendships, the one area that they don't feel comfortable talking about and really getting into is how lesbians fuck. And I've found that particularly problematic around HIV because the work I do is lesbian HIV work. And so it's been interesting to me that I have felt a need to defend things like issues of public sexuality and HIV as part of that debate but they haven't felt a need to defend lesbian sexuality against state intervention or even know what it is.

And the idea that they could, as a normal part of their lives, say *clitoris* or *vagina* as something that, in an HIV context, they actually need to know, like I need to know about their desire and their practices and stuff—it astounds me every single, solitary day. I work in an AIDS organization that runs one of the major nonprofit AIDS hotlines, and when somebody calls to ask a question about HIV, until fairly recently the practice was that if it was a woman calling to ask about any kind of female sexuality, they would wait until they had a woman on the line to answer her question, regardless of what she was asking. And the assumption was that there wasn't anything men needed to learn or know about women's bodies and desires.

JG: Is this not traditional in a male-dominated society? Gay men tend to be not any different from straight men in their unwillingness to know the female body more than superficially, whether it's dating or drag.

AH: Well, I just don't know what it's from. I'm sure that's part of it, Jewelle. But, given that I feel like I'm incredibly interested in their sexuality, because I really feel like it's information about my own— I mean, I see my connection to gay male sexuality. I feel like a lot of the themes of sexual desire are similar, even if the sexual practices are different. Like semen is not the same. But my girlfriend fucks me, and we talk about her cock getting hard. It's like an important piece of our lives. And it's amazing that there's nothing correspondingly interesting, intrinsically interesting to men or worth investigating about my sexuality.

GR: If it's true that gay men are not interested in lesbian sex, is it because they think only penises have sex?

AH: But, at least in my partnerships, one of us has a penis. But that's not even interesting to them.

GR: Now why do you think that's different among s/m folks?

AH: My assumption is there is a lot more freedom to play with ideas of desire that cross gender.

GR: I do think that in leather and s/m communities, there is a lot of communication about sex. This is partly because the things that are sexualized are so much more numerous and varied than genitals and bodies. If you know how to tie a knot in a rope, you can show somebody else how to tie a knot in a rope, whether you're a woman or a man. There's this body of technical information and technique that's highly eroticized but does not have much to do with reproductive anatomy.

I also think there are certain common dynamics. There's been a lot of communication in leather communities in the last twenty years or so between women and men, gay, straight, bi, and transgendered, about mutual interests such as bondage, boot care, dungeon design, or relationship dynamics. For example, top burnout isn't gender specific. In s/m, there are areas where the genders can tend to fall away.

I think the bafflement about female sexuality tends to increase as sex gets more genitally focused. Some gay men just don't get what's happening with female bodies.

JG: In contrast, what is biologically a physical manifestation of desire, since it is different, between male and female—in some cases, not so subtle, but in most cases, more subtle in female arousal than male. The manifestation of having a penis that is erect and solid and present that you hold onto outside the body. As I grip my hand this way, I remember how that feels. And a female's body, the arousal process is so different. So much of it is internal or about wetness, softness.

Granted, there are women who have clits that are hard as a rock. And I want their phone numbers. But—

AH: I love you.

JG: You know what I'm saying? It's like an "in" kind of thing. The sensation is kind of "in," as opposed to out and projectile and all that kind of stuff. So maybe that makes it so subtle that men can dismiss it.

GR: I'm going to argue the other side now. In the late 1970s, when I first attended gay male fist-fucking parties, the guys were doing a lot of drugs and so often didn't get hard-ons. There would be a roomful of guys fisting, having a grand old time. There usually wasn't an erect penis to be found—at least until about three in the morning when the drugs started to wear off. The active sexual parts were hands and holes. I saw a very male sexuality that was nonetheless oriented to orifices and arms. Before I went into this environment, I thought, "Oh, this is going to be very difficult. All these guys getting naked." And then I looked around, and it reminded me of lesbian sex.

AH: You know one of the places I've consistently experienced problems with gay men around erotic identities is with gay men's hostility toward butches. It's really been interesting to me that often gay men liked feminine women and femmes. But butch women, the more butch they were, the more stone they were, the more hostile.

Although I've seen some cruising. There have been crossovers. When Leslie and I were together, that was definitely true because men and women didn't know what gender she was, so it opened up the world of possibility. So a lot of gay men wanted to be fucked by her. And it was faggot to faggot. But they made her a faggot. They didn't make her a butch.

When I've been a femme alone, by myself around gay men, that's often been easier than when I've been with a very butch lover. Gay men had trouble trying to figure out how to treat the butch and see who she was. Was she a guy? Or was she a girl? And the gender has a lot of nuanced meanings in our own communities, both the lesbian communities and the gay male communities. It wasn't as though butches were seen as gay men by gay men; they were seen as somehow "other."

GR: Well, some of that may be erotic tension, some of it may be gender discomfort. And that may be a different issue.

AH: Yeah. I think it's confusing because I think of butch as much as an erotic identity as a gender identity. But I wonder whether gay men see it as a gender threat.

GR: As an appropriation or as a gender confusion, perhaps? Some gay men are comfortable with gender crossing and gender confusion, but others are not. Just as some lesbians are.

AH: What Gayle was talking about, having fantasies that you didn't necessarily have to do—that's an idea that seems to me to be severely limited in this culture, even more severely limited for women. And that any place that you can break those lines, open up, can give you an opportunity to open up your own erotic imagination—even though you may use what you take in very differently from what the people doing it, you know, in front of you mean it to be. It doesn't necessarily mean that what you do with what you see is literal. But what it does is give you more to draw on.

And I feel like one of the things that is most tragic in the culture in general—but for sure with women—is the lack of sexual repertoire and terrain, imaginative terrain for women. But that's been one of the ways that we've been most controlled, punished, and restricted in the culture.

GR: To some degree, I think that gay men in this culture, like straight men, tend to have a fairly narrow definition of what constitutes sexual attractiveness. There's a tendency to value certain body types, which are mostly young, thin, and/or muscular. One thing I like about lesbian sexual culture is that there truly is an appreciation of the beauty in a wider range of body types. There certainly is looksism among lesbians, as well, but there's also a very profound countertendency to celebrate a diversity of body types.

It's true that gay men have bears and chubby chasers, for example, but I think in general they tend to be more intolerant of people who are considered to be fat or overweight. And I wonder whether some gay men haven't picked up on the way lesbians value different physical types as something to appreciate. It's certainly something I love about lesbian culture.

JG: Me, too. Me, too.

AH: Thank God.

GR: There's also a distinction between appreciating diversity and sexually fetishizing particular types. There's a difference between a fetish and a kind of cultural norm that limits beauty to a very narrow range of acceptable bodies. I'm much less upset, for example, by a personal ad that specifies "I want a skinny butt" than I am by the notion that everyone should have a skinny butt.

AH: I know the other area that really has been interesting to me about gay male sexuality—that has really challenged my own thinking a lot—is how they organize relationships around sex. That they have a lot of different kind of arrangements around friendship and sexuality. That two men who are lovers can go someplace and each fuck other people.

GR: Lesbians do that, too. We just talk about it differently.

AH: No, we break up over it.

GR: Not always.

AH: But there's a cultural acceptance among men. The concept of betrayal usually is based on very different kinds of ideological assumptions, and a partner being sexual with someone else is not an assumption of betrayal or lack of commitment.

Those kinds of ideas, regardless of how I organized my own love life, challenged my thinking about how I wanted to think about commitment and about friendship and community. It just gave me some different ideas to work with. I think especially because, much of the time, I have lived in a female world—that is both what I've been blessed with and what's been the problem. It was wonderful to have a whole set of assumptions—whatever I wanted to take of them or not take of them—be operational.

So, you know, gay male friends of mine would look at me like, "Why would you break up with her because she slept with someone else?" Just incredulous about why I felt betrayal, for instance, or how I organized friendships. And that I thought friendships could never be sexual. And they would have these really fine distinctions between a fuck buddy, a lover, and a partner.

I really do struggle with this, and I struggle with it from a lot of different perspectives. I don't quite know what to do with the difference between what I need and what I believe. But it was a place that was helpful to me in recognizing how hurt I had been, young. That's the only way I can kind of think of it, that I carried a lot of baggage into my relationships with women that I then made look as though it was ideological.

Gay men helped me see that by showing me that other people who cared equally about being cared about and loved and sexual, organized it very differently. Differently from me inside a lesbian community, and differently from my mother and father. People were trying something else, and it wasn't just to be radical. And that some of the privilege of gender also allowed them to think about organizing relationships differently. And, again, it was another place to breathe.

GR: I always wanted to organize relationships differently, but perhaps you're right. There is not as much precedent in lesbian culture, but there is some. For example, look at Natalie Barney, one of our lesbian foremothers, who believed in multiple simultaneous relationships, sleeping with her friends, and overcoming sexual jealousy.

Another example pertains to lesbian-feminist communities in the early 1970s. There has been a lot of revisionist history portraying such communities as asexual or puritanical. The one I lived in was neither. It was a hotbed of passion, and there was also a politics that saw sexual jealousy as a manifestation of partriarchal property relationships. We argued against monogamy and the assumption that sex with others should break up couples.

JG: Nonmonogamy was a good thing.

GR: Nonmonogamy was a crusade! There's a continuity in the slogans, from "Smash Monogamy" in the late 1960s, to "Monogamy Is Monopoly" in the 1970s, to "Monogamy = Death" in the 1990s. There was a lot more variety in actual lesbian populations than the stereotypes would suggest. When I found gay men who actually had an institutionalized etiquette for nonmonogamy, it was a relief, but it was not all that different from my experiences in lesbian life.

JG: I think it goes back to what you were saying earlier about normalizing sexual experience, putting it in the context of "This is acceptable, and this is what we do, and—"

AH: No big deal.

JG: Right, right, which I think for lesbians has always been problematic. And will always be until we find ourselves, individually and as a group, less prey to the idea of ourselves as victims in the culture around our sex and sexual desire.

GR: And less subject to punitive measures for our sexuality.

JG: Less subject to other people's vision of what we should be. I don't think I'd say it's healthier to use male models of sexual/emotional relationships. But the strength comes from feeling able to make a choice, based on our own desire.

GR: When women can have sex without losing their chance of economic security, without necessarily having to bear children, without losing their chances to go to school, without taking a lot of risks, then I think we'll have a different attitude toward it.

JG: Having once had a conversation with a gay man about why I felt the lesbian and gay community, a particular organization of the community, should all come to a prochoice demonstration was like—

AH: Swimming uphill.

JG: It was. I kept saying, "But it is connected to women's sexuality. It is connected to your sexuality. Control of your own body. And women who decide to have sex with men are making a choice that puts them at risk. Because then do they have a baby? What do they do about that? Do they take birth control in order to not have babies and risk their health, long term?" And all of this. And it was really interesting for me to see a gay man totally unable to see the connection.

GR: Women have been dealing with the issue of "safer" sex for—

JG/AH/GR: A long time.

GR: That's why these things continue to be so important, not just for straight people, but for lesbians and gay men, too. Without reproductive choice and good access to contraception and sex education, women are going to continue to be sexually disadvantaged in a very profound way. And it's also about educational opportunities and economic opportunities and more. And some people think that's all a done deal and a done fight, that it's over. And they're totally wrong.

It is really about us: every single person on this planet who cares about sex in any way. We need to protect and expand reproductive rights and work for civil and economic conditions that make reproductive choice meaningful and possible. Many people don't realize how much even small gains around reproductive choice that were made years ago have now been systemically eroded. There are vast forces in this society continuing to try to raise the costs of sex for women, gay people, and young people of both genders.

AH: And until the lesbian and gay male communities see that as a fight about ourselves and our own sexuality and that the deepest meaning of sexual liberation is a very different autonomy, body automony, and sense of responsibility and instrumentality. And those things like reproductive rights are not somehow a "girl" thing or a child thing or any of that. They are at the heart of the battles that have been going on about HIV. They're often at the heart of ideas about "welfare cheats" and many of the kinds of ideologies that are so damaging to other cultures that are abused in this world. That those issues aren't somehow separated from their lives.

JG: Who is defined as promiscuous, and whose promiscuity is defined as a problem?

AH: And who is considered to put who else at risk around sexual desire? All those things.

GR: They're key issues right now.

AH: For our survival.

Femme Fables

These are three of the pieces ("The Gap She Fostered" "A Barren Expanse of Loneliness" and "Intimate Signs of Wear") that were written for my column in the New York Native *in 1983–84. I called them "femme" fables as a way of publicly claiming my high femme identity. It was also a way of creatively linking the various parts of my life. No longer so terrified of penning my thoughts, I also began, for the first time, to try writing about my early life and to use printed words to link that life, racially, culturally, economically, and sexually, with the life I found myself currently living. Each of the issues I took on in the column—issues of home, sexuality, class, etc.—were and are ongoing themes in my life and work. It is especially interesting to reread my thoughts as a thirty-seven-year-old* now *as a woman in her fifties!*

THE GAP SHE FOSTERED

I have lived in New York for two years, and this weekend I finally set up my office. It terrifies me to put together my own space, to set up the books, construct the desk, arrange the files and papers I collect with such greed. It seems pretentious and outlandish, a crazy fantasy gotten out of hand. In the hours between midnight and dawn, it is exhilarating to imagine myself a writer, to dream myself a passionate, creative figure in the privacy of my own imagination; in daylight, it seems preposterous. It makes me sick to my stomach when I try.

I am the first in my family to finish high school. Two of my cousins got their high school equivalency in the Marines, and my father has now gone back and finished, but I was the first. Growing up, I read *Reader's Digest* condensed novels and *Love* comics. There was a copy of *The Prophet* by Kahlil Gibran and a full set of encyclopedias. My father read *Hamlet* and loved it. There were a million auto-mechanic books, carpentry manuals, and issues of *Popular Mechanics.* The bathroom held a book called *Jokes for the Pot,* and there were *Family Circles* and cookbooks. But it is fair to say that respect for books is not the same as possessing them, and we had only a few at that.

As a child I was the "bookworm" of my family; everybody talked about it. I read everything in sight: milk bottles and mayonnaise jars, the Bobbsey Twins and the Cherry Ames series. I was as passionate about books as my family was about cars, motorcycles, and Friday night pinochle. It was through books that I first began to see a world different from my hometown—it was not so pretty where I come from. The magic of books took me away from the fights and the dirt, the cars in the front yard, the too-little money, and the worry which filled the rooms we lived in. Nothing about my life seemed so bad when I had a book to read. Books could be borrowed from the library or stolen from the drugstore. I never cared whether I had "taste." I read them all.

It was the opening up of a novel that brought extraordinary people and events into my orbit; it was in books that I found people who felt things no one in my family admitted feeling: emotions and conflicts, sex, wrongheaded passions. People in books talked differently and scrambled my notions of normal or right. Books held promise. I was an addict at an early age, and I fought for the right to read more desperately than I struggled for anything in my life.

No one in my family could figure out where this love of books had come from and what had given me a craving for words. It was their considered opinion that it happened because I had been a sick child, premature at birth, not even walking until my second birthday. I had asthma and colds more than I didn't. I was badly crossed-eyed and would run sideways when I caught adults watching me play. They looked in my direction first when they heard a child fall and were always shaking their heads over my clumsiness.

But I also scared the hell out of them. To them, I was emotionally out of control. I lived in the world of feelings, they in the silent world of work. I wanted to talk; they wanted to do. I said out loud what everyone had agreed not to notice. I was dangerous to them and to the place I was to inhabit as a grown woman. They held that my moods were caused by reading too much, "getting ideas," and living in a dream world. They thought it was crazy, unsafe, and a dead-end. They did not want to see me disappointed, and there was no way to make a living from my passion for books.

Back then, my mother did not have abstract concepts like *class*, but she damn well understood what was possible and what would break my heart. I was her baby, and, proud as she was of my reading and dreaming, she could not afford to encourage a fantasy which would leave me unprepared to face what she knew awaited me. A survivor herself, she meant me to be one, too. Truth is, I was as afraid as my parents were when I tried to see where it was leading. They were right; it didn't make any sense for me. I could be the best-read waitress in Roseville, the best-read wife, the best-read biker chick, the best-read teenage mother.

I was queer, and I wanted a "better" life. In books, I met people who had both. I read the whole encyclopedia many times over, fascinated by the wheat crop figures in the USSR, the kind of snakes in Japan, the reason for the speed of light. I tried out new places to live and other languages. I was a child in the Himalayas, and I first met lesbians in the soft-core porn I was stealing from the place next to Woolworth's; books gave me ideas.

Meanwhile, my mother and I were at war. I was at an age where I would brook no interference from her. She didn't agree. In my senior year, I was sent away on scholarship to an upper-class school to create some peace for us both. I returned home without many clothes and a suitcase full of books. I brought them all back, including the most pretentious I had read that year. I had been introduced to "good" books, and I took to them with the same stubborn determination which had kept me reading bad ones.

That year in boarding school had been terrible for me. I was different and stupid seeming to most of the students, and, most of the time, I agreed with them. I felt ignorant and unpracticed in all they took for granted. But the one thing they had that I could figure out was books. I was being introduced to a literature that I could never have discovered or understood in my hometown. Night after night I stayed up after curfew trying to catch up. I tried to span the distance between the other kids and myself in eight months, a difference created by the years when they had been surrounded by literature, poetry, and music alien to my world. In the end, I couldn't cross that distance, but the race between me and words set in motion a flight from the deadening effects of too much hard work and a rush toward learning which I had been fearing and desiring all my life.

I came home awkward and bitter toward my parents; I saw that they couldn't give me, ever, what those kids' parents could grant effortlessly in a month's allowance or a well-placed phone call. Humiliating as the year had been, it made it impossible for me to stay in my hometown for good, impossible to forget the other ways I could be in the world. I had been *away*. I had been a learner, a student of great ideas and powerful thinkers. I had taken the trip outside and was forever changed by it. Now I had to leave.

In that first strange month of my return home, my parents built me a desk and shelves for all the books. They framed a map I brought back of the Parthenon and got me bookends and a study light. None of us knew what I was to do with these things; it just seemed required now that I was the owner of such large, impressive-looking books. They were awed by them, held them in reverence and dread just as I did—though I wouldn't admit to it. These were my trophies, the stuffed animal heads on my wall. This was the proof that their sacrifice to send me away from the place where I was raised had been worth it.

We all circled those bookcases like hounds after an animal we had never come upon before. I, as their owner, would shut the door to my room and open their pages again and again. They were proof to me that I had been somewhere, and to my parents they were a sign of how I had become different and unknown to them, how I had traveled without them to places they could not imagine. It was a sign of how we had changed and grown apart.

I was not duplicating the motions of the women in my family, each female child moving slightly away from the woman who birthed her, though less than it seemed initially, once she became an adult and settled in. I would rechart the map my family and I had propped up in our minds. I had been born to grow up to have children, marry, and live out my life as a modern version of the women who had come before me. Now it was clear I would not. I was becoming another kind of survivor.

A week after the shelves were put up and the books put in place I returned home in the middle of the day to find my mother in my room, surrounded by them. They were spread all around her, some half open, some sprawled across the bed as though they'd been thrown. She was crying—my mother who never cried in front of me. I stood at the door of my room, too stunned to speak. We stared at each other and those books, not talking, her crying. And, finally, she turned toward me and said, "I don't understand any of these books, nothing that's in them, nothing they say. How can you read them, understand them, if I can't? How can you still be my daughter and have these on your walls? Who do you think you are to have these in my house?" And then she left.

I have never put together an office when I haven't fought against this sense of betraying my family. My mother's terrible pain when she sat on the edge of my bed envelops me whenever I try to start. I see her grand intelligence and the terrible price she was forced to pay to offer me hope. I feel her wounds at being so cheated of any chances of her own. Her only hope had to rest in me and what her determination could wrest from a poor start. I see her face, the slope of her shoulders, as she cried and touched the books around her and faced the difference she had helped foster between us. It is a terrible thing that the world is so weighted on the side of wealth and privilege.

This is a pain I cannot avoid each time I sit at my typewriter or assemble my office. The ghost of her narrowed options and all the dreams she had to defer to me, the confusions and bitter separation between us, are shapes which hang in my house now and live with me. In order to give me a chance, my parents had to create a child they did not understand; they had to endure my shame of them. The pride we carry about each other is surrounded by a sadness none of us can dissolve.

A BARREN EXPANSE OF LONELINESS

This weekend my lover saw her ex for the first time since we had gotten together, and every specter that could haunt me came out in force. For weeks I had been dreaming of it, imagining that the worst might happen: she would compare me to her, and I would be tarnished in the comparison; I would lose her to this former lover. I would be told Sunday night it was done between us.

I've always hated my jealous side. The high-drama fix is never satisfying enough to compensate for the times when my hysterics shove me so deeply into despair that I go out of control, spinning at the end of my own rope, even occasionally swinging face to face with my desire for death.

When I was younger, I played with it, using it to get me in and out of the crazy situations and settings of my life. I was fond of calling life an "adventure," one that I intended to live out with the best of them: Marilyn Monroe would never have anything over me, and neither would the Hell's Angels. I intended to live my life hard because at the core I didn't expect it to last very long; I wanted to go out in a real blaze of fire and defiance. At that point, sexual jealousy was a stage set to portray myself as sufferer or betrayer, and it was relatively safe because I was straight. I had great power over my emotions, then, since I wasn't feeling much. I could indulge my theatrics, an indulgence I enjoyed and milked for all it was worth. I had also noticed that people who appeared to be suffering or feeling great emotion seemed more interesting to everyone else and were pursued and talked about with admiration or awe.

After high school and still straight, I nurtured my addiction to jealous dramas. I was bored with heterosexuality; heartbreak and jealous betrayal made it a hell of a lot more impressive. It also kept alive my hope that there was still a chance for me; I wasn't quite the freak I thought myself to be. My explosive emotional life covered the genuine drama I was avoiding.

When I fell in love with a woman that first time, the sensation drove right to the center of me. I was shocked and terrified of really feeling. And almost immediately I came up against my first adult confrontation with passionate jealousy. The cards had turned, and I was forced to navigate from actual vulnerability, from aching possessiveness for another person.

That first love taught me a quick, horrible lesson on how jealousy operates when it's really out of control. I was enraged daily by our having to be in the closet, but it wasn't until our relationship began to falter and my lover began to sleep with men that I saw the barren, violent dimensions of my own character. I wanted her dead rather than with a man, and I intended to be the one who killed her. I was so beyond control that, after I found her with a man, I left her in three weeks, afraid every minute I would lose all restraint. It petrified me then. I could be the person on page 1 of a sordid tabloid: "LESBIAN SEX CRIMINAL KILLS LOVER AND FATALLY WOUNDS LOVER'S MALE BEAU."

I have been thinking about jealousy ever since. It has occurred in some form in nearly every relationship with a woman. But it is most powerful with lovers who involve my sexuality deeply, the ones who have read my needs and pushed me to admit my own desires and weaknesses. It is those few women who dare to move me beyond reason through sexual barriers into the basin of my feelings. It is those women I fear, those women I've been least able to accept leaving, and those women who, while our relationship continued, often filled me with wild, jealous passions.

It is this that led me close to suicide, unable to accept that the woman who had first reached through my sexual stop signs could move on to love other women, could make love to them, could move her hands over their bodies the way she had once touched mine. Her leaving exposed me to the horror of the years of barren expanse stretching ahead and laid bare the degree of my own deprivation.

I am rarely touched for long by sex in most relationships. Pretty soon it has become routine; often it has not been the most significant aspect from the beginning. I am profoundly alone most of the time; I feel trapped and caught inside myself. That another woman could release me, even for a minute, also releases richer passions. Her breaking through my sexual isolation allows me to feel all my feelings more vividly, gives me access to the best in my own abilities to reach a lover, to share and listen and roll back her loneliness with impulses that heal us both. I am, at that moment, capable of great love.

But that's the trick. Those feelings make me dependent and raw, wide open to any demand a lover might make. They shift my balance, make me compromise to avoid conflict, and seduce me into not struggling against any difference which comes up between us. I desire unity at any cost, sometimes at the expense of my own independence and needs. I am in a panic to not be walled in alone again. I feel my body to be without its own engine; I am plugged into her desire for me and cannot operate without it. I feel like a beggar, released from bondage for a moment but threatened with return to it if the relationship ends, if I am inadequate at holding this lover in a spell of desire for me. I see how little control I have over the life of the relationship, even with hard work and commitment.

Hard as it might be to allow a lover to be sexual with someone else, I can fight that through, but not the emotional jealousy that desire creates in me. I do not want my lover to share intimate moments with another woman; I do not want to take the chance that, even by accident, another woman might touch her so deeply that she might leave me, that someone else could displace me and I could wake up alone again. I do not like needing another person so deeply. I do not want to know how delicate and uncontrollable this loving another person can be, how little our promises can protect either of us or make it safe to play with these feelings we rouse inside each other.

The looking is never easy; the material of my jealousy is not what I want to understand about myself. But the examination changes me, makes hope possible, gives me reasons behind the fears. I need reasons to keep moving through this knowledge, reason and comprehension. Monday, I will read this to my lover.

THE INTIMATE SIGNS OF WEAR

Already at thirty-seven, I examine my face each day for evidence of the deepening creases; has this one widened? Are the edges around my eyes softening? Has anyone noticed yet that my skin creases at the wrist, neck, elbow, waist? Each day I look for intimate signs of wear, of how I'm holding up, how I think I'm changing.

I look different to myself now, actually older. My expressions don't shift in the same inexperienced sequences. I am no longer called "Miss" by clerks in the stores. It is evident now that I don't need to worry if I forget my ID—my age will not be questioned. My face is catching up with my life and showing through. New York has finally refused to fall for a mythology of innocence I could previously create with my features. Each day it has become harder for me to remember how to spring forward as sharply, to look as intensely into another's face, to be as generous and open in my physical actions toward others.

I have begun to pull my body in around me. I look down at my hands on the subway and realize they're clasped tightly over each other, forming a knot that I have never seen myself make before. I can remember watching this gesture in older women with purses, handbags, and wrinkles. Now I sit with my arms protecting my chest or rigidly poised at each side of my legs. I am not even sure when I began this, but it is happening more and more frequently.

My body is refusing to stay young, refusing to allow me a poise of innocence even as I am aging underneath. That is how it was in my early thirties, my body still with the particular vibrancy that youth bestows. And I was proud of it; I had a kind of cultural arrogance that was, like other forms of passing that I practiced, a mark of my difference from the community of women who reared me, the women who are tired at fourteen and look middle-aged at twenty-three. Those are the women I come from and whom I couldn't afford to look like. I wanted to escape. I had to change how I spoke, which words I selected to explain color and thought and texture. It was like losing my tongue. But my body also had to cooperate in the deceit lest I end up one of the women who works the lunch counter at Woolworth's with swollen legs and face powder that stops at the chin.

Middle-class women look untouched in their twenties and thirties. Their hands have not been burned by a restaurant's deep fat fryer or wrinkled from daily plunging into ammonia and baby shit. Their hands have opened books, sold blouses in the summer, written college entrance exams, washed out their own underwear and nightgowns.

At eighteen, I was cleaning office buildings at night, wringing mops and scrubbing endless corridors with huge pails of ammonia and waxing machines. Then, starting at 9:00 or 10:00 P.M., I would dance in a club, lighted low enough that the condition of my hands didn't matter, only the quantity of bare skin that was showing. I worked in restaurants, hamburger joints, A&Ws, donut shops, cocktail lounges, if I wasn't dancing or stripping. And all of it, in one way or another, depended on my youth and quick thinking—for tips or hiring or getting by. Back then, it was my insides that felt old. The tiredness was in my legs from working two or three jobs at a time, the weariness that settled in young from the worry and the hustles. Still, my body got me by—my body and my wits.

My looks were important because they allowed me to choose which coffee shop I worked in or which bar. But, when things were bad, it was my strength and stamina, that gift of being young, that got me through. I could dance, clean houses and office buildings, and work the graveyard shift at the ice-cream-cone factory, all three if I had to. It was my only safety net. I could make my body work. It would get me a paycheck week after week.

Now I can feel it slowing, tiring, not recovering as quickly when I get sick or depressed. I can't stay up all night and go to work looking all right; in fact, I can hardly pull off getting there at all. My body is refusing to move without subtle pains and creaking. It takes more effort to climb flights of stairs now or help a friend move. These are the symptoms that I can still control. But my face and aging skin have their own timetable and are refusing any longer to cooperate in the lie of ageless years.

I am horrified to be aging, to be entering middle age. I care about my youthful appearance and my sexual desirability, much of which I attribute to my looks. My feminism, I had hoped, would protect me from caring about such things; I would stride right up to middle age and wear it proudly. But it is not proving so simple. I care passionately about my looks. More deeply, I am terrified of what this aging means for me as a survivor, as a woman who has traded in elegance to "get over," attempting to live outside her own people. I haven't the comfort of being surrounded by "my own," and my elegance is slipping.

I have a nightmare that happens too frequently. I am at a dinner party, an elegant intellectual supper. Everyone is female, and everyone there is doing something creative or challenging. I am there in a long creme silk dress; I smell sweet, my hair is perfect, my perfume subtle. In conversation with women around me I am interesting and easy. Then, as I sit there, my hands begin to change and age, my hair turns dull and greasy, all the color disappears from my face, and it becomes lined and pouchy and very tired. My body loses definition, slumping forward at the shoulders while my belly grows folds. My clothes dissolve, leaving me with nothing on except a half-buttoned housedress, ripped under the armpit and unhemmed in the back. My mouth changes shape; my teeth are now cracked and yellow. The words that I had learned to use fluently disappear. I can only talk about television shows, soap operas, ex-lovers. Before those savvy, self-satisfied women I have become my grandmother, a shrunken Irish washerwoman, bitter at taking in other people's dirty clothes seven days a week.

Standing at the edge of the table, I try one last time to talk with the language of their class but cannot remember how. I finally excuse myself and go to the kitchen, where I begin to clean their supper dishes and prepare their desserts.

I do not want to go into my forties and fifties, and yet I am powerless to refuse it. Each day I speak to myself about not allowing the fear, the vanity, the uselessness of this worry to eat at me. But, like other fears planted deep and early, it refuses to negotiate. My own body is going to betray me, and I must live in it daily as it does. I see clearly that my need to be young and attractive is tyrannical, forcing me to reach for a steadily diminishing possibility. But the appeal of beauty and the obvious advantages I reaped from it are "oppressions" I have used to survive. Having my stamina gouged by standards only youth can meet is, to me, bitter. My lover also fears the passing of time, but her fears are about her strength, her continued ability to play racquetball; she worries about needing reading glasses or becoming forgetful. Though she doesn't like how her looks are changing exactly, she is not obsessed with each nuance of skin tone and flesh color. She is butch and middle class. Her career is settled, and she is not dependent on either her looks or the physical strength of her arms to eat. She will age with distinction, not losing her right to sexual territory or image, trading in for a salt-and-pepper look and a low-set stride that gives her body substance and power. As a femme slipping into middle age, I must truly face the rigid standards of female beauty and become increasingly pathetic.

From childhood, I—like so many other women—used desirability as part of getting by. And as an exit from my class. Though I no longer care very much what men think of my looks and believe that lesbians will continue to appreciate me, it is myself that I can't come to terms with. I have a fear of becoming useless, unable to take care of myself, and I fear becoming undesirable and the loss of whatever edge good looks may have gained me. It is my own gaze at my own image in the mirror that frightens me and fills me with loathing. I am the judge I cannot face.

But there have also been moments, recently, of real exhilaration, feeling that my face wears the evidence of my history. There are times when I am sure of myself, confident. I see that my face is lovely as it has never been. There is in me, at those moments, a strange eagerness to see what sort of woman will emerge with the passing of time. There are days of pleasure at who I am becoming and how well it fits me.

But the fear never really goes away, the terror that, without my youthful strength, youthful body, and a fresh young face, I will not have the tools to take care of myself. I feel I am in a race to establish my identity strongly enough to secure a ledge not built on smooth, unlined hands and round, tight buttocks. A spot that can balance the bitterness I feel at these changes with the self-knowledge that comes with age—and with the risks that knowledge allows me to take.

Sympathy of the Blood

I wrote this in 1984 for the Village Voice *gay pride issue. Here, I really did use writing to confront the family I came from, to discuss what it meant to me to be who I was, what it meant to try to go home (although I have changed all the names in the article). This was writing done so that I could see the lines on the faces of the women I grew up loving, so I could remember the sounds outside the trailer parks where I grew up. Along with "What We're Rollin' around in Bed With," it became my best-known piece of work.*

The bus was hot going over the Grapevine toward Bakersfield. The smell of southern California growing valleys, of the dry land between rows of crops, and the low glaze of heat holding in the fever of the earth were drifting toward me. Images of the slightly leaning houses listing from the dust storms, the rains, and the lack of money to keep them perfectly upright, and of the people who were bent over the lettuces or strawberries, reaching up for the beer hops or oranges, were rolling past my eyes like I'd never been away, like I'd never made an escape.

My mother's side of the family came to the United States after the potato famines in Ireland. Later, my grandmother was forced to uproot again, this time from the devastation of the Midwest's dust bowls. She ended up in this semidesert town with her children and her willpower, raising her daughters alone, first as a servant and cleaning woman, and then as a washerwoman to the emerging upper class that was making it on the oil that had been discovered here.

Oildale, just outside Bakersfield, is a town of car mechanics, oil workers, and migrant laborers. It is made up of poor white trash like my family or Mexicans who have settled here, many marrying Anglos. This is Steinbeck's Hoboville, the town I was born in. I am Edna McCune's lesbian granddaughter, and I was finally going home.

I hadn't been to Oildale in twenty years, not since I had first made a break for it, running from the heat and the dead-ends that seemed inevitable if I stayed there. Through twenty years I have dreamed this land, smelled it, hated it, wanted it, and been afraid to return. The running from it caused a hollowness which stretched across most of my adult life, invaded and seduced my dreams, weighed on my mind, and been a part of all I feared as a radical and as a dyke.

I needed to see my grandmother before she died. She was on the critical list, and I had been her favorite granddaughter. Though I had half brothers, first, second, and third cousins, aunts, and uncles, I was the only girl to survive childhood.

I broke with this side of the family when my grandmother, watching the evening news, saw me in an early anti-Vietnam protest march. I never went back after that. But the rift could be traced much further back to a struggle between me and my family over class and hope and the women I desired.

I am not the middle-class woman generally described in the literature used to teach women's studies classes, not like many of the new generation of lesbian feminists. The history of my brand of lesbianism is the story of women who ran from towns like the one I fled, who joined the army, navy, or air force, or who were busted when discovered with another girl and thrown into juvie hall. Or it is a quieter story of women who form a culture different from the feminist one—a life led in gay bars on Friday and Saturday nights if you have a lover, every night if you don't. It is about drinking too much and playing pool with style. It is an underground that runs through the phone company, the Teamsters' Union, the Bank of America, and the grocery counters of this country. It is made up of women you never notice, women who pass as men, and women who are femmes to butches whose bar names are Jesse and Sandy and Paul. I have lived a double life, seducing butches from the bars while working long hours writing, speaking, organizing in the feminist community. Most of the material that I write I have created so that I would see my own life on a piece of paper, see the lines in the faces of the women I grew up with and the women I have loved.

Although I had told my mother and father early on that I was a lesbian, my homosexuality and radical politics were hidden from the rest of the family. "It would hurt them," we said, masking our pain and confusion at what I was: lesbian-Marxist-organizer-feminist. My mother would return periodically to Oildale with vague stories about the city I lived in and how happy I was, but her stories were empty of any details except my general health or weight. After a few years, the family stopped pressuring her about when I was coming to annual family get-togethers, stopped asking for a phone number and address my mother could never produce.

This was the distance I had to travel to protect myself from discovery, a bitter irony of safety and sadness: I had been forced to create this wall between us in order to pursue my life, and, in doing this, I had become other, unknown to them, different from anything they had thought my life would be. Yet they continued to be the people who lived in my mind; their voices were the ones I tried to answer and to write about through all the years of separation. Their fear of my queerness came as much from my moving outside the expectations of our family as it did from sex. They generate their dignity, their lives, through the power of the family and a sympathy of the blood. It was their sense of my betrayal I most wanted to speak to.

The trailer park was very bare. It was a new one, and the concrete slabs which people put their trailers on had no shrubs or trees to soften the hot, cement-grayed earth. Oildale is not very green; it takes too much water to keep lawns lush and flowers healthy.

From the moment I arrived, between visits in the morning and afternoon to the hospital, I worked with the women in my family, piling bologna and lunch meat onto trays and setting them next to loaves of bread, making potato salad, iced tea, and Kool-Aid for the kids, while the men were building a wheelchair ramp at the side of the trailer. I washed Grandma's glass figurines and folded her "company only" tablecloths. I went with everyone to my niece's eighth-grade graduation; I had my picture taken with the rest of the family outside the Sizzler. No one spoke of their despair at Grandma's worsening condition; no one spoke of my return. We worked with the radio blaring and the kids ducking in and out of the trailer. Like always, if it wasn't said out loud, it wasn't there.

Sunday was my last day there, time to break the silence our work could not obliterate. We told stories of our childhoods together: of Jeff cutting up bumble bees on his plate during camping trips; of how we had locked all the grown-ups outside one night until my father finally broke the door in, caught all of us, who got beaten and who got blamed. We remembered secrets we had sworn never to tell and instead had just forgotten as we got older.

We began to speak of getting older. All my cousins are cops or ministers or prison guards; all came back from Nam, married, and had kids. They pulled out old pictures, early baby shots, the guys around Hank's pickup truck at the rifle range, the kids at their baptisms. Wayne had finally joined AA after twenty years of being drunk—a habit he acquired trying to kick the drugs he'd gotten hooked on in the Mekong Delta. Artie had come back from the war and worked at the B. F. Goodrich plant, gotten sick of it, and become a county sheriff. Jeff had come back angry, tried being a cop, then settled in as a Seventh Day Adventist minister. Wayne came back in bad shape. He had trouble keeping a job and ended up a guard at the county prison.

We each dated our lives around Vietnam, they telling war stories, me trying to talk about why I'd joined the antiwar movement. Until two of the boys ripped off their shirts to expose jagged, deep pink scars and even the shrapnel still in their bodies. They asked me, yelled at me, "What do you think of these—do you think we're killers? Do you only cry for Commies when they die?" I yelled back, "Fuck you, that's what I was trying to stop. Do you think it's an accident you were drafted instead of some middle-class college kid? You had no business being there; it wasn't your fight."

I brought out the picture of my woman lover. I had told them all I was a lesbian before making this trip. Now they all stared, embarrassed, at her picture. Aunt Bev said, "Very handsome." Aunt Vera thought she looked "stern." None of the boys called her butch, which she is; they just thought it. "Do you think its hormonal? Were you 'one' when we were kids? Couldn't you find a guy to marry? Were you ever arrested? Does she wear men's clothes? Don't you feel you owe something to the family?"

"What did you think we were doing all those years you were gone? Did you think it was OK to just disappear and never let us know a goddamn thing? Didn't you think we would worry? What do you think we told grandmother? We thought you had joined the Weathermen or something after a while, and we never heard. Did you think it was just all right to disappear from everybody? Or did you think we were too stupid to be bothered with?"

"If I had come back with my antiwar buttons on, would you have let me in the door? If I'd stood in front of the Bakersfield City Jail protesting racism, would you have busted everyone but me? If I'd ridden up on the back of my dyke lover's motorcycle, would you have asked us to stay overnight? If I had come home that way, would you have been asking when I was coming to the next big family picnic?"

We could not have talked before. We had been too arrogant, too sure we were right. But, since then, we had all been pulled apart by inappropriate desires, defeat, illegal abortions, and bullets still lodged in the hip—the unexpected circumstances and forces we could not control. Finally, we could accord each other our differences.

In the last visit before I left, my grandmother didn't remember the television newscast of so long ago. She held my hand and told me stories about what kind of kid I'd been, how I'd caused her a sleepless night or two. She told me about how hard it was for her getting old.

Strategies for Freedom

My ten-year relationship ended in 1990. By 1993 I was still in New York living on my own downtown, doing full-time community organizing work as the director of the Gay Men's Health Crisis (GMHC) Lesbian AIDS Project — the first such project of its kind anywhere in the world — and I was coproducing/directing a documentary film, The Heart of the Matter, *which won the Freedom of Expression Award at the Sundance Film Festival the following year. I wrote this article for a special lesbian/gay edition of the* Nation, *in response to the fact that* Newsweek, Time, *and other mainstream publications were featuring gay material on their covers for the first time in history. The straight world's brief flirtation with what we had begun calling "lesbian chic" was in full swing.*

The good news is, We finally exist to people other than ourselves. The bad news is, On what terms? It is giddy to be written up as "the new power brokers" in *Newsweek* or *Time* magazine. To have the cover of *New York* magazine read, "The New Lesbian Chic." To be invited inside the White House rather than carrying signs or lying down outside it, to be consulted as the experts on our own lives and about our own needs. This is heady stuff. A million strong, marching on Washington. It is a piece of what we have fought to accomplish, what we have literally struggled and died to achieve, and it is momentous and valuable.

But, in this new period of returning Democratic Party dominance, the temptations for us to "go straight" also seem tremendous. Already we are being asked to clean up, dress up, compromise, bargain gratefully with the boys already at the table, the boys who *own* the table. Our agenda, the issues and passions that more truthfully reflect our own needs, like ending the AIDS epidemic, having our partnerships named and valued, assuming our right to be safe, out, and open at work, on the streets, and in the schools of this country, of being allowed to parent if we choose and to create our own kinds of families, all rest on a set of questions deeper than any single issue or session in Congress, and yet each of our issues can be radically affected by what happens there.

We are at the tip of a fragile inclusion that has taken twenty-five years of constant battle to achieve. We are watching as majority culture takes its first baby steps to say the *L* or *G* word out loud and in polite company. This faint call to finally be included and respected, to be allowed to return home from the exile that straight America has set down as the price of being lesbian or gay, is like a siren song to those of us who have been written out of history, forgotten, or hidden in the attics of a heterosexual, white, male closet.

That intoxication makes it even more vital to sustain a long view of the struggle. To be saying to ourselves, in our own voices, *what is key to us,* where are our commitments as a movement to the deeper boundaries that block our liberation as gay people. Lesbian invisibility and the hatred of women in this culture. The struggle against racism and the imperative for significant inclusion and leadership of lesbian and gay men of color. The need to construct a radically queer politics that celebrates and encourages our wild, beautiful, not-like-straight-culture differences; the campy, the butch/femme, the androgynous, the transgendered, the sexual, the willfully queer. When we sit at the inclusion table in this hard-time economy, whose gay battles to survive will be remembered and prioritized? These questions seem to me much more to the point. But, in that bigger world, we are still fighting to control enough power to determine and set our own terms, to lay out the fights as we see them. And to resist the attacks from the Right, which escalate daily.

Our movement is a liberation movement, nothing less. We are a profoundly beautiful people, capable of joy and intense determination to survive. Our roots are deeply placed in every community in this country, and that is our unique strength and peculiar power. When we said twenty-five years ago, *We are everywhere,* we believed it was true, though we couldn't prove it yet. This period is visual proof of that belief, the deep understanding every gay person carries of how many of us there really are. We need to build on that belief and on a commitment to value and respect each other, even as we differ in our understandings and approaches. The attacks from the New Right are insignificant in comparison to the attacks we often launch against each other. The caliber and success of our struggle will be vitally affected by our ability to value each other's lives and thoughts. This is an incredible time, and we are completely equal to the tasks ahead—making ourselves heard in the insider straight boy's world that dominates the headlines and statehouses of today and the bigger fight to build a global movement to be a free and openly gay people. It hinges now, as it always has, on how big we dare to dream and whom we are committed to including. It is up to us and no one else to decide whose voices, whose stories, whose passions, whose hopes and fears and dreams will be at the heart of this fight in the next five or ten years. Our absolute commitment to each others' survival and to leaving none of us behind will change not only us but America itself. And that is really heady stuff.

Sex Work Notes

Some Tensions of a Former Whore and a Practicing Feminist

This is a compendium of things I wrote and thought throughout the 1980s, as I began to reflect on the impact that sex work had had on my life. At this time, I was settled in New York City and was in the middle of a deeply involving, stormy, decade-long relationship. I'd become professionally involved in TV and film, directing and producing. And I continued doing political work— primarily in the area of AIDS activism and as the video producer–educator with the AIDS Discrimination Unit of the Human Right Commission of the City of New York.

Why did it take so long for the women's movement to genuinely con- sider the needs of whores, of women in the sex trades? And why did it take so long for the movement to produce writings by those women? Maybe because it's hard to listen to—I mean really pay attention to—a woman who, without other options, could easily be cleaning your toi- let? Maybe because it's intolerable to listen to the point of view of a woman who makes her living sucking off your husband?

Many sex workers, of course, were and are feminists. And some feminists have long personal histories involving sex work. But, over- all, few movement feminists have had direct experience of the sex-for- dollars world. And everyone in the feminist movement learned how vast the differences between women can be—how all the cultural bar- riers surrounding each of us keep us from stepping easily into another woman's world. The resulting isolation, the narrowing of vision and options, has often forced us to speak only to others like ourselves— despite the fact that the movement always did make prolific use of that universal feminist *we*. But, once acknowledged, the presence of women who earned a living in the sex trades led plenty of feminists to ask, "Who the hell are 'we,' anyway?"

The bottom line for any woman in the sex trades is economics.

However a woman feels when she finally gets full tilt into the life, it always begins as survival—to pay the rent, buy medicine for the kids, buy drugs for yourself, go to college, purchase prenatal care, finance an abortion, run away from an abusive home, live despite lack of documentation, live out a "bad" reputation, flee from incest. Yes; it always starts with just trying to get by. What happens after you enter the world of sex work usually comes as a surprise. At least it did for me.

The personal toll for a woman who goes into sex work quickly becomes painfully clear. All the issues of daily life are complicated immeasurably. How to have and raise children, love a partner, be accepted in the lesbian or the straight world, care for an ailing parent—the list goes on ad infinitum. All these activities are constantly mediated and negotiated through the "crime" of prostitution, with its legal and social fallout. Gail Pheterson, an organizer of the first World Whores' Congress and cofounder of the International Committee for Prostitutes' Rights, links cultural ideas of impurity and defilement with systems of racism, anti-Semitism, class, and "the whore stigma." She chooses these dimensions because, she says, each exposes the social justifications for silencing and degrading women who work as whores.

From my teens through my early twenties, until I suffered serious illness and injury and had to stop working, I was an "exotic" dancer, a stripper, and a hooker. This was something I rarely discussed until the late 1980s. When I did start to speak and write about that part of my past, it was as an attempt to bridge my own history—as a sex worker, a political organizer, a lesbian, and an ardent feminist—to embrace everything, to come to an understanding that would encompass and somehow unify all these seemingly disparate elements of my life. I came to believe that, if we are not to sacrifice some essential part of ourselves or our community, we all have to go through the grief of genuine exposure and struggle, often banking on only a thin line of faith or trust that we will emerge whole and unbroken. The only way I knew to begin this process for myself was by saying, "I will give up nothing; I will give up no one."

In 1984 my mother became very ill. I went back home to see her. But before I entered her hospital room, my father pulled me aside and said, "Someone sent your mother an article where you talked about having been a prostitute. I don't know who sent it, there was no name on the envelope, but your mother is very, very upset. I just wanted you to know in case she brings it up." That article was a review I'd written for the *Women's Review of Books*—a discussion of two books about sex-trade workers. In it, I'd written about the tensions I felt as a former prostitute and a practicing feminist; I'd written about the silence that fear of exposure can impose. I was referring, then, to my fear of rejection by the feminist community; but, of course, my deeper fear was of facing my own family. At the time, though, I had decided not to be paranoid and had gone ahead and published. The package sent to my ailing mother was a reminder that my paranoia had been based on something very real. It was also an intentional threat. The whore stigma is not imaginary; it underscores the "good girl/bad girl" dichotomy we all grow up with and pinpoints the punishment in store for any woman who "slips" from being madonna to being whore. It reinforces the fear that, once you have crossed over to the world of sex work, you will never be allowed back into the straight, "moral" universe. The package sent to my mother spoke volumes about the impossibility of leaving one's past behind.

If the world of sex work is usually concealed, the world of lesbian sex workers is completely invisible. Throughout every part of the sex-trade business there are lesbians working as hookers and dancers, as dykes who function in massage parlors and as the lesbian madams of brothels and escort services—and as prostitutes' rights organizers around the world. Especially in the working-class world of butch and femme life and in working-class gay and lesbian bars, these spaces operated as one of the few safe locations for many lesbian sex workers. It was one of the infrequent places where as a sex worker I could be open about the butch women I desired and the work that provided my living. It remains one of the few access points where those worlds meet and merge.

Women who have worked in the trades have different feelings about the experience of their work. What a woman must do to be paid, the conditions she has to endure, on the streets, night after night, in freezing cold or rain, in bars and filthy massage parlors, the endless confrontations with brutal cops or dangerous johns and madams or abusive pimps or vice squads, the constant fear of arrest—all these elements complicate how you feel about the work itself. If sex work is work—and I maintain that it is just that, wage labor, service for a fee—then the issue of working conditions is something that a movement dedicated to the liberation of all women cannot choose to ignore. Over and over, sex workers have begged the feminist movement to support them as they struggled to organize and control this aspect of their working lives. Because, first and foremost, the way the work itself is structured forces the women (and the men) who do it to live outside any established legal or community framework that could protect or empower them.

The greatest dangers, of course, are faced by street workers. These are the people most vulnerable to violence—from trick, pimp, or police. It's no accident that the majority of women who work the streets are our society's poorest women. Often, they are women of color. The dual impact of poverty and race on sex work is enormous; statistics alone make that clear. In the United States, while about 40 percent of street prostitutes are women of color, 55 percent of those arrested are. The overt racism of the state, when it comes to prostitution, is even more apparent when you look at the figures on who gets jailed: 85 percent of prostitutes sentenced to do jail time are women of color. These least powerful, most vulnerable of women are the ones who suffer the brunt of this culture's overt hatred for all women. And it is these women who are most vulnerable both to the violence of the trick and the power of the police. Because the fact remains that prostitution laws can be used against any woman, at any time the state wishes to. When women are out alone on the street, in a bar, at a bus stop, or when we are being sexually assertive on our own terms, we are all vulnerable to being crushed under the same whore stigma that is the unspoken basis for those laws. The *whore* label is attached to anyone who works in the sex industry as a prostitute, pornography model, striptease dancer, masseuse, sexual surrogate, or other provider of sexual service for entertainment. The whore is the prototype of the stigmatized woman or feminized man. But it's important to keep in mind that not only prostitutes are labeled *whores.* Any woman may be designated a whore within a particular cultural setting.

The control and organization of prostitution varies greatly from country to country and even from region to region within a country.

This depends on factors as ephemeral as the individual "moral" beliefs of the local police chief or as concrete as the way certain streets are structured in a particular city or town. But the common denominator internationally, despite all the differences in working conditions and settings, is the fact that almost nowhere are prostitutes organized to represent their own interests.

I don't have any idea what the sex trades would look like if women could consciously choose the work, or if they had a whole slew of other really viable options going for them. Class, race, age, and physical appearance all intersect in the sex trades. It's a world of hierarchies, with street workers at the bottom. But some concerns affect everyone: control over working conditions, access to health care, Social Security, worker's compensation, and the ability to avoid continual prosecution. It's clear to me that (1) decriminalization of prostitution in this country, (2) an organized international prostitutes' rights movement, and (3) becoming a recognized part of the global drive for workers' rights and unionization would begin to positively transform some of the most dangerous aspects of the work. If we want to respond to and support women in the sex business, the women's movement must also ask why we have failed, so far, to advocate for and build strong and lasting ties to women in prison and more generally to other classes and communities of women altogether. We must stop ignoring the issues these women need recognized: drug addiction, the creation of more women-specific drug-recovery programs, HIV risk and prevention money for hookers, the repeal of HIV testing programs for pregnant women. The problems specific to immigrant women, to women on welfare and workfare, also fall under the constellation of concerns that often influence the lives of women who are sex workers. Consciousness is a starting place for support of prostitutes' rights, but the nitty-gritty of that support—especially as it might help street workers—needs to be looked at more closely. Street workers face a deadly fight to wrench control of prostitution away from the dangerous, unwanted pimps and dealers, from the police and the courts. And no group of sex workers will ever fully welcome feminism, or its questions about the meaning of sex work, in the absence of such comprehensive support.

As long as prostitutes' lives are so devalued that we can be killed at will by anyone at all while few protest, as long as these murders go markedly unnoticed when the victims are black, brown, red, yellow, or white, as long as women can be forced against their will to engage in sex anyway, as long as young women can be forced to sell sex to survive, we in the feminist movement need to respond. Working conditions, health, AIDS risks, violence against prostitutes, police refusal to believe a prostitute can be raped—all these things demand our attention. Debates about representation and sexism, or violence against women and pornography, or the meaning of sexual autonomy, or the struggle to get rid of the internalized sexism that we have each absorbed, all need to continue, but so does organizing for survival. No matter how much any of us agree or disagree on the meaning and significance of prostitution, none of us can afford not to support prostitutes' rights.

The world I lived in as a lesbian whore and exotic dancer was a world full of men who dropped in, from positions of power or relative powerlessness, to visit the gendered environment of prostitution. They came for sex, they came in need, they came for conversation, they came for solace, they came to ogle me, or they came in anger and with the desire to shatter and destroy. They entered a realm full of women who had no ability to resist whatever they chose to bring. The work itself was hard, but it wasn't the work of sex that made it dangerous—it was that no whore could ever hope to have an authentic female voice with legitimate rights if she came from this discredited place: an underground world that depends on keeping all its activity outside the verifiable world of labor and of commerce and, therefore, outside society's laws.

One night, at an International AIDS Education Conference in Yaounde, Cameroon, in 1986, a theatrical group of female sex workers, all of whom were still in the life, appeared as part of an evening of drama. These women were deeply funny, very savvy—detailing their clients' fears, their own sexual sophistication, the comedic elements of the business, the subtle camaraderie they developed after deciding that none of them would take on a customer without using a condom. Later, I sat in the dark thinking about all that would be destroyed if we don't finally lay the whore stigma to rest. Even more urgently, I thought of all those women who would be lost to the movement if we didn't finally come to terms with it.

Lesbianism Is Not a Condom

Facing Our Risks for HIV *in the Middle of an Epidemic*

Dedicated to Gail Pheterson

This is one of the first pieces I wrote about lesbians and AIDS *when I became director of the Lesbian* AIDS *Project at Gay Men's Health Crisis (*GMHC*) in New York City. From 1990 to 1998, I was deeply involved in organizing around* AIDS*, women's issues, and lesbian issues. Very few white lesbians were talking about the impact of* HIV *and* AIDS *on the lesbian community or in the lesbian health movement. Except for those of us already doing* AIDS *work, or those lesbians already infected with* HIV*, women-who-slept-with-women (*WSW*) were a completely invisible cluster within a still-marginal group in the epidemic overall.*

I was deeply frustrated at this point in my life with the direction the women's movement was taking. I was tired of the sex wars' legacy of bitter fighting. As an organizer, I also wanted to see what would happen to feminist ideas and feminist theories if those beliefs were presented to a different community of women who had no relationship to the women's movement: primarily poor and working-class lesbians, often lesbians of color. What would happen to feminism, what elements of feminist thought would still be found useful, if enacted and understood within the contexts of different cultures, filtered through different class, race, and sexual systems?

Much of my writing during this period was a way of sorting out what I was seeing in my work. It was a way to respond to the kinds of questions I was being asked, the kinds of answers I was beginning to form in active response.

The invisibility of lesbian risk for HIV is a classic example of the greater sexual and social invisibility we suffer in the world at large. Women who sleep with other women, no matter what we call ourselves, exist in every community of this country, yet we remain stubbornly unseen or unrepresented in the larger AIDS blueprint. Thirteen years into the epidemic (an epidemic marked by discrimination and government in-action) an entire community of women as diverse in our sexual and social habits as the broad lesbian and female bisexual communities remains marginalized or absent altogether from any basic, integrated awareness of HIV transmission, risk, and prevention.

For many women who are sleeping with other women, this invisi-bility leads them through a maze already marked by confusion, denial, and fear about AIDS. For lesbians who are HIV positive, this confusion and panic leaves them even more vulnerable, often forcing them to exist without community support, respect, advocacy, and inclusion in the broad lesbian, AIDS, and women's community. Yet questions con-tinue unanswered:

Is AIDS really a lesbian issue?

Is there risk of sexual transmission between female sex partners?

How prevalent is our drug use, and how much does that put us at risk?

How many women who are sleeping with other women are also having unprotected sex with men (or have had in the last few years)?

These questions and the doubts they raise refuse to go away. Yet reli-able information about these issues, issues that profoundly influence our communities' survival, remain unavailable.

The lines linking our various and intricately connected communi-ties of women who sleep with women are very obscure. And the world through which most lesbians openly travel is very restricted. It is a geography rigorously determined by background, by class and color, by rural landscape or city streets, by whether we are politically active or spiritually inclined, by the narrow confines of age and health, by lives defined by lesbian bars, gay studies programs, or the military, by how we each came out and with whom, by our status as lesbian mothers or our decisions not to have children, by our dreams and aspirations, by our very ability to have dreams or hope for our own futures.

As lesbians in this culture we suffer from the same lack of power and resources common to all women. In the midst of that oppression we must also navigate our health, sexuality, and social existence in an environment committed to imagining all women as heterosexual. In a universe without voice or presence, lesbians and our particular risks for HIV have remained submerged inside a "straight" female landscape, keeping us ignorant and uninformed about our own risks for HIV. We are a specific population of women with high numbers of HIV-positive members but no official recognition or accounting.

In the midst of this blank space, the "secret" of lesbian risk and lesbian death due to HIV spirals. This spiral magnifies the confusion among us, leading the entire community into doubt and anger. Some lesbians deny all vulnerability to HIV, making the question of risky behaviors, especially safe sex between women, appear dangerously unknowable. For lesbians who are HIV positive or have AIDS, the gap becomes a gulf marking them outside the status of "real" lesbians by behaviors other portions of our community disown as an integral part of the accepted lesbian landscape, like sex with men, drug use among us, or the possibility of sexual transmission between female sex partners.

It is here that race and class background becomes a particularly vicious component of our risks for HIV. For middle-class lesbians, the margins we have from birth can slip quickly away when (or if) it becomes known that we are sleeping with other women. For working-class women without any buffers, the picture is immediately more fragile, yet our need for our communities of birth is accentuated if we are women of color, women whose first language is not English, or we are poor or working-class women who are responsible for and committed to the survival of our extended families. In this already contested setting, HIV/AIDS is often devastating, while our resources remain scarce. We are often forced to lie and hide our sexual desire for other women so that we can access the health care or social services we need. We also hide in order to guarantee the commitment and support of our biological families, our jobs, our neighborhoods, our children, our language, and our access to valued cultural institutions. Medically, socially, and economically, the less room we have to turn around, the more problematic our crisis becomes as we balance precariously between the women we desire and the help and support we need.

The crisis is compounded by the lack of decent, nonjudgmental information about lesbian sexuality. Because it remains unacceptable to love and desire other women sexually, we are also left with little sub-

stantial information about what we do in bed with each other, including what might put us at risk. Sexually transmitted diseases of all kinds
are little understood or discussed between women partners, and the
fear and ignorance surrounding HIV compound the already existing
blank space encircling our sexuality. Like all prejudices, homophobia
hurts us profoundly, leaving us unarmed and unprotected, as though
forbidding the word (*lesbian*) of our existence could stop the act of our
love. It doesn't, of course; it just leaves us vulnerable and uninformed.
Our communities' confusion about whether AIDS is a lesbian issue reflects these biases.

The denial of our risk for HIV is often supported by a circumscribed lesbian sexual border we have constructed, refusing to acknowledge or accept that we sleep with each other in many, many
different ways. We are butch/femme women; we are queer or androgynous; we are lesbian feminist; we don't believe in labels; we practice
s/M; we use our hands, our mouths, our bodies, sex toys, to pleasure
and please each other; and we may also sleep with men, whether we
call that *bisexuality, coming out, economic necessity,* or we don't dare talk
about it. Drug use and alcoholism in our communities has always
been an unrecognized crisis, compounded by our invisibility and our
lack of political clout. And suicide, especially among young lesbians,
is another epidemic in this population of women who love each other.
All these activities and identities are components of our communities'
sexual and social lives. While we have taken an extraordinary risk in
daring to love another woman, this has not guaranteed that our judgments against each other's erotic or drug choices won't be as cruel as
the general culture's judgments about us. Our understandings of the
reasons many of us shoot or snort drugs, drink till it harms us, experiment with substances that can hurt us, are stories that we have
not let surface enough inside our community, hoping to not be hit any
harder by social condemnation than we already are. It's as though we
think by disavowing a set of activities (and the women we stereotype
as doing them) we can protect ourselves from even more homophobia.
We carry those prejudices into our sexual judgments as well, thinking
that, if we don't enjoy a particular sexual activity ourselves, no other
lesbian will either. If another woman *wants* differently, she is in danger of having her credibility as a "real" lesbian questioned. Yet we are

women who are sexual originators and social inventors, leaping across the sexual and emotional silences surrounding women's desires for other women, daring to touch and possess each other sexually, daring to claim our right to be sexual, to love and want another woman.

Our right to be sexual with each other and to struggle with the issues of our daily lives is, like drug use, just one piece of the lesbian puzzle. Whether or not the larger culture acknowledges us, we must recognize each other and our different struggles. The lesbian map is very large, our numbers are significant, and we must pick up this fight to protect ourselves and each other while we fight to be seen and respected. We can't wait for other people to see what is right in front of our noses—that we are an integral part of this world, not outside it, and that so is a potentially fatal virus, HIV. Our community is not immune, and lesbianism is not a condom for AIDS. Like everyone else, we are vulnerable and must take the steps necessary to learn how to protect each other's lives. No one else will do it for us, and no one will do it as well. We have been taking risks to love each other for millennia. Now we need to expand our understanding of who we are and what we do in order to understand the many ways we need to go forward. Our communities are fabulously sexual and inventive, and we can support each other in taking the steps each of us needs to be safe, erotic, and powerful.

Transmission, Transmission, Where's the Transmission?

This essay was my way of trying to answer the question people always brought up whenever the topic of lesbians and AIDS arose: Can unprotected sex between two female partners transmit HIV? It was as if the credibility of the entire issue of lesbian vulnerability to AIDS hinged on the answer to that question. The fact that a lesbian remains a lesbian when she shoots drugs, or when she has sex with a man, seems to amaze people—even other lesbians. This is one of the reasons why it has been so difficult to do education work in communities of women who sleep with women about their risks for all STDs, including HIV. No education, no prevention.

I was angry when I wrote this, tired of middle-class lesbians acting as though the world of lesbianism—and of sexual risk—was only important if it was about them, because they were the only authentic and "real" lesbians in the world. The experiences and daily realities of working-class lesbians— lesbians of color, immigrant lesbians, homeless lesbians, lesbians whose first language is not English, lesbians in prisons or in drug and rehab centers, lesbian single moms struggling with workfare or welfare, transsexuals and their female lovers, teenaged lesbians, lesbian sex workers, drug dealers, and street women—these were the women I wanted to speak to, to reach. And it was how HIV and AIDS affected this group of lesbians that I was trying to comprehend and convey.

At a health forum about HIV-positive lesbian health-care needs, sponsored just last week by the Lesbian AIDS Project (LAP) of the Gay Men's Health Crisis (GMHC), of which I am the director, two women in a room of 150 people finally spoke out late into the program. Each unknown to the other until that night, first one stood, then the other, and said, "I am here as an HIV-positive lesbian infected through sex with my HIV-positive female partner. I have been ridiculed and dismissed in talking about this, but I am here to say that I am not a liar or an exception. Before I was infected with HIV, I did not believe that lesbians could get AIDS. And like many of you in this room I didn't believe that women could pass this virus sexually to another woman. But I know differently now. The question for me is, How many more of us will have to stand up and testify about our own lives and our histories of sexual transmission with another woman before we are believed? Two of us know more now. And so should you." Their eloquence silenced us all.

I am the director of the only, to date, lesbian-specific AIDS project in the world, but I work with a network of over a hundred frontline lesbian and bisexual health-care and activist women who confront, in similar ways, what I see daily. And each of us has been appalled at the growing number of lesbians with AIDS or HIV with whom we work while the consciousness about this in different segments of our communities remains so low. And though we often don't agree among ourselves on the exact or most probable sexual routes of transmission among women, we all agree that we are seeing the numbers grow in all categories of risk, including this one.

When the project began, I felt it was vital to reach and serve lesbians with AIDS, regardless of our numbers; today I have met hundreds of lesbians with AIDS. The LAP HIV-Positive Lesbian Leadership Project has just begun to organize the first conference only for HIV-positive women who partner with women, and we expect this local, one-day conference to have 100–150 HIV-positive lesbians, and we're already worried that we are undercounting. In story after story and conference after conference, each of us doing this work recounts a local horror story of who in our own communities still discounts the expanding reality of lesbians and HIV while we see the crisis broadening.

Our government also continues to confuse visibility, identity, and behavior—this same government that brought us the idea that a woman is a lesbian only if she has not slept with a man since 1977 and the same government that refuses to recognize or track our behaviors, rendering us paralyzed when we try to figure out exactly what is going on and why. We are in two-sided trouble—no serious help from the outside and a resulting debate and denial inside some of our own communities about these issues. The consequence of having so little to go on when we struggle to create sound, conservative, clear-eyed descriptions of our risks as women who partner with women and to quantify our numbers for HIV is that many of us who are doing the work are left angry and bitter. We know that listening to the government is always tricky, though necessary, but that, in this as in all else concerning our survival, we have to use every tool at our disposal. But what many, many of us are seeing, we fear, is just the lesbian tip of the HIV iceberg in our communities—a warning that we can pay attention to or dismiss at our own eventual peril. This is not about scare tactics; it's about survival.

Still, from its beginning two years ago, I have resisted LAP being pulled into the woman-to-woman sexual transmission debate because it was clear to me that people wanted to define our vulnerability and need for recognition, research, and AIDS services solely through this one question, rather than understanding that whatever we eventually learn scientifically about sexual transmission between unprotected female partners, lesbians as a people are uninformed about all the ways we may be vulnerable to HIV and consequentially our communities lack vital and lifesaving information that would prepare us to adequately assess all our risks and vulnerabilities to HIV.

This continuing misguided and entrenched polemic concerning woman-to-woman sexual transmission, which is still positing that lesbians cannot transmit the virus to each other sexually, has had broad and terrible consequences overall in our communities. We have been told we are not at risk for HIV sexually and therefore are the "lowest" risk group overall for contracting the virus, which has then led to many erroneous and tragic conclusions and confusions when each of us tries to understand her own personal risk for HIV.

When a lesbian says that she doesn't know how she could have contracted AIDS because she *only* shared needles with other lesbians and that, since lesbians are not at risk for AIDS, she thought she would be safe from the virus, or when another dyke says that she and her HIV-positive female partner called the AIDS hotline for safer-sex information and were told that there was little to no risk in "regular" lesbian sex and now she too is positive, or when a woman calls crying that she is a lesbian, really, has been all her life, and has slept only with other women, many of whom were HIV positive, though she was raped once and can't get the CDC or her AIDS provider to not list hers as heterosexual transmission because of the rape even though she has buried two female lovers to AIDS—then the catastrophe is laid bare. It means that, as a lesbian body politic, we remain unreached and untargeted as a people trying to confront the intricate truth of our own histories, memories, conversations, accessments, knowledge, and geography.

In the midst of this tragic confusion, with little official or community recognition regarding all our risks (including our primary exposure for HIV still being drug use and unprotected sex with infected men), it is important to point out that the third and smallest category of women who attribute their HIV infection to HIV-positive female sex partners continues to grow. Though these women have been vilified and belittled in many AIDS and lesbian communities and disbelieved by many health-care providers, and when most of the research to date was set up explicitly to try to discount their knowledge and clarity about how they became infected—in the face of such impossibly huge roadblocks, more and more lesbians continue to stubbornly report woman-to-woman unprotected sex as their only or primary risk for HIV.*

This fight about HIV transmission sexually between women calls up so many simmering issues in our communities and needs to be seen for what it is—a political battle, often between friends, about what we are seeing and hearing and how we interpret that information between us. I was equally confronted immediately by a set of ideological questions that could not be shoveled under the "scientific" or "HIV medical expert" rug and which are painful to discuss and hard to bridge. How do we talk class and race in our various women-who-partner-with-women communities? Who are the *we* when we generalize the demographics of our lives and activities vis-à-vis any risk, and where does that leave us when we try to understand something as complicated as HIV jeopardy or even try to grapple with what "we" do in bed. What meter are we using to talk about *us,* and how can we generalize and differentiate in this and other significant arguments within various lesbian communities?

Bottom line for me is I don't believe the unspoken construction of

*J. D. Rich et al. "Transmission of HIV Presumed to Have Occurred via Female Homosexual Contact," *Clinical Infectious Diseases* 17(6), 1993.

"our" lesbian community and "our" judgment about the implications for or against our HIV risk as it's presented, that we are a nearly monolithic, mostly middle-class, mostly white, serially monogamous group of women who sleep with each other and rarely or ever do the things that are identified with AIDS risk—not much shared-needle drug use or unprotected sex with men and certainly not much "rough sex," whatever that means. Do those assumptions really serve us well? Is that really who we are, or do we need much more rigor when any of us writes or speaks about HIV risk so that we call forth the range and complexities of the many ways we present ourselves as a group, that breadth and combinations of ages and identities and colors and behaviors over time and class stratifications and coming-out histories that all but disappears?

Who is being spoken to or about, and who is being included in the construction of community and HIV risk? And who remains invisible or has been removed and dismissed with a sentence or a footnote as unimportant or not significant to this discussion? Do the places we can most easily document HIV among lesbians, such as prisons, outpatient clinics, shelters, and drug-recovery settings, mean that many other lesbians who don't come out of these experiences can dismiss any significance for themselves and their own HIV risk because they see themselves differently from "those kind of women" because they are much more middle class and/or white and don't have to also take on the issue of lesbian HIV?

These acted-on but usually unstated prejudices have led to a kind of lesbian sexual apartheid when we talk about HIV—"it's over there, for those kinds of dykes, in those bars or those outside communities, but it is not about 'us,' and therefore we have nothing to learn from those others because we have named ourselves out of danger, hiding or not encouraging discussion of our many similarities as well as the differences." And it has made most conversations about this issue nearly impossible to translate through that passion because at the core we are fighting out the race, class, and sexual differences between us, which are often based on our own opinions and prejudices but which we are reluctant to openly state.

I think this conflation of demographics, preconceived ideas, and risk significantly influences the overall understanding of HIV in various lesbian and women-who-partner-with-women communities. Research of any kind to this point is painfully scant, but what we do have simply indicates the frontline vulnerability of various parts of our communities—young lesbians, women who are coming out, poor, working-class lesbians, and/or lesbians of color—and cries out for a passionate insistence by all of us for more research, more inclusion, more inquiry, and more subtle tracking mechanisms that can begin to unlock the rich, tangled meanings and significance of behaviors, activities, orientations, identities, and demographics. When we are asking about all those categories and crossovers among ourselves, who are we asking about, who are we describing in our mind's eye? We have so little information or data about ourselves that, when we come up against any of these big topics—parenting, breast cancer, chemical dependence and alcoholism, suicide, sex with men, sex with women—we have the skimpiest information to draw on. This, sadly, is a literal reflection of our oppression and our need.

This leaves us staring out at an uncomfortable reality: we have no power to demand the research we need in order to understand what's happening in our communities. We have no long-range, significant research into the possible transmission activities that might be suggestive when looking at the arena of unprotected sex between women and HIV. No research on the different progressions and intensities of HIV viral load in a woman's bodily fluids over the course of HIV infection through to AIDS. No research to see if there is any corollary intersection when a woman is HIV positive and has a yeast infection or a sexually transmitted disease (STD), which often causes an increase in the white blood cells present in vaginal secretions and could lead to a concentration of HIV in a women's vaginal secretions while fighting off that yeast infection or STD. Where is the research we need on cervical warts and cancers and their impact on virus distribution in vaginal fluids? What of HPV and HIV? Where is the research helping us determine the potential impact on an HIV-negative female partner if she has herpes simplex and her lesbian lover has just contracted HIV?

Where can we find the work we need that reflects the reality of how few lesbians access any kind of health care preventively, let alone get Pap smears or pelvic exams? What do we do when a lesbian's own medical provider tells her she doesn't need these procedures "since lesbians don't have sex with men"? What to do when chlamydia, so hard to identify and so often remaining hidden without specific testing, is being endlessly passed between female sex partners without adequate medical interventions? When will it be stark enough that, as lesbians, as women, we are not generally taught how to understand our own bodies or our own sexuality?

It is a perfect circle back to the magical-lesbian-free-of-contagion message reflected in the simplistic and dangerous representations of "the healthy vagina." True, both saliva and vaginal secretions are structured to fight infections. But there is an important piece of counter-information any woman can access for herself. Simply consider your own pelvic history—for most of us it is a history of cyclic yeast infections, tric, chlamydia, bacterial vaginitis, herpes, endometriosis, PID (pelvic inflammatory disease), interrupted menstrual cycles, and unexpected spot bleeding, to name just a few.

Sometimes I think our vaginal and pelvic histories are like our phenomenal ability to "forget" when our periods are coming, month after month, year after year. As women, we have vaginal memory loss and the feminist and lesbian health movement struggles against this year after year. It is like pushing boulders up a hill.

There is also little relevant and useful research about all our "cross-over" activities which begin reflecting an accurate representation of the varieties of our sexual activities and of our shared drug use and which would begin to sketch out a more elaborate map of who and what we are doing sexually and socially and how that may contribute to or mask our risks for HIV. In this debate we are shackled with dead-end codes like *lesbian sex* or *rough sex,* which tell us nothing, in lieu of a demand for serious, multifaceted sexuality and drug-use studies which know how to ask a complicated trajectory of questions in order to capture the web of actions, desires, identities, and ideologies we practice in bed or put into our bodies.

We must also address the bitter history of the sex wars and the correspondingly lost or hidden sexual narratives in many lesbian communities. These wars and their earliest foundation in our female socialization are the chronicles of our painful legacy as women kept ignorant about our bodies and our sexual options. When we speak of who we are and yet fail to mark out the tremendous effect of this silencing and lack of knowledge and the corresponding issues of needing a lesbian sexual language and how that scarcity affects our abilities to talk openly about what we really do in bed with another woman (or with a man), let alone speak about the impact of the stigmas attached to openly acknowledging substance use or dependency, when these are hardly mentioned or mentioned only in passing as though very unimportant, then the complex lesbian needs for "safer sex for lesbians" have not been substantially addressed. What the sweeping dismissiveness of the lesbian risk of HIV does encourage, though, is the refusal in the different parts of our communities to recognize that we are in a world forever changed by AIDS, and we merit more than simplistic "don't worry, we're really safe" messages as we confront the complicated nature of our lives as lesbians and bisexual women in the middle of the epidemic.

I think the bottom line of crisis and difference between different lesbian communities is reflected more realistically in the speed with which we can adequately address our individual health-care needs, not whether any of this can or does happen to each of us similarly. And it is the same with HIV. The question isn't how we are different from each other, and therefore not at risk, but only the actual distance between the most vulnerable among us and the most sheltered.

SO WHAT DO I THINK ABOUT OUR SEXUAL RISKS?

Simply, what do I think about transmission of the virus sexually between women? This is only my opinion, and I won't try to represent it as "fact." It is based on the best thinking and research I can bring to it, but there is still much we need to know to come to any final answer, as I tried to suggest earlier. But here goes—

I think this virus is much harder to transmit to a woman having any kind of unprotected sex with another woman than to a woman shooting drugs and sharing works with another woman or to a woman having unprotected sex with a man. But I do think the virus can be transmitted through our vaginal secretions in high enough concentrations and over time, especially if there are existing cofactors, as well as through going down on each other when there is menstrual or any kind of blood present. I don't think that "rough sex" has much to do with it since vaginal "trauma" occurs with any penetrative sexual act: fingers, fists, or dildos. I think, given the just-analyzed data in the LAP sex survey, that women are practicing a wider range of sexual activities than we previously thought, from rimming and sex-toy play to vaginal and anal fisting and group sex. The key factor in this, I think, is repeated exposure, and, given the ways we partner (even casually with fuck buddies, whom we often see more than once), we have many community patterns that support our repeated exposure to HIV with a female partner who might be infected.

I also think that any yeast infection or STD compounds our risk dramatically. I am worried that we have no idea how widespread this crisis is in our communities and that, when cofactors like STDS, HPV, herpes, and yeast infections are combined with the notion that we aren't at risk for HIV (or can't spread it sexually between women), our chance of exposure increases again. It also seems to me that lesbians don't often know their antibody status until very late in the progression of the disease and cannot therefore protect their partners or even recognize the need to do so. I would also guess that transmission is more likely at the beginning of HIV infection than later in the disease, though it continues to be possible. I think that as more and more of us are infected, in whatever ways we are, the chance of using, sleeping with, or being lovers with an HIV-positive woman, whether she or her lover is aware of it, is increasing. And, finally, I think the amount of crossover activity, both sex with men (often gay or bisexual) and our sharing of needles, is still very underreported and underrepresented in our communities, all our communities, and that, too, increases the number of us who are being infected with HIV. In every study that I have seen to date about various lesbian and bisexual women's communities, we are the group who accesses any health care last, and with good reason. As lesbians, as women, often as poor or working-class women, as women of color, as lesbians struggling with addictions in an often homophobic recovery environment, as women who are "coming out," as mothers who fear the loss of our children if we self-disclose or are brought out, for all these reasons we use health-care services last, and this, too, increases our risks for STDS, HIV, cancers, and many, many other illnesses.

Is saying this "erotophobic" (ironically, a term I created in 1981)? Or are we trying to say that, as sexual adults, we need to look frankly at what we are grappling with, in bed and in our heads, as women, as lesbians, and that those things factor in when we are sexually active with anyone? If we are still at the point in our communities where we often cannot talk to a woman partner about much of anything sexually, of what would delight us or what isn't working when we are making love, if it is still hard to say, "Lower, darling, and harder," where are we when we confront our risks for HIV? If many of us have been systematically excluded from the medical information we need to help us self-diagnose yeast infections and other sexually transmitted diseases and so can't tell when we have these medical problems, this also increases our sexual vulnerability. If talking sex is still hard, than thinking hot and thinking safe is a wide stretch for most of us. It is for me. I am forty-seven years old, and I am still struggling to bring voice and sexual awareness together with my desires and actions.

To know that HIV is in our communities and that it is growing, and to know that working-class lesbians, most often African American and Latino dykes, are being hit hardest right now, is not to deny HIV's eventual power to affect and infect any of us. As a very diverse set of communities of women who love and have sex with each other, are we going to believe numbers only when it is too late to get in here and tackle it directly?

Finally, none of the lesbians I know who are doing this work are trying to suggest that what is happening to us looks like the devastation now visible in the gay male communities. But I have been surprised and moved that, when I say to gay men, "We need help precisely because it is still possible for us to reach our communities before the scale is tipped from prevention to fighting brush fires, and if we get in here quickly enough, we might be able to be one of the few remaining communities who could still turn this around"—when I say that, they are right there. This battle for recognition of our risk of HIV and of the number of lesbians now struggling with AIDS is not "virus envy" or victim gliding, and it is not trying to scare our various women's communities. But it is saying that, in a culture that hates and reviles us, refusing to recognize how and where and in which ways are we being affected by HIV, and then pointing out where that will ultimately lead, is mandatory. We need to learn from the powerful histories of women and gay men that surround us and name this crisis now.

When I said lesbianism is not a condom, I meant exactly to confront what many in our communities won't—that we are not immune to this virus, that our communities and behaviors and identities are extraordinarily broad and complex and HIV/AIDS is not insignificant in our communities. The number of lesbians and women who partner with women continues to grow, while our access to health care and diagnosis remains minute. We can no longer afford to hide behind the false shelter of our identities while we watch our numbers grow.

Lesbian Denial and

Lesbian Leadership in the AIDS Epidemic

Bravery and Fear in the Construction of a

Lesbian Geography of Risk

I wrote this piece in an attempt to improve my own genuine understanding of the politics of lesbian invisibility; to communicate how I see the realities of class, race, and sexual desire as lived outside the boundaries of middle-class lesbian feminism. As literally hundreds of HIV-positive lesbians and their partners and families found their way to the Lesbian AIDS Project in New York City, the heretofore missing stories and textures, the voices and materialities of these women-who-desired-women became wonderfully distinct and visible.

I was writing to portray how this previously invisible community of lesbians was at risk: working-class and poor women, lesbians who were not feminist-identified, women who were or had been IV drug users, who had a history of incarceration and sex work. These women and their children, I believed, would comprise the next great tidal wave of AIDS casualties in this country.

This essay is also a continuation of writing that represents my own attempts to decipher the impact of the AIDS movement on feminism, the Left, and progressive queer movements. It is an attempt to bridge the extraordinary gap between the political reality of one vociferous class of lesbians and that of a voiceless "other" group, a group representing the "wrong" sexual and erotic histories. This was an exhilarating and painful time, because the truth is that when you live and speak through the experiences of a group that is considered peripheral, every struggle becomes a battle for credibility; and, in this case, lives hung in the balance.

During this time in my life, too, I experienced my own personal struggles around lovers and relationships. I suffered a health crisis when I collapsed, nearly died, and was diagnosed with Type 1 diabetes. And I struggled at work, trying to convince the powers that be at GMHC that my vision of the epidemic's changing face was, in fact, accurate. Sadly, time has proved me right.

Wanted: Attractive feminine woman for romance, pleasure and possible long-term relationship. No HIV+s need apply.

Looking for serious relationship with womyn-loving-womyn — no butches, druggies, drinkers or HIVs.

Lesbian looking for lesbian love, hot sex, good times, great partner . . . Could be permanent! Femmes, fatties, HIV+s, don't bother.

These are all current personal ads running in lesbian newspapers around the country. I found them in lesbian papers published in San Francisco, Los Angeles, New York, Illinois, and Michigan. These magazines ran the gamut from lesbian-separatist newspapers to sex-positive lesbian mags like *On Our Backs*. And, while they contain many descriptions that are awful, each contains one identical and terrifying disqualifier: no HIV-positive lesbians wanted here.

How can lesbians' risk for HIV/AIDS still be debatable thirteen years into the epidemic? How can some lesbians still not know any lesbians with HIV? Yet the debate continues. I spend an incredible amount of my time as the director of a lesbian AIDS project disagreeing with other lesbians who are still repeating the dyke mantra, "Real lesbians don't get AIDS," while listening to the numerically spiraling voices of lesbians who are HIV positive or have AIDS (or talking to their friends and lovers). In between these two groups of women is a third chorus of female voices full of panicky questions about risk, about who to believe and how to think when they look at their own behaviors as lesbians.

LESBIAN LEADERSHIP IN THE AIDS MOVEMENT

Lesbians have been leaders in the AIDS movement since its earliest breath. We have influenced and shaped the discussions, outreach programs, demonstrations, services, and prevention drives since the earliest moments of this crisis. Working early on with gay men, we were often the first women to see how broadly different communities were being impacted by HIV and to use our political histories as organizers and health, feminist, civil rights, and Left activists to inform the creation and responses of this new movement. It is hard to write this history to show our powerful role and at the same time credit the broad leadership of so many and varied men and women fighting against HIV.

Many of us doing this work, together with the HIV-positive lesbians we were beginning to meet, first began to talk among ourselves about the risks lesbians were facing in the epidemic. But for many years it was a quiet discussion between lesbians doing AIDS work and HIV-positive lesbians, all of us coming up against growing numbers of HIV-positive dykes every day. This was happening at the same time we were being told that lesbians are not at risk for HIV. We would meet in small groups together to repair ourselves from hard parts of doing AIDS work or to get away from the sexism or racism of this new movement, but we would quickly move into talking about how many lesbians, how many women who sleep with other women, we were seeing who were HIV positive. We would compare notes and shake our heads. It did not add up. We would talk late into the night, trying to unravel the keys to our risk at the same time we remained completely invisible as a community at risk for AIDS.

MY OWN HISTORY, COMING HOME

I have been organizing and writing about sexuality for fifteen or twenty years and doing work around HIV for nearly ten. I have been a part of the large contingent of lesbians who, from the earliest days of the epidemic, began to do AIDS work and became AIDS activists. And through those years I have talked to lesbians about what compelled us to get involved. For some of us it was the shared gay identity we felt with gay men that brought us forward early in the epidemic; for some of us it was the dramatic increase in the already devastating daily occurrences of homophobia and gay bashing that occurred because of the government's misrepresentation of AIDS (or GRID, gay-related immune-deficiency disease, as it was known then) as a gay disease. In that increased violence, "all gay people, both gay men and lesbian, looked alike." For many gay women and men of color, the devastation in their communities and the need for their engagement and activism were urgent and obvious to them; for many progressive lesbians, the communities most under siege were exactly the communities we were committed to working within (women and men in prisons, poor people, communities of color, young people, women, etc.). And many of us were losing friends every week, every month, more each year. Our reasons as lesbians were numerous, varied, and passionate.

I was motivated by all of these—and one other, which I have seen clearly only in the last year or so and which I speak of much less openly. I was deeply disillusioned and bitter at the horrific fights about sex that had erupted so viciously twelve years ago in the feminist, lesbian-feminist, and antipornography movements of the early 1980s, the fights that have now been called the *sex wars* in the feminist movement. I come from a poor white-trash working-class background, and I am a high femme dyke passionately committed to butch and femme lives. The sexualities that I defended in those bitter fights and the sexualities that I wanted to continue to explore were drawn from all the ways women (and men) feel desire. But I was particularly driven to explore a woman-identified sexuality that was risky, smart, dangerous, often secretive, and often capable of encompassing great variation and erotic need between women who sleep with women. And I wanted sex to have a right to its own history without forcing some women to hide or reinterpret their past (or ongoing) desires through a constantly shifting lesbian ideology. I was also tired of trying to say that the political lesbian community was only the smallest tip of the lesbian iceberg, with the vast majority of lesbians still an uncharted, vastly different set of groupings of desires, identities, contradictions, and sexual dynamics. Many brave feminist women spoke against the right-wing drift of the sex wars and the porn fights, but we were a minority in a feminist and lesbian movement already beleaguered by Reaganomics, Christian fundamentalism, and the fight to keep open women's ability to control our own reproduction. The times were hard.

THE WOMEN I COME FROM

Finally, I wanted to return, to go home again to the women I came from. I longed to build a new revolution, made up of lesbians who had mostly been left out of the current feminist explosion: working-class women, women in prisons, reform schools, and juvie halls, women locked down in mental institutions for being too queer, women of color, women in the military and in the bars, women surviving in "straight" marriages and dead-end jobs who longed each day to touch another woman, women who were peep-show girls, sex workers, carnival strippers, women who shot drugs and women in recovery from those drugs and the streets, women in trailers, small towns, and cities across America, women who filled the floors of the factories, fast-food restaurants, and auto plants of this country, women whose lives were situated in PTAS, shopping malls, and Teamsters' unions. These were the women I came from, and they were the women I longed to build a movement with. It was here, with these women, that I hoped for the possibility of a new political dialogue about sex and desire and power. They were also, I quickly realized, the women most immediately at risk for HIV.

The struggle against AIDS brought (and brings) all my worlds together, instead of being barely tolerated because of my sex politics and my sense of urgency about the meaning and power of erotic desires (was that really political?). Here, in this movement, I was welcomed. In those early years, when the government refused to take on the leadership of this battle (we still have to wait and see about Clinton), it forced us to create a movement based on grassroots organizing, word of mouth, and long-range goals. Each day we had to bite back our urgency and despair at how to get the messages out quickly enough. It was a movement that understood the critical need to talk about the uncomfortable or ragged edges of our sexualities and desires and that wasn't fooled by what we each called ourselves, as though those identity words would explain what we did in bed (or who we do it with) or who we were on the streets or in our jobs.

My first paid job doing AIDS work was as an HIV pre- and post-test counselor and hotline worker in New York. It was a revelation. To talk to people on a phone often frees them up to tell you more honestly what they're afraid of, what their risks are. You couldn't see anybody's face on a phone, couldn't trace them after the conversation. It radically shaped what I understood about the epidemic, about how enormous the groups of people affected were and the gaps between people's perception of what constituted their individual risks and their understanding of how that translated to their personal lives. Each day I listened to voices and stories, and each day I took people by their numbers into a small room to reveal to them their test results. The pain and shattering of people's hopes (often regardless of the results) I heard on that phone and saw in that room, and the bravery, changed me like I hadn't been changed since the early civil rights movement.

My second job was with the AIDS Discrimination Division of the New York City Human Rights Commission. The work was to intercede against the fear and stigma that had arisen so violently around HIV. The work relied on, demanded, a sharp understanding of class and race in this country to know where to find those among us most vulnerable to HIV. And as an educator and filmmaker for the AIDS Discrimination Unit, I was organizing at a community level around my passion to bring forward the voices and stories of the women (and men) who lived in long overlooked communities, letting them and their stories finally stand center stage where they belong.

When I wasn't at a paid job, I was an AIDS activist. And in spite of the difficulties that are always a part of building an imperfect movement, of the sexism that was often there, and in the face of the government's locked-tight doors, in spite of the times there was racism or fear of us as women and a refusal to understand or support women and men whose risks were different than the ones generally understood as gay, still, it was work where everything remained to be done and anyone willing to confront those obstacles could join.

And my heart was breaking from the deaths of those I loved. I could tick it off on my fingers: life and death among my friends and in my communities, the urgency of people struggling to live with HIV, the need to integrate sex issues through a grid of race, class, and gender, my love as a filmmaker for working-class people's stories, each of these pieces added up in ways that compelled me forward.

As time went on there was one other reason that moved inside me. *At some time in my life (and into the present), I had engaged in every one of the behaviors that I knew put lesbians at risk.* I heard my own personal and often secret, unspoken narrative in the stories and histories of the lesbians who I met with AIDS or who were at risk for HIV. I was a lesbian, and I had been one for twenty-seven years. Through all those years I had engaged, frequently, in every risky activity associated with AIDS, regardless of what I called myself at the time I was doing it. If that was true for me as a lesbian political organizer and activist, what was really happening for the vast majority of lesbians, bisexual women, young lesbians, transgendered lesbians, lesbians who were "coming out," passing women, and women who partnered with other women? What about the hundreds and thousands of women who used none of these words as they loved and desired another woman? What was happening to them? What, finally, about the huge unseen us that resides primarily outside the confines of our political networks, that vast geography of women building their lives against or with their desire for another woman that runs like an underground river beneath the "straight" female landscape of America?

Creating the Lesbian AIDS Project at GMHC (Gay Men's Health Crisis) has been a major part of that answer for me; it is my own history coming home. And, because I see the issues of HIV for lesbians totally intertwined with the issues of sexuality, class, race, gender, and erotic desires which I have spent much of my political life working on, it has both combined and thrust me back into a level of organizing I haven't been involved in since the early civil rights and antiwar movements of the 1960s and 1970s. It is an organizing project that engages me with a breadth, depth, and diversity of women who sleep with women both powerful and engaging. Going back to this work with my history as an organizer committed to a politics of inclusion, returning as a forty-six-year-old lesbian who has been doing this political work since I was seventeen, allows the richness of my own life history to illuminate the gigantic map of our actual lesbian world, a map with sharp relief and global scope and a map which I see as a tool we can use to grasp and then chart the wildly disparate universes of queer female lives and communities in order to understand our survival.

LAP (the Lesbian AIDS Project–GMHC) is an organizing project with two core ideas: lesbian HIV visibility and lesbian sexuality. Lesbians at risk of or with HIV have been "the disappeared" lesbians in our communities for too long. Wrong class, wrong color, wrong desires, wrong histories. But these are the women who need to become the center of the lesbian movement, not just the AIDS movement, and their stories, struggles, and issues have to be integrated throughout our understanding of which women are lesbians, whom we count when we ask that question, and which women will have the voice and power to determine our overall political direction. And sex, our sexuality in all its variety and contradiction, needs to be opened up, aired, and considered as a major component of the unique political understanding we bring to all other social change movements.

WHO IS THE *WE* IN OUR SISTERHOOD?

But the lines of the map linking our communities of women who partner with women are very faint. The terrains through which most lesbians can openly travel are very restricted. It is a geography rigorously determined by our backgrounds, our class, and our color, by rural landscape or city street, by whether we are politically active or spiritually inclined, by the narrow confines of age and health and physical ability, by the marks on the map that identify us as lesbians from the bars, the trade unions, the military, from gay studies programs or art history departments, by how we each came out and with whom, by the shape of our desires and our willingness (or ability) to risk it all on our love for a woman, by our status as mothers or our decision not to have kids, by the nature of our dreams and aspirations, by our very ability to nurture and sustain hope for our futures.

As lesbians in this culture we suffer from the same lack of power and resources common to all women. Within that oppression we must also navigate our health, sexuality, and social existence in an environment committed to imagining all women as heterosexual. In a universe in which we have no voice or presence, lesbians and our particular risks for HIV have remained submerged inside a "straight" female landscape, keeping us ignorant and uninformed. We are a specific population of women with high numbers of HIV-positive members but no official recognition or accounting.

In the midst of this blank space, the "secret" of lesbian risk and lesbian death due to HIV spirals. This spiral magnifies the confusion among us, leading the entire community into doubt and anger. Some lesbians deny all vulnerability to HIV, making the question of risky behavior, from shooting drugs to unprotected sex with men to safe sex between women, appear negligible or unrealistic and unknowable. This guarantees that lesbians who are HIV positive or have AIDS will fall through this crack of fear and denial and be marked outside the status *"real" lesbian.* Our openness about our histories as women engaged in these activities and behaviors works to disown us as an integral part of the bigger lesbian landscape.

And it is here that race and class background becomes a particularly vicious component of our risks and our understanding of HIV. For working-class women without any buffers, the picture is immediately fragile; our need for our communities of birth is accentuated if we are women of color, women whose first language is not English, or we are poor or working-class women who are responsible for and committed to the survival of our extended families. In this already contested setting, HIV/AIDS is often devastating, while our resources remain scarce. We are often forced to lie and hide our sexual desire for other women so that we can access the health-care or social services we need. We also hide in order to guarantee the commitment and support of our biological families, our jobs, our neighborhoods, our children, and our language and our access to valued cultural institutions. Medically, socially, and economically, the less room we have to turn around, the more problematic our crisis becomes as we balance precariously between the women we desire and the help and support we need.

It has also become clear to me that the process of "coming out," one of the most celebrated aspects of lesbian myth and queer storytelling, is often a "high-risk activity." I meet too many lesbians from lesbian/gay/bisexual student unions on their campuses who have become HIV positive during the period they were "coming out." Or women who have struggled to leave small towns and come to cities, where they moved in and out of many social networks before finding community or identity. Think of it. This is often the time when confusion and silence about desire for another woman is the most terrifying to come to terms with. It is often a time of lots of sexual experimentation; often, for women sleeping with other women, their partners are gay men, and that is often combined with drug use and drinking. It is a period when we fall between communities and identities, and it can often be a time of isolation from or shame in the face of former friends, our families, and the figures of authority or support in our lives. For middle-class lesbians the margins of their privilege from birth can slip away quickly when (or if) it becomes known that they are sleeping with another woman. For whatever age, "coming out" is a highly charged and often dangerous path each of us walk. HIV magnifies that risk a thousand times over.

WHOSE VOICE, WHOSE LEADERSHIP, WHOSE MOVEMENT?

HIV makes a mockery of pretend unity and false sisterhood. Though the women now affected come from all classes and races, the majority of lesbians right now who are HIV positive are predominantly lesbians of color or poor white women, usually struggling with long histories of shooting drugs or fucking men for the money to get those drugs. These are not the women usually identified as the primary voices of feminism or the women the lesbian movement most values and tries to organize to create a progressive political agenda. The HIV-positive lesbians who continue to come forward as leaders in the lesbian AIDS movement have histories and lives lived in neighborhoods most gay studies courses rarely identify as lesbian, let alone use as the bases of understanding queer women's lives and experiences.

The question of HIV, of race and class, becomes a question of whose movement and whose leadership. Will lesbians who shoot drugs or are in recovery be the women turned to to speak for the movement? Will categories that depend on the construction of "real" lesbians disappear and reveal instead the incredible numbers of women who hold another woman in their arms, regardless of what each woman calls herself when she does this, no matter who else she may be fucking? Will histories of low-paying jobs, the revolving door of prisons, the military and bar life, the sounds of kids playing while the lesbian consciousness-raising group convenes, become common and ordinary occurrences within our movement? Will the power of being butch or femme, the stories of life as a lesbian mom or a runaway teenage street dyke predominate? When will femmes with long nails and sharp-assed attitude be the voice heard leading Gay Pride Day marches? Whose movement, whose voice, whose stories, whose hope for transformation and change? Whose? These are the questions I see in front of me every day.

SOME COMPLICATIONS ON OUR WAY TO UNDERSTANDING LESBIAN HIV

The crisis for lesbians struggling to understand the impact of HIV in our communities is compounded by the general lack of decent, non-judgmental information about lesbian sexuality. Because it remains unacceptable to love and desire other women sexually, we are also left with little substantial information about what we do in bed with each other, including what might put us at risk sexually. STDs (sexually transmitted diseases) of all kinds are little understood or discussed between women partners, and the fear and ignorance surrounding HIV compound the already existing blank space silencing this discussion in our communities. Homophobia, like all silences and prejudices, hurts us profoundly, leaving us unarmed and unprotected, as though forbidding the word (*lesbian*) of our existence can stop the act of our love. It doesn't, of course; it just leaves us vulnerable and uninformed. Our communities' confusion about whether AIDS is really a lesbian issue reflects this oppression.

The denial of our risk for HIV is often supported by a circumscribed lesbian sexual border we have constructed which refuses to acknowledge or accept that we sleep with each other in many, many different ways. We are butch/femme women; we are queer or androgynous; we are lesbian feminist; we don't believe in labels; we practice S/M; we use our hands, our mouths, our bodies, sex toys, to pleasure and please each other; and we may also sleep with men, whether we call that *bisexuality, coming out,* or *economic necessity* or whether we don't dare talk about it.

For a small, though growing, number of HIV-positive lesbians, their only (or primary) risk for HIV was that their female partner was HIV positive when they became lovers. When these lesbian couples looked for good information about woman-to-woman transmission, they were rarely successful. And, when they went to other lesbians to try and discuss it (if they dared), few other lesbians could help. Like so many other people before them, the lack of adequate and specific information to help them assess their risks was unavailable. This third group of lesbians, though by far the smallest subset of HIV-positive lesbians, is growing each year. But, like all the other risks in our communities, woman-to-woman sexual transmission remains scientifically undocumented or to be reliably researched. This combines dangerously with the general denial of HIV in our communities and with the crisis of our drug use and the alcoholism which continues throughout our communities. This crisis about our risks is compounded by our invisibility and our lack of political clout.

All these activities and identities are components of our communities' sexual and social lives. While we have taken an extraordinary risk in daring to love another woman, this has not guaranteed that our judgments against each other's erotic or drug choices won't be as cruel as the general culture's judgments against us. Our understandings of the reasons many of us shoot or snort drugs, drink till it harms us, experiment with substances that can kill us, are stories that we have not let surface enough inside our communities, hoping that by not telling aloud those pieces of our lives we will not be hit any harder by social condemnation than we already are. It's as though we think by disavowing a set of activities (and the women we stereotype as doing them) we can protect ourselves from even more homophobia.

We also carry those historical silences into our sexual judgments as well, thinking that, if we don't enjoy a particular sexual activity ourselves, no other lesbian could either. If another woman *wants* differently, she is in danger of having her credibility as a "normal" lesbian questioned. Yet the irony is that we remain women who are sexual outlaws, sexual originators, and social inventors, leaping across the sexual and emotional silences surrounding women's desires for other women, daring to touch and possess each other sexually, daring to claim our right to be sexual, to love and want another woman.

SO THE VOICE ON MY PHONE MACHINE SAID,
"WHAT'S YOUR PROBLEM ANYWAY?"

One of the first things I did when I created the Lesbian AIDS Project was develop a sex survey. The survey is very explicit and was done to try and determine how we are really having sex with each other, how often, in what combinations and with whom, and what we think of ourselves as we do it. This was not a survey primarily about relationships. It appeared in the 1992 *Lesbian and Gay Pride Guide,* which annually produces sixty thousand copies for the June Gay/Lesbian March and which is picked up and used as a resource book by a wide variety of lesbians, including women who don't necessarily hook into the gay bookstores and lesbian political organizations in New York City. When the survey appeared, my answering machine was suddenly full of "anonymous" messages from "normal dykes" suggesting that what I really needed was to go "fuck a man." Sometimes the messages were from "regular" lesbians telling me how sick they considered some of the categories and activities that I had included in the survey. Usually those messages ended with a free-swinging interpretation of what they imagined "I was into." These anonymous messages always hurt. They made clear to me again how problematic the real world of female sexuality is for all of us and what an added minefield being a lesbian could be when it was thrown into the mix. Sex in our community remains our smoking gun, and the fight for whose hand is on the trigger continues.

Still, many women were thrilled by the survey, and over sixteen hundred women filled it out and sent it back. These numbers were very high. Women wrote their opinions in the margins and on Post-its stuck over the sections they loved or despised. Lesbians said, "Congratulations. I've waited a long time for someone to care enough about our survival to finally ask us what we do sexually." Women who answered used exclamation marks and red pens to write their ideas and express their opinions. "I didn't even know lesbians could do this!" "I love these questions. My girlfriend and I are going to try them all before we finish the survey." "Hot survey! Getting steamy just answering it." But other women wrote, "I didn't even know that lesbians could get AIDS."

In one of the surveys, I found this note attached. It said, "I am glad you're doing this survey for those lesbians that can use it, but my lover and I don't really have any use for these questions. We are both women, and because of that, we understand each other's bodies and desires. Maybe women that are more fucked up don't understand this, but for us it's really just natural. Thanks anyway."

In anthropology, this is called *magical thinking,* and this magical thinking is rife throughout the communities I have to speak with every day. It is the most common idea I hear across the wide groups of lesbians I talk to. The notion that, because we are women touching other women, we automatically understand and empathize so totally and therefore we know intrinsically how to caress each other, how much pressure to use when we suck or lick each other's bodies, how to stroke or fuck each other to climax, is very dangerous and very widespread. If that's where we're beginning, it is hard to imagine how to start discussing safer sex, negotiating up front and directly with a lover, to talk openly about HIV and STD protection methods, or discuss our drug or sex-work or sex histories.

Magical thinking also leads a lot of women I talk with to assert that they don't think we can transmit sexual diseases (or yeast infections) between each other. And it leads to other dangerous and incorrect sexual notions. One of the most common is that, if STDs are transmitted between women partners, it's probably due to a lesbian sleeping with a "bisexual" woman. In this lesbian worldview, men are dirty, women who sleep with them are contaminated, and only lesbians who sleep with other "real" lesbians can remain safe. I hear these stories and watch us say these things as yeast infections spread back and forth sexually between us and STDs remain out of control in our communities and still are not discussed regularly. How can safer sex ever be a regular part of our lives when we are literally forced to risk our right to community in order to tell the truth about what we do and who we do it with. The legacy of being women in this culture, of being denied decent, nonjudgmental information about our bodies and our desires, is multiplied for lesbian women.

Still, in the face of this culturally imposed ignorance, I see women who love other women trying to carve out an erotic terrain of our own which claims and encourages all of us to explore and reckon with our desires for each other. It assumes that there are thousands of complex ways we each feel desire and passion. Especially in younger lesbians I have seen a much more matter-of-fact acceptance of HIV risk for lesbians. These are women who have grown up sexually in the first decade of AIDS, and they are much less resistant to the idea of lesbian risk and HIV safety. And, in lesbian communities already hard hit by HIV, the question of safer sex, regardless of presumed mode of transmission, is also different and more open. It is there, in working-class lesbian political and social organizations, that I see the most innovative and least judgmental struggle to integrate HIV knowledge into daily lesbian life. These are often communities of lesbians that have had the tragic example of numbers and the powerful voices of HIV-positive lesbians to reckon with and to lead the discussion. There, HIV is no stranger. In these communities, HIV-positive lesbians are lovers, mothers, sisters, best friends.

Growing numbers of HIV-positive lesbians are regularly speaking out. More than anything else, it has been their bravery and their insistence to tell the truth of their own lives (and histories) that has cracked the silence and denial in the larger lesbian communities. Like the role that HIV has played in other settings, AIDS transmission always exposes the gap between who we want to believe ourselves to be and what we really do in our regular lives. The leadership of lesbians who are infected with or affected by HIV is a powerful and original model for the building of a new, more inclusive movement of women who partner with other women. It brings into one dialogue the lives of all of us throughout our evolution as lesbians. The work being done by these lesbians in AIDS organizations, women's outpatient health clinics, detox centers, youth programs for runaway lesbians, prisons and recovery programs, and in neighborhood organizations, is rarely documented, but it is some of the most powerful lesbian activism happening. And it is building a new foundation and a different class base for a larger lesbian political movement.

Our right to be sexual with each other, our right to struggle with the issues of our daily lives, like our drug use and the sex we have with men, are all pieces of the lesbian puzzle. Whether or not the larger culture acknowledges us, we must recognize each other and our different struggles. The lesbian map is very large, our numbers are significant, and we must pick up this fight to protect ourselves and each other while we fight to be seen and respected. We can't wait for other people to see what is right in front of our noses, that we are an integral part of this world, not outside it, and that so is a potentially life-threatening virus, HIV. Our community is not immune, and lesbianism is not a condom for AIDS. Like everyone else, we are vulnerable and must take the steps necessary to learn how to protect each other's lives. No one else will do it for us, and no one will do it as well. We have been taking risks to love each other for millennia. Now we need to expand our understanding of who we are and what we do in order to understand the many ways we need to go forward. Our communities are fabulously sexual and inventive, our lives and histories varied and full of meaning. We can support each other in taking the steps each of us needs to be safe, erotic, and powerful. And we can build a movement, starting here, that refuses to privilege rigid ideological categories over the truths of our lives and finally build a lesbian movement that bases its theories on a more complicated and unreduceable map of lesbian desire and lesbian voice.

Sexuality, Labor, and

the New Trade Unionism

The new activism to build and revitalize the union movement constitutes some of the most important and exciting organizing going on in the United States today. This interview was done in 1999 for a book about gay people in the labor movement. Together with Nikhil Pal Singh, I make the argument that issues of desire, sexuality, HIV status, gender, and passion are fundamentally important to the "new unionism." Sexuality and desire cannot be removed from an understanding of activism and union building based on class.

A CONVERSATION
Amber Hollibaugh and Nikhil Pal Singh

Amber Hollibaugh is an organizer, writer, and filmmaker whose work centers on HIV/AIDS and sexuality. Nikhil Pal Singh is assistant professor of history at the University of Washington in Seattle.

NIKHIL PAL SINGH: We want to discuss the relationship between sexual politics and the labor movement, a subject that you have given a great deal of thought and active effort to. Perhaps you could begin by telling us about some of the organizing work that you have been doing around issues of sexuality in the workplace.[1]

AMBER HOLLIBAUGH: About ten years ago, I was at the AIDS Discrimination Unit of the New York City Human Rights Commission. At that time, we were already looking at discrimination issues and the union movement. The hospital workers' union, 1199, was concerned about HIV, but the only way they knew how to deal with it or think proactively

---

1. This discussion took place on 30 April 1999 in Singh's office at New York University.

about it was in terms of safety or barrier methods for health-care workers. They talked about needle sticks and those kinds of issues. They thought their members should be trained about safety measures, but—as in most unions at the time—there was a deafening silence about the fact that union members were dealing with HIV in their own personal lives. HIV only made it more obvious that people had to choose between their private lives and the way they saw themselves as workers. It was profoundly isolating. Everything that put them at risk was considered a part of their private life, and the only thing that could be dealt with in the public sphere was a risk in that workplace setting. Union officials always thought the conversation was about homosexuality—that we were trying to tell them there were closet cases in the union movement. Well, yeah, that was true. But what we were really trying to talk to them about was class, sexuality, and what had been considered privacy. It was an almost impossible conversation.

I remember meeting a business agent who had worked for years in one of the municipal unions. He was terrified because he wasn't out about his sexuality. He didn't actually identify as a gay person, but he had sex with men. He was HIV-positive at a time when one's health was vulnerable very quickly, and he didn't know what to do. He had to have health care, but he was terrified to have his HIV status known. When he came forward to talk to other union officials about it, they laid him off but agreed to continue paying his health care. He was isolated and so didn't feel he could challenge it. And I thought, Oh, this is really horrifying. This can't be allowed to stand.

I asked myself, How could we begin to have a different conversation about drug use and sexuality inside the union movement? How could we challenge the union movement? I think that challenge needs to start by saying that our understanding of human experience is fundamentally different than it was twenty years ago. Then, private life was not really seen as a component of organizing work, whether it was organizing from the Left, from progressive movements, from the antiwar movement, or from the civil rights movement. Since then, we have learned that if you can't talk to people about the literal lives they lead, you can't convince them to see the union movement—or any other movement—as a community. If people are terrified of speaking out, of ever articulating the particularities of their own lives, they won't sign a union card. They won't speak up when there's a grievance. They won't shut a line down. Their spirit is broken precisely in the place where they need to have a voice.

The newest and most interesting organizing strategies of the AFL-CIO are not just economically based. They are very specific, long-term, community-building strategies. They're based on a very different understanding about immigration, gender, and race—and race not just as black or Latino but also as South Asian and African. Given who labor has now identified as the people it wants to organize, issues of sexuality and HIV status become fundamentally important as clues to what a new and revitalized union movement needs to take on pro-actively and progressively. Sexuality and HIV are the life issues that those people are dealing with. Good organizing needs to speak to the complexity of private life as well as public life. If you can't speak to that, you can't create a space where people can acknowledge what things they struggle with, and ultimately you haven't created a space that makes it possible for people to talk about what affects them as they try to survive economically. That to me is a bottom-line consideration for the new union movement: Will it build a different sensibility and a union culture that's deeper and richer?

NPS: We're talking about a fundamental distinction that organizes modern capitalism: the split between private and public and the ability to cordon off *the private* as a preserve of sanctified property and self-possession, justified and buttressed by forms of ascription that aren't named or identified but rather naturalized. The most historically notable forms of ascription (maleness, whiteness, straightness) have thus been located (along with the property relations they uphold) "outside" power or any kind of public accountability or political contest.

The greatest achievement of social movements in the 1960s, it seems to me, was that they offered unprecedented challenges to the public/private distinction, in the recognition that "everything is political." They did this not only by rejecting the stifling economism of the existing trade union movement. In fact, in some ways they challenged the private/public distinction in terms that may have been closer to the old Communist and radical Left than we now realize. The latter, after all, attacked the validity of private property, but without fully recognizing the forms of proprietary individualism and ascriptive logic that underpinned the property system. In some ways, what we are talking about today is bringing together forms of radical theory and practice that have remained separate for far too long, in effect bridging the Old and New Left divide.

AH: Yes. To look at it from the other side, some of us have been trying to challenge social identity–based movements to take on class. As much as the union movement is conflicted about taking on "identity politics," identity–based movements have been terrified to take on class. There's a reason that lesbian AIDS is invisible in the self-identified "lesbian community." Why? Because those working-class dykes with AIDS were never the dykes that the white, middle-class, identity-oriented lesbians wanted at the table. They never wanted butch/femme dykes with two years of high school to be the people who articulated the political agenda of that social movement.

NPS: When social identity movements do not interrogate class, their goal in some ways becomes being able to enjoy the same privileges of privacy, to have a kind of sanctified, legitimated identity that is ultimately no different from any other, basically to enjoy the same kind of proprietary privileges, protected and insulated by property and well-being, that so-called straight people, or other people who are similarly placed, enjoy. So, ironically, social identity movements come to be about class aspiration. In certain ways, what we're doing in this conversation is showing what it would mean in a practical sense to deconstruct what we mean by *class* and thus to begin to really recognize the universality of class struggle with all its deviance and with all its material messiness.

AH: Yes, the real point is that deviance isn't something that's homosexual. Deviance or difference isn't something that can ever be bracketed or privatized. Difference, including differences that are problematic and that people don't know how to talk about, are embedded in the way that individually we come to understand ourselves. It may be a fantasy in our mind, a way we dress, a place we go to, a set of people we love. These are the kinds of things that actually are the most unique qualifiers about how we live as working-class people.

To take another example, the Black Radical Congress was extraordinarily influenced and fundamentally affected by the fact that a lot of

the organizers were in the union movement. They were union organizers who didn't say that somehow their union work was outside their
black community work or their radical politics. They brought union-
ists into dialogue about the need to create a progressive black voice
that could speak to the issues and the class base of that black community. The reason I feel strongly about the union movement—despite
my criticisms—is precisely because I know how necessary it is. And it
cannot be bypassed. You cannot take class out of sexuality. You cannot
take class out of race. You've got to insist on the right to the real differences that someone understands within her or his lived experience as
a working-class person.

NPS: One question that immediately comes to mind, though, is the
specificity of sexuality—and of gender, I suppose, as well. It does seem
that the new union movement, which is rooted in social movements, is
taking off in all kinds of ways. There are many examples of how union
organizing has been very effective in incorporating questions of race
and ethnicity and even the private and the domestic—the various aspects of people's "identity" or embodied subjectivity. At the same time,
it seems to me that there's still often a normalizing impulse at work.
For example, there's a willingness to talk about "women's issues" so
long as they're cordoned off from anything that might be outside pre-
scribed ideas of gender. Or there's a willingness to talk about issues of
concern to a particular racial or ethnic community, but within terms
that are already defined by that community. In this way, oppressions
that may already exist within communities are in certain odd ways reproduced.

One of the striking difficulties of the sexual liberation movement
—which, in certain ways, took the personal as political to the farthest
degree it could be taken—is the extent to which that movement is not
really identifiable with community as such. The movement cuts across
self-identified communities and communities of interest, sometimes
presenting itself as universal, as something like the economic. So I
agree that issues of HIV status and sexual practice pervade people's
everyday life. But what happens when you're organizing in a community that also wants to repress these questions? Isn't it still necessary
to organize around the specificity of HIV-positive people and gays and
lesbians in the workplace?

AH: It's going to be interesting to see how the new union movement takes that on. Twenty years ago, hardly anyone was out in the workplace. Now, people are out. To my thinking, labor needs to be provocative and brilliant about taking the reality of lived experience as the basis for doing its organizing work. If you take that on, you take on a combination of issues, seeing them as different but profoundly important and influential in the way the workplace is organized and the way people understand themselves in the workplace.

If I'm a single mother and raising kids, everybody gets it that I'm going to have a very different kind of life than I would if I had a permanent partner who's employed. Organizers probably would be willing to bring that situation up. But people seem to think HIV status should be kept outside organizing work. Maybe some unions will take a liberal "don't ask, don't tell" attitude. They might say to organizers, "You can be queer, but you don't have to talk about it when you're out there doing your work. You don't have to bring it up unless somebody asks."

But why do you have to leave it at the door—your health status, your sexuality, the way you parent, the way you partner, whether you're monogamous? If these are things you never bring up at a union meeting, then to me you're not building a different kind of union movement. I think the only reason people believe in the union, rather than just need it, is if it literally empowers them to understand and take charge of their own lives. I don't think any union movement can survive if people don't see it as a part of their culture. By that I mean a *class* culture with very different dynamics for the various people in it. They don't have to be identical to each other, but the issues that are specific to their individual social experience have to emerge. The class reality of the workplace is a commonality. If that's the principle that generates organizing, then unions don't have to tell their organizers to leave a part of themselves at home.

NPS: I've been reading about a Service Employees International Union (SEIU) policy directive in the aftermath of the fantastic victory in Los Angeles County in the organization of home health-care workers.[2] The

2. A struggle for unionization that began in 1987 came to victory in February 1999 when seventy-four thousand home health-care workers in Los Angeles won representation through the SEIU.

directive said something to the effect that male organizers couldn't have visible piercings—pierced ears, pierced tongues, or pierced eyebrows—and that women organizers couldn't have any multiple ear piercings. It also specified a dress code: male organizers had to wear jackets and ties and so forth. All this was based on the idea that, well, the workers they are organizing are mainly Latinos, they are Catholic, socially conservative, churchgoing people, and so on, so the organizers need to present themselves in a quiet, nonprovocative, well-dressed manner.

Although it may seem trivial, to me it is an interesting example of both the potential cultural radicalism of the new labor movement (who are all these pierced organizers after all?) and the way that radicalism gets normalized or new barriers get put up, in part because strategic calculations are made. I think these calculations are often made by union leaders on the pragmatic, if not cynical, basis that winning the loyalty of workers is in part a negative process of not giving offense, of meeting workers where they already are, of not issuing any challenge beyond the wage demand, rather than a more radical project of activating people to ever wider imaginations of their circles of affiliation. Organizing should be based not on reductive notions of sameness but on a sense that, while we live our experiences differently through different modes of representation and desire, fundamentally we're engaged in a common struggle. We should not, in order to be sympathetic and understand each other, have to imagine ourselves as the same.

AH: Having done AIDS work for fifteen years, this is what I heard about AIDS work, too. You had to be really cautious; you couldn't be too explicit; the only way to be respectful was to leave out anything that could be considered provocative or challenging, anything about yourself that might upset the people you were speaking to. I have to say that that is the most useless kind of strategy. To think that HIV somehow isn't there, that piercing isn't there, that homosexuality isn't there—that it's somehow in somebody else's community, in somebody else's neighborhood, that it's somebody else's issue—is not to get what's really going on. All the things that put people at risk or that make people exciting and interesting and sometimes vulnerable are present in every community.

NPS: The lie of normalcy.

AH: Right, the lie that it happens only to certain people or under certain circumstances. Sometimes organizers don't want to deal with AIDS — not because it's not going on in the communities, but because they don't feel capable of talking about the fact that a woman they're trying to convince to join the union is fucking three guys and doesn't have a clue about how to insist that a man use a condom. That organizer doesn't bring it up and never talks about the kind of issues that put that woman at risk. In the meantime, the workplace may be the one institution she pays attention to—the only place she gets information. If that place isn't giving her information about her private life, she has no access to it.

NPS: I would like to throw out a parallel example, which comes from Yale, where I organized as a graduate student. We couldn't talk about abortion there. "It's going to divide the union down the middle if we take any 'official' stand on this." That kind of sentiment is about effectively curtailing the union as a political entity in the public domain. According to this rhetoric, a union can't act politically because—for its members—the union isn't political, it's economic. But, at the same time, by staking a claim for yourself in a radical democratic culture, and in doing this kind of organizing that you're talking about, you're taking the path of most resistance in certain ways because what you're suggesting is that the union should take on every issue that affects the quality of the lived, embodied experience of people who are working.

AH: One thing that blows me away about the Left—not just the union movement—is its inability to understand how *desire* affects the workplace. So someone will say to you, "Sexuality doesn't have anything to do with the way you organize a workplace." And then you think about all the eruptions that happen in the workplace because somebody gets pregnant, somebody has an affair, somebody finds out she's HIV positive, somebody is having sex with somebody else behind the factory building. These are the kinds of explosive issues that actually animate most people's human experience. The one place where they experience the most hope and the most despair is at the level of their personal lives—it's about the quality of their relationships with their children, with their partners; it's through their sexuality—because this personal life is one of the few things that isn't entirely negotiated through economics.

NPS: The perhaps more vexing question about what it means to practice an antiracist, antisexist, antihomophobic political agenda is trickier in the context of organizing if only because your proposal of bringing desire into the workplace and being sensitive and attuned to difference is a nonlegislative model, whereas we have generally tended to understand these questions in terms of legislation, prohibition, and censorship. Thus, to be antiracist means saying that racial jokes, stereotypes, and caricatures are not acceptable in our workplace. Now, obviously, gross racial caricaturing still goes on. If anything, it's on the rise in a lot of workplaces. Sexism clearly doesn't disappear with sexual harassment legislation. Homophobia, if anything, remains the absolute norm. So how, as an organizer, do you root those things out? How do you foster a different culture within the union while continuing to insist, "This is not acceptable; we cannot have this as part of our movement"?

AH: I don't think these are easy questions. The union movement reflects the contradictions and complications that everyone in our society is trying to deal with. The union movement is neither responsible for, nor the exception to, any of these rules. It has always been confronted with where it draws the line. Does it take on race and racism? Does it take on gender and sexism? Does it take on sexuality? Does it take on provocative issues that are considered political? When it has failed to do those things, it has paid a terrible price.

NPS: It's still paying a terrible price.

AH: Nonetheless, very few institutions operate the way the union movement does, representing diverse constituencies and organized around class. For that reason, I think unions need to grapple with the question of sexuality and sexual behavior. That makes me ask of any organizing drive whether it will be prosex, whether it will understand that human desire is fundamentally organized around the hope of how you partner or how you feel about your body. That includes abortion, pregnancy, reproductive health, and all kinds of homosexuality, not just the kind that looks like heterosexuality except that it's between two girls or two guys. I'm talking about the things real people do. Those things are not marginal. If labor can speak to them, then it's a movement that also can understand how deeply rooted those issues are in people's lives and how people are vulnerable in the workplace because of them.

A lot of people think of these issues as social, but to me a revitalized union movement has got to be a social world.

NPS: Right. It's about constituting a genuine alternative, one that really does, as you say, construct an "alternative social world." Given the impoverishment of the discourse of class in this country, there's a way in which the images we have of class are holdovers from antecedent times. You're talking about reimagining solidarity, outside reductive ideas of class that have been inherited from older models where the typical worker is a male industrial worker and the head of a family. When we're talking about organizing around class as the site of materiality, we're required to talk about all the things you have mentioned. It's not about a bunch of different issues that add up; it's about the fact that material, embodied reality is lived through all the things that we're talking about. In a sense, it's about what class is.

There's a lot of talk about union democracy right now. The fact of the matter is that the ossification of the trade union movement in this country during the cold war, the growing impoverishment of internal democracy in the governance of many unions, the acceptance of an economistic compact with government and corporations, all these things were integrally connected to the failure of the AFL-CIO to fully confront the contradiction of race in the 1950s and 1960s and, beyond this, the failure to take on the range of issues that have stemmed from the contradictions to democracy in American life. So what we're talking about is the failure of the American labor movement to develop as a significant counterculture, a "parallel civil society," as Mike Davis suggests.[3] It has not developed as an alternative space for governance of the pressing social questions and needs that are not dealt with by corporate culture, that are not dealt with in the Beltway, that are not dealt with by local government.

3. Mike Davis, "Why the U.S. Working Class Is Different," in *Prisoners of the American Dream: Politics and Economics in the History of the U.S. Working Class* (New York: Verso, 1986).

There has to be a way of thinking and talking about these questions within the union movement. There are real signs of that, but still tentative ones. As soon as those signs appear, there also seems to be an impulse to retreat. I guess what bothers me is that there is still some way that the discussion of the "new union movement" betrays a failure of imagination. It's as if the revitalization of American labor is something that comes from on high—from John Sweeney's election and so forth. This ignores all the energy that's been infused by rank-and-file organizers—many of whom were active in other arenas. You see this activist energy on every college campus today—around labor and employment issues, the no-sweat movement, student radicalism around education and access, the new abolitionists working on race and incarceration issues, the anti–police brutality protests—

AH: And that's also been generated by the activation of new immigrant populations like New York City taxi drivers.

NPS: Yes, and generated by organizing around race and ethnicity, sexuality and gender. I think it's a fascinating question because it turns the "identity politics versus class politics" debate that we've heard ad nauseam from the old New Left—mostly white men—on its head. It says that the reinvigoration of class politics has derived from all those places where innovative, interesting organizing has been going on.

AH: The question is not whether a flat, unimaginative definition of *class* will engender organizing because it won't. It may succeed in a particular drive because there's a particularly good organizer or because there are extreme needs at that moment, but, over time, it will fail. The ability to create new conceptions of organizing and union building will depend on a much more dynamic understanding of *who* is in the class.

The union movement needs to acknowledge the complexity of the material lives people lead. It needs to recognize that identities are not rigid or always obviously defined, to have a complex understanding of diversity. If you want to bring all the players to the table, then you have to understand who the players are, what their issues are, and how their own issues color the way they see issues of commonality. When the union movement fails to recognize that, it is, in effect, containing the workplace. Frankly, it's operating like the employer, who does not want difference and uses difference only to divide people. Employers want the generic worker they can control and manipulate.

If you think about who should be targeted in new organizing drives, the demographics are almost identical to those people the CDC (Centers for Disease Control) identified as being most at risk for contracting HIV. It's the working poor. That's where HIV is, where parenting without marriage is, where having kids or trying to get abortions is, where racism and illegal immigration are.

NPS: That's where issues of criminality come up as well. Here, again, we have come up against a very sharp boundary and test for the new union movement. Today, illegality and incarceration are principal sites for perpetuating both racialization and forms of civil death that have primarily affected African American people in this country. As attacks on the working and workless poor, these kinds of things are clearly an immediate threat to any viable working-class movement, especially insofar as quasi-forced prison labor is on the rise. And yet it seems that these are the things that most unions don't want to touch with a ten-foot pole. Criminals are really beyond the pale.

AH: I've done prison work for thirty years now. Working with women in prison, you see the hopeless lives that people lead when they have no choices. "Let's see, what shall I do? I will let my kid starve, but I won't try to get $250 off a blow job that gets me busted." That's what you see. When people are poor, they're one step away from incarceration. That's what they know. If we're going to build a new understanding of race and gender, then we have to come to terms with that.

Again the questions are, Will the union movement be an institution that understands the nature of economic justice and economic injustice in all its nuances? Or will it have a more limited understanding? Will labor shy away from the issue of prisons and say, "That's not about us. We don't have anything to say about it, nor do we want to intervene in it"?

NPS: When you put this together with what you said earlier about CDC statistics, it's a remarkable convergence. Sex work and street-level drug dealing and drug use are the places that produce the most risk around HIV, and they are also the places that have been targeted for the heaviest forms of policing over the last two decades. It's the place where we have concentrations of women and people of color in the greatest numbers. Actually, it's not a remarkable convergence. It's terrifying.

AH: The women's side of Rikers Island prison has five hundred inmates, and 60–70 percent of those women are HIV positive. They're all going back into the community, and they're all going to be looking for work. They are the people the union movement will be organizing. What will unions do about these women's HIV status? What will they do about foster-care programs that have custody of these women's kids?

It's interesting to me that in Mexico, in the border towns where U.S. industry has gone, so many of the women who work in *maquiladoras* do sex work to supplement impossibly low wages. Frankly, that doesn't happen only on the U.S.-Mexico border. It happens in Albany and in the South Bronx. You do what you need to do in order to put a roof over your head or buy your kid some shoes. Unions have no choice, it seems to me. If they want to organize people in industries that suffer the most from not being organized, they've got to deal with race, immigration, HIV status, and sexuality.

Most recently, I have been doing HIV prevention work with women, as national field director for Women's HIV Prevention Services at the Gay Men's Health Crisis (GMHC). But when prevention work is embedded in an AIDS organization, it is already too late. By the time a women gets to an AIDS organization, she's already positive. In order to do prevention work, you've got to partner with the primary institutions in a women's life that are not connected to HIV—the church, the union movement, the hair salon, the neighborhood park, the dry cleaners. You've got to go to the places where people live their lives. If union training programs included issues around health care and positive preventive health maintenance—if that training included discussions of sexual partnering, sexually transmitted diseases, HIV, pregnancy, and options to pregnancy—then HIV would be a discussable topic in the workplace.

NPS: Health care is a frontline issue in employer-employee battles right now. A radical health agenda for unions is crucial, not only in securing benefits that are being eroded, but in safeguarding the health of workers. If it were possible to wage a deeper battle against the corporate culture that we all live in, it would save a lot of people a lot of money in wasteful, unnecessary medical expenditures.

AH: It would save a huge amount of money, and it would save a lot of lives. We need to take on mental health, for example. It's one of the things that people don't want to talk about. Admitting that you have an alcohol problem or are depressed is difficult and also provocative in terms of taking these issues on in the workplace. But alcoholism has always been acknowledged as a problem in white working-class communities. So, in the last twenty years, alcohol rehab programs have become fairly common in unions. When it comes to more socially controversial issues of substance abuse, HIV, or domestic violence—issues that are deeply connected to race, gender, and sexuality—unions have been reluctant to give those problems a high priority. Domestic violence, for one thing, has to be part of the union agenda in the same way that racism has to be—because it divides a workplace. If a guy treats his wife like shit, trust me, he's not a nice guy to the woman who works with him. These are not separable issues. Social attitudes are reflected in human relationships. If I'm a racist at home or in my neighborhood, then I probably am at work, too. If no one calls me on it, and if the union lets me get away with it, then the union movement has lost an opportunity.

When you speak up, people may not agree with you. But if you've built real relationships so that people respect who you are, then they will engage in discussion with you about issues on which you may disagree. That's the kind of engagement that needs to happen. It won't be simple or easy.

NPS: Again, we're talking about creating a transformative political culture in the union movement. It's like radical teaching—you provide a kind of "exit" for people from various kinds of behaviors, attitudes, and identities that are crippling or damaging to themselves and to other people. An exit is the representation of some credible alternative, the sense of a different, more enabling way of being. That exit is something that you have to be able to show, represent, and constantly rearticulate. But you have to have real credibility yourself to be able to do that. It isn't legislation. It's persuasion.

AH: It's persuasion and also engagement. People don't have to agree with me, but they do have to engage with me. That's why I'm a good organizer and can do what I do. It's not because I have all the answers. It's because I'm willing to bring up the things that are difficult and make it possible for people to talk about why those issues are both so profound and so troubling at the same time.

NPS: It's a missed opportunity when unions don't engage people. When you're organizing people, and when people are challenging power around economics, it's the scariest thing anyone can do. And there's an assumption that, when you're doing it, you have to keep everything else constant; otherwise, you won't be able to fight the battle. But in fact the opposite is true. It's amazing how our personalities can be reshuffled in an instant. People can be completely transformed when they're fighting. They see other people on the picket line, for example, and suddenly the whole world is reorganized. Then you do have an "alternative social world"—assuming you've managed to articulate things like race, gender, and sexuality and show that they're central, as opposed to trying to reprivatize them and push it all away. If you just say, "We're all here because we're fighting the same thing and we all want the same thing," that's an immensely squandered opportunity.

AH: It is. The union movement saw what trade unionism at its most literal and pragmatic led to. It led to racism and sexism—where a certain sector of white men were seen as the only credible and important speakers for union politics. What I always found interesting was that the union movement wanted to reflect its radical past without having any of its radical politics. For example, people would talk about the Flint, Michigan, sit-down strikes. But if you ever suggested sitting down at your own plant, your union would tell you all the reasons you couldn't do that, that you had to be in conversation with management. But, you know, if you want to be a voice for economic justice, then you have to take on the forces that create injustice. That means you have to be willing to speak to those injustices as they are lived by the people in the workplace. A union movement that doesn't have a vision may still be able to obtain something for workers who have no economic power. But the only way that movement can last and grow is if it gives people genuine hope for improving their lives.

Most of us will never be creative workers, who can find satisfaction in isolation: we can't all make a movie or write a book. Most of us live engaged lives where we work, and the quality of our job has a lot to do with the quality of our life. When our labor is something that gives us honor, we are really proud to be workers in the places where we do our jobs. We don't have to go somewhere else to feel decent about what we do. To those of us who come from backgrounds where we were poor and scared, the union movement represented a way we could begin to speak for ourselves—in a place where we thought we had no power. Why would we want to ignore all the other places that represent us but where we have been silenced against our will? If the labor movement can encompass all those sites of personal identity, people will stay when things get hard. They will help build belief in a union movement that can organize a workplace—organize not around the bitterest antagonisms but around the most generous of our common experiences. In that kind of movement, no workers have to be humiliated when they're forced to take a job because they have to pay the rent.

The union movement has to be brave enough to have a vision that individual people often are afraid to hold out for. The politics of such a vision is not just little variations on a theme. It is not about whether I get to hold hands with my girlfriend at work—not that that's small. It's not the symbolic acts; it's about being a movement that reflects the best about human life and human possibility. And you have to ask yourself, Where else but the union can that happen?

NPS: I think we have been rightly focusing on the state of the current trade union movement and all these issues on the assumption that this is an extraordinary and incredibly exciting moment. It has emerged out of new thinking in the labor movement and new behaviors and new identities, which in turn are being encouraged by the labor movement. At the same time, we still have advocacy politics, with different agendas, outside the scope of trade unionism. Given the work you've done around AIDS and sexuality, how do you see these other sites operating in connection to these issues and to the union movement? To what extent does the current incarnation of the gay rights movement take on issues of class politics and employment and see them as central? Do they need to?

AH: The reason that you and I are having this conversation is both because the union movement has created a new dialogue about hope and organizing and because the limits of the class, race, and gender politics that drive social identity movements have become more and more obvious. These things have become especially obvious to those of us who were in those social identity movements because we didn't know how to be in the union movement and be out sexually. Social movements that are advocacy movements—the queer movements, the sexuality movements, the HIV movements—have been articulated more and more fundamentally by the class of people that dominates them. So those movements advocate for their own class agenda in an endlessly infuriating way. Take the way the military issue was dealt with. The queer organizations in conflict with Clinton's "don't ask, don't tell" policy said the policy discriminated against gays at West Point. They didn't ask, Who are the majority of gay people in the military? The majority are poor, of-color women and men who joined the army or navy or air force because they had no job options where they were. Policy on gays in the military is most felt by the foot soldier, by the guy who is a faggot who flies a helicopter or a dyke who drives a supply truck. Not having those people represented as the driving force behind an agenda for gay rights in the military reflected the class politics of those movements and the economics that fueled those campaigns.

Many of us did AIDS work in reaction to the class politics of social movements because in AIDS work you have to be able to deal with the complexity of race and class as well as sexuality. Much of the gay movement, in my experience, has been willing to forgo substantive discussion about anything of concern to anyone but a privileged and small part of homosexual society in this culture. The politics of these gay movements is determined by the economic position of those who own the movement. You see contradictions over and over again in what they think a gay issue is. Is immigration a gay issue? Oh no! Is workplace organizing a gay issue? Oh no! Are prisons a gay issue? Absolutely not!

For a lot of us, the reason we are so fierce in our hope for this new union movement is because we need to come home. We need to bring the skills and gifts we possess into the bigger organizing drive that has to embrace working-class communities because we are part of those communities. At least in my life, if you were a lesbian, the only choice was to be quiet or to leave. In the trailer parks I came out of, man, those were the options. You could be a homosexual and get the shit kicked out of you at work all the time, or you could leave and try to have a life with other gay people. That no longer is true. It's not the same dynamic any more, precisely because we have done so much to change the dialogue about lesbian and gay life. Now it's really embedded in a much bigger world. Most gay people are working-class people. All the issues they have in their lives are working-class issues. They need to be able to bring their queer, working-class selves out to the unions, out to the workplace, out to HIV, out to sexuality. We are not outside agitators. We're absolutely the backbone of those movements, in terms of our gender, our color, and our sexual orientation. Does the union movement want its children or not? That's the real question. If the union movement wants us at home and out, it's got to see that our identities reflect the ways in which we are also working class.

Organizing sex workers—that's got to have a home in the labor movement. Issues like that are not irrelevant issues that concern only a small number of people. They are broad social issues that engage many working-class and poor people. We need to be able to represent ourselves as we are and as we live. Most of the women with whom I do HIV organizing are precisely the women who are organized in the home health-care movement, who are doing the poorest-paid jobs in hospitals, who are trying to figure out how to get a GED because they spent six months in jail instead of in high school. That's who they are. They are also dykes. It's not either/or: they need decent-paying jobs; they are lucky if they have a high school diploma; they have two kids they had before they were eighteen; they are trying to figure out how to survive in families that are conflicted because they are lesbians. The union movement's got to help them in all that. These are people who have no idea about the Human Rights Campaign or the National Gay and Lesbian Task Force. Maybe they come to Gay Pride once a year because, well, it's not in the Bronx, so, fuck it, they can go to a march. They're lucky if they even know there's a gay and lesbian community center.

NPS: It seems very important to recognize the fact that the forms of cultural innovation and identity performance that the gay and lesbian movement and the black movement pioneered as a part of the dynamic of protest have transformed the public sphere by creating much of the emotional and dispositional space for "difference" to appear in public. That's a huge, undeniable achievement. At the same time, it is amazing how the political movements have narrowed to things like defense of marriage, affirmative action, and the most watered-down kinds of nondiscrimination politics.

AH: If we're going to have progressive politics, the union movement has to be a part of the dialogue about what progressive politics means in this current historical moment. Part of what progressive politics now means is engagement around things like affirmative action and nondiscrimination, to be sure, but also an engagement around the ways this culture more and more rigidifies, reduces, and alienates the possibilities of human expression and experience. I think there is going to be an explosion in this culture over exactly these kinds of issues. The question is whether the union movement will capture the power of that explosion and give it voice.

NPS: Underneath the veil of normalcy is the culture of racial hatred and violence, self-hatred and despair, the inability to deal with difference or fathom difference, an absolute obsession with militarism—

AH: And it's all killing the cultures and communities that the union movement knows it has to organize. For that reason, unions have got to take on HIV—and prisons because prisons reflect the racism of the culture. It's how racism is practiced daily.

NPS: And that's why we are talking about things that of necessity must go beyond affirmative action. It's not just about developing a response that's adequate to the reactionary constraints of the late twentieth century. It's about identifying the modalities of racism and sexism in the current moment because they have also shifted and changed.

AH: They have shifted and changed globally. There are very few institutions in this country that can speak from a global perspective and represent class. The union movement can because it knows that it's got to deal with the impact of the global market. Organizing in the United States is fundamentally affected by what's going on globally, so labor has to speak to class in global terms. Everywhere, our world is radically altering around issues of race and sexual orientation and gender. And it's not happening just in the United States. The developing world is being devastated by HIV. The workforce is being wiped out in South Africa because it's working-class people who are dying of AIDS. The trucking industry across the Middle East is dying from HIV. The wives of HIV-infected workers are giving birth to kids who are HIV-positive. All this is reflected here in the United States, and it's reflected elsewhere. There's a way in which these complex issues can be made to appear as if they are outside the limits of general discussion. In that context, AIDS isn't anything except a set of secrets and taboos. That's all it's about—*powerlessness engaged in desire.* Why do we think it's so different—what you do in your workplace and what you do in your bedroom?

It's always amazing to me. People tell me things because I'm gay and because of what they feel about homosexuality. They feel homosexuality is forbidden. So that allows them to tell me about what they feel is forbidden for themselves. What you learn from that dialogue is that everybody has something forbidden. That's what you learn—not about your own homosexuality but about how much people live inside a forbidden subjectivity. That's what they carry, whether it's a fantasy or a secret. I want to create a political movement where that kind of understood, lived experience can have value depending on whether it's relevant to what's going on but where a priori it won't be decided that it's not a part of the dialogue about the workplace. If this experience could be engaged in the workplace, then deviance wouldn't be about homosexuality; it would be about desire. What you have to understand about desire is that this culture has given people no rights around desire, although it's given some men power. But it's given nobody any intelligence or training or education about their bodies, the way they live in their bodies or how they feel desire through their bodies. That has meant that women have always paid, poor people have always paid, and queers have always paid. If that's who the union movement wants to organize, then it has to speak to the bodies that it's organizing, the ways that these bodies are acted on by the culture and the expectations that people live through their bodies. It can't be separate from that— it can't be.

NPS: That's wonderful. Let's stop there.

Gender Warriors

This 1997 interview, which appeared in Femme: Feminist Lesbians and Bad Girls, *touches on some of the issues that I've always cared about: class, race, sexuality, gender, and—more currently—aging. Also, I see it as a valuable discussion I had with a much younger femme. So here are two self-identified femme lesbians, of very different generations, talking about the things that matter.*

AN INTERVIEW
WITH AMBER HOLLIBAUGH
by Leah Lilith Albrecht Samarasinha

Amber Hollibaugh is a powerful woman. When we were setting up this interview, I joked about her being one-third of "the holy trinity of high femme," along with Joan Nestle and Madeline Davis. And she has been central to the struggle to reclaim and validate femme/butch gender and sexuality during the feminist sex wars. She is also a lot more: old-school femme, working-class woman, labor organizer, sex worker, writer, and filmmaker. More recently, she's been known as the founder of the Lesbian AIDS Project, the first organization created to fight for the needs of lesbians with HIV. She is a smart, passionate, and luscious survivor who continues to live the struggle. For me, a young femme, Amber is what I want to be when I grow up. One afternoon, we talked real loud about femme identity, gender, sex, loyalty, AIDS, race and class, youth and age, whoring, and everything else under the sun, as the straight women at the next table tried to figure out whether we were drag queens or not.

A Lifetime of Femme Identity

LEAH LILITH ALBRECHT SAMARASINHA: So has your femme identity changed over time?

AMBER HOLLIBAUGH: Oh, yes. You do change over time. The things that you considered fundamental to the way you constructed your femme identity when you were twenty don't seem really important after a while. It is intriguing to be in your own life when you're not scared of it. That has taken me fifty years to get to. Now, I am no longer afraid that the choices I make somehow threaten an essentially important identity. I do not walk around saying, "I do this; am I somehow more or less femme? Am I more or less the erotic person that I imagine myself to be?" I am. I am that person. I have been that person for a very long period of time.

LLAS: I doubt myself like that all the time. I think, "I have been wearing pants a lot lately, so maybe I am not really femme."

AH: It is all a process of maturing and coming into yourself. But you do get there, even though it is a struggle. When the woman I was with for ten years and I broke up—and she was very, very butch—I was forty-five. I was a middle-aged femme. I didn't have a lot of preparation for what that was going to look like, and not very many people talked about it. Most of the middle-aged people I knew who were in butch/femme relationships were settling down, buying houses, just what we had done. Suddenly, in the midst of this coupled butch/femme world, I was by myself and not into the bars any more. And I said, how am I going to find lovers? How am I going to be a femme *here*? When I'm no longer young and sexually adventurous and out there?

LLAS: Which is where I'm at right now—I go to the bar in a miniskirt and sit on a stool and feel like I can take home anyone in the bar. I'm enjoying it, but I also know it is for a limited period of time, and I wonder about what comes next.

AH: It is a fabulous time period, but, as a forty-five-year-old, you don't really want to go do it any more. And, even if you did, would you want to pick up someone who is twenty-six? That's the question when your body doesn't look the same, when you don't feel the same way about your body. I've got a long history now. I'm experimenting in different ways. My sexuality is permeated by age and how I feel about age. As femmes, I think, we get the same old shit that all women in this culture get. Butches get some of the privileges of men in the culture: they age better.

LLAS: So how do you handle this?

AH: Well, for one thing, I decided not to stay in that relationship when it was really in trouble, like I had seen femme friends of mine do. They stayed because they were so terrified. They had no alternatives; they basically waved their butch lovers off to go have flings because they didn't think that anyone wanted them as older femmes. I thought, I'll be single for the rest of my life, by God, before I'm going to wave anybody off.

LLAS: Before you sell yourself short like that.

AH: If we decide to be nonmonogamous, that's fine with me. But, by God, I'm not going to do something because I am so terrified about whether or not I have an erotic future. I'd been in a relationship for ten years, and I was confident about myself in a way I had never been. I no longer thought it was an accident that women desired me. I'd been proud, I'd been cocky, I'd been like, "Yeah, honey, come and get it." [*Laughter.*] But I'd also been afraid. I had been afraid that, once they discovered the real person, somehow I would not remain that kind of instrumental fabulous hot femme that I like to put myself out as. Well, I lost that fear, and I could go forward.

LLAS: I think that confidence in the reality of yourself is what femme is at the core. That confidence that your body is femme — but not "beautiful" in the killing way the culture and the ads put out there as an archetype — it is fucking gorgeous.

AH: That's right. That's exactly what happened to me. As a femme, it is very necessary that you develop that arrogance, just so you can get by in the world and wear that really tight black dress down the same block every day. That confidence is something you have to struggle toward and grow into.

LLAS: If you're straight and looking in from the outside, butches may read as tough and femmes as vulnerable. But, if you're in the life, you know that femmes are much more ballsy — much more brassy — than butches. Something I say to my friends is that I am "a high femme with the heart of a stone butch." Under that really tough bitch-goddess exterior I have most of the time are all these vulnerabilities. I don't know how to show them to people, especially the butch in my life, who I get all caught up in taking care of and healing and making a home in my arms for. Do you see this dynamic playing out in your life?

AH: Yes, I do. I think that part of the magic between high femme and stone butch is precisely the understanding of that invincibility and that vulnerability, in combination. Although we present and project ourselves very differently, in order to have our integrity, we have a complicated set of standards around what we will and will not tolerate. I think that what that means for a lot of femmes is that we have a kind of integrity—if we survive—about holding onto our own erotic identity, refusing to give up any piece of ourselves. I know that's what butches do all the time and also that it is visible on them in a different way. There was a point a few years ago when there was this button that said, "Butch in the streets, femme in the sheets."

LLAS: They have one now that says, "Femme in the streets, butch in the sheets." We've come so far.

AH: Yeah, right, what progress. Part of what was so painful to me about that statement—besides that it was idiotic and completely demeaning to the way that people live butch/femme identities—is that it assumed somehow that being tough on the street was butch. It did not understand that the power you have to insist on as a femme to survive with integrity on the street is a real kick-ass ballbuster attitude. I don't think it is an accident that so many femmes I've known have histories of sex work because we have the attitude to pull it off. It took me a long time to realize that I walked down the street very differently than other women, not because I was femme, but because I used to be a sex-trade worker. I didn't drop my eyes. As a prostitute, if you can't make eye contact, you can't get a customer, so you really have to keep your head up. Once you've done that as a professional, you keep your head up. Part of the reason why men look at me is that I don't drop my eyes. If I dropped my eyes, it would be clear to them that I saw myself as a veiled woman, and that would create a kind of I'm-a-good-girl, I-don't-look-at-men identity.

LLAS: When I was nineteen and living on Avenue B and wearing my mini and garterbelt, that was one thing I learned. If I looked men in the eye, they would not harass me, which is the total opposite of the good-girl-ignore-it message that you are taught as the way to deal with being sexually harassed. I saw that my attitude freaked the men out even more than my young butch friends did. The men had no place in their heads for a woman in heels and a tight dress who wasn't scared or threatened by them, who was wearing all the cultural signifiers of sexual vulnerability but was not someone they could fuck with.

AH: To be a femme who cares about her erotic identity on the street, who does not drop her eyes, but who does not meet men's eyes for erotic charge, the question becomes, How do I keep my head up? How do I walk the way I walk, dress the way I dress, feel my body the way that I'm feeling, desire the women that I desire, and appropriate the street? How do I do that with the partners that I'm with when just the existence of our partnering is going to bring a concentration of hostility down on us? The butch because she's gender inappropriate, and me because I'm a gender traitor. I look like the right kind of girl, and I chose the wrong kind of "guy."

LLAS: It is very interesting when people get so furious that they don't know where to start. [*Laughter.*]

AH: I think about it a lot now because I think about how to age, as a femme, and keep on being able to appropriate all that I need to. I want to address it in this interview because one of the things that terrified me as a younger femme was thinking about getting older. I didn't see femmes around me as they aged.

LLAS: Did you see them defecting back to heterosexuality or just not coming to the bar or what?

AH: I just didn't know what happened to them. The only life I knew was within a certain kind of age period, bar life, and political life. But I do think it is very complicated to age with butch/femme sexual identities. Many butch women I've talked to have had real trouble trying to figure out how to navigate when they were no longer instrumental, when they could no longer open a door, when they had trouble making it up stairs, and when they couldn't be gallant with their girlfriend. That instrumentality was very compromised by aging. Femme identity, it seems to me, has many of the same permutations. As an older femme, you can't pull it off in the same way. I mean, you've got a back-ache, the sexual positions are just not as easy to get into when you're older, so what are you going to do?

LLAS: Advil?

AH: Advil, and negotiation. The problem for me is that I don't see women older than myself who I can relate to saying, "This is what femme looks like at sixty. This is what you can do at seventy." And that's really hard. A negligee doesn't look the same on you at sixty. You may still *want* to wear it, and you may still wear it, and your lover may think it is fabulous. But it is not fabulous in a culture that fetishizes youth.

LLAS: You're going to have to completely renegotiate your relationship to your body and to all the femme style and artifice you've used all your life.

AH: We both know that butch/femme is something much more than style, but it is often negotiated through style; it is created through the appropriation of very specific gendered appearances. Butch/femme is created through playing with these artifices. So, if that style is not as available to you because aging modifies your own relationship to your appropriation of those symbols, we're really talking something that's complicated. Aging is about watching yourself grow old, and that's not really very much fun. I mean, I'm sure some women have a fabu-lous experience doing it, but some women say they enjoy having their period. I have never found that I like my period; I didn't like it when I was twelve, and I don't like it now. It surprises me every month; I don't celebrate it with the moon.

LLAS: That's the thing about being femme; you don't enjoy *everything* about being a girl.

AH: That's right. You're always trying to figure out what part of female experience you're going to appropriate and what part of it puts you in a compromised position. So you are *constantly* in an internal struggle: does this hairdo, this dress, this mannerism, this way of sitting, speak-ing, this eyeliner, in any way compromise my femme position? Femme identity is as constructed as butch identity, and not a lot of people talk about it like that.

LLAS: Can you talk some more about that?

AH: The difference between myself and many of the straight women I know is that they think that they are normal and natural. They believe in girl-ness, that girl-ness becomes woman-ness, and that woman-ness becomes old woman–ness. They believe in a gendered system that they flow through. But my role models for being femme have been drag queens because drag queens construct female identity. I look at drag queens, and I think, That's how I feel as a woman.

LLAS: Drag queens and femmes both have that blatancy, that in-your-face outrageousness and sense of being too much.

AH: My femininity is about irony. It is a statement about the construction of gender; it is not just an appropriation of gender. It is not being a girl; it is watching yourself be a girl. I go to drag queens as my mentors and my role models because they were the ones who believed completely and passionately in their femaleness. The better they were as drag queens, the more they were completely 120 percent girl when they were in persona. They knew exactly the work it took to get there. They could take the dress off and be the messiest looking guy in a coffee shop, but in twenty-five minutes they could be the most ravishing beauty. They made femininity make sense to me.

Femme, AIDS, and Activism

LLAS: Speaking of outrageous women, do you see femmes playing a specific role in the lesbian AIDS movement? I see a lot of women I would call femmes in the AIDS movement—Lani Kaahumanu and Cynthia Astuto are two who come to mind—who have been key people because of their ability to talk very explicitly about sex. I see that as an extension of a typical femme role, the outrageously sexual woman who is not afraid to talk about it.

AH: I think that is true, and I don't think it is an accident. When you look at what the issues are for a lesbian dealing with HIV, they are sexuality—often butch/femme—class, race, substance abuse, and incarceration. For HIV-positive lesbians, their histories are going to be already centered around butch/femme issues, such as the oppression of forbidden sexual desire and questions of how to live their life without giving up their sexual community. Femmes have taken these issues very seriously over a long period of time and long before HIV.

LLAS: How do you see butch-femme and class playing out within the lives of lesbians with HIV?

AH: When I started doing the Lesbian AIDS Project, it was like coming home. The women that I deal with in the Lesbian AIDS Project who are HIV positive and affected by AIDS are working-class women. Since my own personal and social life is constructed around those lines, when I look at lesbians with HIV, they're completely understandable. The question is how you lucked out and ended up not positive, how you avoided addiction or somehow avoided a dirty needle, or how you were a sex worker who used condoms enough to protect yourself. Because you were in a privileged enough setting that you could do that or had enough skill that you could do that—there's a couple of ways you can pull that off.

LLAS: Like a sex worker would learn to put some lube on her hand and slip it on real quick.

AH: Exactly. The women in the Lesbian AIDS Project are often women who have been punished for enormous amounts of their lives for being gender inappropriate. They are not women who have lived in the closet and were afraid to come out. Often, at least for the butches, they were women who were punished at twelve, at eight, at three, who always were different in communities that were very intolerant. The issues of survival in these communities are *so* delicate that, if you have a daughter or a son who is too queer, you're terrified. So, when you look at the Lesbian AIDS Project, you see women usually with very strong sexual identities.

LLAS: Because they were strong enough to survive?

AH: Right. But they are not necessarily comfortable with those identities; some of them feel that their butch and femme identities actually had something to do with their addiction issues, their lack of feelings. It is a complicated history. I don't want to present it like everybody is a happy butch or femme.

LLAS: How do you, as the head of the Lesbian AIDS Project, deal with their butchness and femmeness in your work?

AH: My job is figuring out how to mentor women who have never been valued for the kinds of gifts that they bring around their identities. These are women who have never been praised for their sexual choices and have never been appreciated for how they desired women. Often, their story is that they felt ambivalent even if—at the same time—they were acting on those identities. They felt they were paying a terrible price. But once diagnosed, their attitudes often changed. They felt like, "I have got no time to fuck around here, so, if my mother doesn't like my sexuality, my mother just doesn't like it."

LLAS: So they think, "I've got five years left, and it's just too bad, honey."

AH: Yes, and they want to have an erotic identity of their own. That's a pressure on all women with HIV—to stop being sexual. There's a cultural weight that goes against all people with HIV. It says, "You're diseased, and you're contagious, and you threaten us." That syphilis model is really at play in the subtext of HIV.

LLAS: Also, specifically with women, the voices say, "You're a bad girl, and now you're paying for it."

AH: Right, and further, "You're a danger to me. You already have a forbidden sexual need, and now you're going to complicate what's already perverse by insisting on that need even after your HIV testing." One of the really valiant struggles women with AIDS have fought is to remain sexual in the face of a life-threatening illness. The reason why I and a lot of the women in the project are there is because we are committed to working to validate the rights of women with AIDS to community and to sexuality. We feel they have a right to work through the complex, maybe ambivalent relationships they have to identities and not have to give up their desire to be sexual in the role that allows them to see themselves as powerful. If that's about being a butch or about being a femme, more power to you, girl; you go. And, if it's not, there's room in the project to struggle through how this works in your life.

LLAS: So, in terms of your work at the Lesbian AIDS Project, your political analysis seems to integrate race and class and sexuality and gender and everything else; you don't prioritize.

AH: I think the success of the Lesbian AIDS Project has been our refusal to reduce any one aspect of identity to the whole. It is not a project that's only about sexuality; it is not a project only about race and class, only about one kind of oppression. It is a project that actually tries to bring them all together, to value the integrity of the women who are at risk and give them a space to find out what their priorities are in a culture that's never given them any room at all. It is about meeting other women like yourself, starting a dialogue about your lives and the forces that got you here in the first place. It is learning a set of skills you've never had in order to mobilize politically to reach other women. It is a place where you don't have to choose one part of yourself to be. Women can be all of themselves at the Lesbian AIDS Project.

LLAS: Is that why you got involved with AIDS activism? You started to get involved after the Barnard conference, right?

AH: AIDS activism as a movement valued my ability to do explicit work around sexuality. If you couldn't talk about sexuality as part of class and race in the beginning of AIDS work, you couldn't do the work. There I was, in a political movement—the sex wars, Barnard, all the controversy around butch/femme in the early 1980s—and people were saying, "Why do you have to keep bringing this up?" You can be in your own movement and completely oppositional only for a while without feeling like a freak. Coming from a family that taught me never to cross a picket line, one of the worst times I ever had was crossing the only one I ever did: a feminist picket line of Women against Pornography at the Barnard conference. I thought to myself, "This is really telling. I'm crossing a picket line, with women carrying signs with *my* name on them, saying that I'm perverted, that I don't belong in this movement." I had to cross a collective line that should have been about rights and freedom but was restigmatizing me for my history. I decided that I needed to be someplace where I wasn't always saying, "Yes, but . . ." So, yes, AIDS activism looked to me like the place that brought together all the social injustices that were stigmatized. It was the place where all the culturally stigmatized secrets—which were what really put people at risk—came out, from race to class to "I suck men off and then go home to my wife."

LLAS: One of those culturally stigmatizing secrets is butch/femme— because butch/femme sexual practices, like using dildos and fisting without barriers, are the ones that transmit AIDS the most easily from woman to woman.

AH: Yes, AIDS activism seemed like a natural world for me, a world that valued and demanded my skills. Finding this world has been one of the most fabulous things; instead of having to say "Yes, but . . . ," I've been in the position to say, "Yes." The project has made race and class and sexuality visible. And, as a femme, it has been fabulous for me. It has been a way for me to go home — to go back to the women that I'm attracted to, that I love, whose histories reflect my own—and not be strange. We don't sit around all the time and talk about sex and work, but, if it comes up, it is not strange. And, because my position at the Lesbian AIDS Project is regular, I become valued. And if I did not have a handle on butch and femme—not just race and class—I don't think I could have done it.

LLAS: Definitely. Cheers, honey. [*Laughter.*]

Femme, the Next Generation

LLAS: What do you see as the next step for femme women who theorize butch/femme within radical gender theory? What do we need to do next?

AH: In the last few years, the transgender movement has insisted that there is another place for queer identities to be named. They have begun to explore what *butch* means in a transgender setting, and it is not the same thing as in a butch/femme setting. But what *high femme* means in a transgender setting outside butch/femme, that needs to be taken on.

LLAS: My God, thank you. When I went to see Leslie Feinberg read at A Different Light at the book release for *Transgender Warriors*, I really wanted to get up and ask her why she left out high femmes and butch faggots from her book. Because, even though we do not cross from our assigned-at-birth gender to the "other" gender—the way transgender is often thought of—we still chose to live a different gender. If a high femme goes to a baby shower and *struts* her stuff, she will be read as being as queer as a drag queen would.

AH: You know that, if you're doing high femme, your femininity is profoundly made up. Femmes make it happen in a way that is not at all natural—it is real but not natural. As a femme, you have made decisions about how you will appear as a gendered person. And, when you're doing it, you don't take a deep breath and say, "Ah, I'm finally me." Instead, you go, "Ha, I finally actually look like the way I think a girl who isn't a girl looks." When I look at drag queens—that's how I see myself—I like looking like a drag queen. It matters to me that I look that way. When I look to and identify with that construction, I am also transgendered.

LLAS: I think that that is a very common high femme experience that is not often discussed. I cannot tell you how many times when I was eighteen my gay male friends would tell me that I looked like a trannie.

AH: Absolutely. I think that people have to be careful not to pose as part of a movement (like transgender) that they aren't primary players in, so I want to be very delicate about it. But, for me, there is at least an aspect, as there is for stone butches, of transgendered experience. When you design girl-ness, when you make up the way you are female, that's a transgendered experience. I think that transgender hasn't been mapped or named in the same way for femmes. That has bothered me because there is that transgendered aspect of high femme–ness that isn't about the erotic relationship, that isn't in relation to butches.

LLAS: I think that's so important. Because, unless we have that understanding of femme as trannie, there will never be an understanding of us as equally queer as butches.

AH: I think that a femme conversation with drag queens would offer some very interesting, very similar experiences. My fantasy has always been to have a femme panel that didn't assume that femme was lesbian. I want us as femmes, where it is appropriate, to insist that we're part of that *queer* dialogue instead of what usually happens, where as we get more feminine we get perceived as straighter rather than as transgendered. I also think that femmes need to become each other's allies. If we do that, we will begin to make it truly safe to be a strong femme in partnership with a strong butch.

LLAS: Our femme bonding will challenge that discourse where butch is the signifier for both lesbianism and butch/femme. There is no such thing in a lot of people's minds as an independent femme identity. If we battle that —

AH: But don't you think that that's what my generation of femmes has done? I think historically what people like Joan Nestle and myself and Dorothy Allison have done is to give the butch icon a run for its money. We have said that we are femme regardless of the butch that we are partnered with. That we are a freestanding sexual signifier that is as powerful an erotic voice on its own.

LLAS: Yes, and a lot of women my age I know revere all of you — and Jewelle Gomez and Chrystos and others. But it still takes a long time to learn to balance vulnerability and toughness as a femme.

AH: It is very hard. I think we don't appreciate how complicated it is to assemble our identities, to let them become shaded and nuanced as we grow. Two things I have very much valued about s/M communities are, one, their members' ability to distinguish *play* from how one lives around butch/femme (among other complicated sexual identities), and, two, their understanding of how one constructs a sexual arena. I think that the s/M community doesn't have the visibility it should have. I have been — and continue to be — extraordinarily influenced by what I see in s/M communities, especially around HIV, around safer sex, around gender, around sexual play and who tops and who bottoms. And what you call yourself when you're in that sexual play is different from what you call yourself in your life. I think that more femmes, whether or not they see themselves as s/M, need to pay attention to the s/M community. Most of us have a teensy tiny little arena to play in and no place to learn. My sexual playground can be literally resculptured by a dialogue with somebody who has done something that I never imagined that I could do. I take that behavior and think about it and worry about it — try it, change a little bit over here, keep this piece of it, and so on — and end up with some new understanding that thrills me.

LLAS: I think it is important for femmes, especially, to learn from s/M communities about topping and bottoming. Power exchange is key to much butch/femme sex, in one way or another. To take one example, there's the classic femme bottom role, which can be a very powerful liberatory strong position. But if you're eighteen and you've struggled to the point where you know that you like being a girl and wearing stockings and a garter belt and being called a slut and fucked till you scream but you don't know how to say no or how to negotiate your limits—my God, you're going into a minefield. If we're going to make the world safe for femmes, we have to know how to negotiate that minefield. I think back to what I went through when I was twenty, and I think it is a wonder I'm still in one piece. And that's a very common thing.

AH: The idea that you can't truly say yes until you know that you can say no is a very true one. You cannot make sexual choices until you know how to orchestrate and control sexuality, from every possible position. One of the things that happens in s/m that is very liberating for many women is that you have to be in your body no matter what. You are expected to participate. You really do call the shots: "No, don't do that," or, "My wrists are numb," and, "Don't hit me on the ass." So your needs, to the extent that you know them, really determine the content of the scene. Femmes need to talk to each other about sexual empowerment and historically remembering sexuality. So that we don't romanticize victimization but we learn to use where it has left us, in our real bodies as we make love. So that I don't live in *or* deny my fear.

Right now, I can actually arrange my world in alignment with what I think should be true. It is both a privilege and a challenge to be all the things that I am, to keep hold of them, remember them, value them, and figure out how to make them work. Even though it is a very difficult thing, we should keep choosing a bigger and bigger picture, even when people want us to be smaller. Femme identity really speaks to that because it cannot be reduced. It is a living, breathing thing that women are a part of, that women play, that many of us are not prepared to give up or make comfortable for anyone else because we want to live it.

LLAS: That's the bottom line: femme is always going to be walking down the street with a bullhorn in her hand yelling at the top of her lungs, "I'm here. Deal with it, goddamn it." Fabulous, huh?

AH: Damn straight.

My Dangerous Desires

Falling in Love with Stone Butches; Passing Women

and Girls (Who Are Guys) Who Catch My Eye

This is the final essay in the book. It is my attempt to come back, in a new millennium, to the issues that have engaged me for so many years; to look at, think about, and again confront the essential place where desire and danger and the need for radical social change meet.

> *She said, "When the door opens, of sensuality, then you*
> *will understand it too. The struggle begins . . ."*
> —Muriel Rukeyser, *"Kathe Kollwitz"*

In 1969 this is the dream I most feared, the dream I denied, dreamed, denied, dreamed, again and again:

I have on a negligee. Its fabric skims my body, drapes my breasts, curves against my hips, catches the shape of my cunt beneath its silky folds. It holds and captures the female shape of me, makes absolutely clear the contours of my expectations.

In the dream, I walk slowly across the room toward the bed, pause, move again, then stay in place for my lover's gaze. As I reach the edge of the bed and drop down, I am urged in against the yearning I have created, coaxed in and down until I blister the darkness. As I am undressed, my body scalds the palms of my lover's hands, pulling her fierce desire inside me, giving it shape, pulling her cock unrelentingly into my body, drawing it deep, holding it there, riding it, molding it, liquefying it inside my cunt. I am overtaken by a woman's hands, a man's cock, a lover's fever. I am possessed.

This is what I wanted. This is what filled me with horror.

My dream lover was no customary female, no "normal" lesbian of 1969, or of today. She was not a woman who is primarily a girl but a person who is a man that is a woman. This is an identity incompatible with girl/guy biology or its specifics, someone whose body conjures both authority and its subversion, who situates her autonomy through a transgressive gender strategy, who does not dread the outline of her masculine differences or shrink from her desire for my woman's form. This was and is a person who does not exist in the domain of the purely female.

I have desired this kind of woman, women who are men that are women, since I first came out as a lesbian and saw a butch. It was the first time in my sexual life that I understood the focus of my precise yearnings, felt my own longing answered, knew for certain that I required this kind of woman with a hunger that would not quiet down—knew that, with her, I could finally be had. And the only time in my life that I tried to kill myself because of my erotic cravings was over a butch lover—though by that time I had been a lesbian for many years. I was filled with the terror of it, as I was filled with its hunger.

I am not sure now which I believed was worse: the fantasy of myself in the negligee or my fantasy about the kind of a woman I wanted to remove it! I was horrified to find within myself the kind of rapturous longing I attributed to straight women. Yes, it was terrifying to recognize my need to be possessed and, furthermore, to be possessed by a person who had the affect of a man but whom I knew to be—whom I needed to be—biologically female. I had no idea how to begin to understand my own complex desires. I had no one to ask.

I'd been having the dream constantly since breaking up with my first butch lover, a woman who often passed as a man. Together we brought each other fully inside the erotic and emotional landscape of queer working-class life as butch and femme dykes. I bought her her first tuxedo; she picked me up for our first date on her Harley. We were a powerful butch/femme couple in the bars and in the working-class social world of ups drivers and hookers. But I was also a part of the independent revolutionary Left and a member of a radical Communist collective.

The questions that that dream corroborated—and which I lived but could not answer—were about which world I would be a part of, which world represented what I believed, which world I would live within, which world I would authenticate and fight for. The world of submachine guns, anti–Vietnam War demonstrations, running in the streets from tear gas and police, joining the newly forming women's liberation consciousness-raising groups? Or a world of nighttime negligees, of living unconditionally for the passion I experienced with women the world saw as men, lovers who rode me on the backs of their bikes to the local lesbian bar? I bought ties and BVDs for them, like I had for the men in my poor white- and Gypsy-trash family. These women who weren't interested in building a leftist political movement, they wanted to join the Roller Derby.

I could not square it.

The entire world seemed, in those days, to be irretrievably dangerous. Not that it had ever seemed safe. But the apparent contradictions in my life were more than I could tolerate or understand. Especially after my first butch lover and I had broken up and I could no longer believe that loving her had been an aberration or an accident. I could not forget her hands, the ways she had touched me, brought me fully alive within my own desire. I already lived on the edge as a political organizer and a sex worker, and I told no one but her about my work as a dancer and a whore. Even back then, I knew that my silence was about class, that I was in a political movement that had never understood my kind of background or its violence and poverty. But the particular meaning of my own passionate erotic need and my resulting queer, high femme, old-gay lesbian identity—this looked suspiciously deviant, even to me.

Facing my profound longings after the breakup meant facing the truth that, erotically and emotionally, I needed to be with lovers who were butch. I required that world, that way of coming together, that environment, in order to sustain my own femme erotic identity. This meant to me that I was a femme.

I knew no other women who claimed that sexuality, that identity, that life. At best, I saw them out of the corner of my eye at the bar on Saturday nights, as my lover and I left the dance floor to reclaim our table. There were other femmes in that universe, sure. But we didn't talk with each other about our femme-ness, didn't speak to each other directly about our identities or the meaning we attached to our perilous relationships with the butch women we desired, slept with, committed our hopes to, betrayed, and adored. We didn't talk much to each other at all. We would look one another over, evaluate the other as threat or friend, then separate to be alone or with individual butch lovers.

At that time femmes were at a premium in the bars, a very desired object in a world dominated by an overflow of butches. But I could find no women there who were like me, who crossed into and out of the worlds I traversed daily, women who lived fiercely as a high femme lesbian hooker and a Commie dyke organizer. Politically radical lesbians or women's liberationists lived in one stratosphere; working-class femmes and hookers lived in another. I appeared to be the only person around straddling both environments. And I feared that, in ways I could hardly imagine but which I dreaded, exploring and living out my femme identity meant going further away from the movements I ardently identified as my own, meant turning my back on the political work that had saved my mind and my life and given me vision, context, hope. It was, at the same time, a confrontation with class, with the very background I had tried so hard to escape. For many years I remained in a state of crisis about which world would define my human life.

Gay liberation was the most passionately personal movement I belonged to. Betraying its values, or disputing its implicit sexual codes, seemed to me then to act against myself, to transgress—and, in that transgression, to become even more marginalized as a lesbian. I had already lived outside my own desires in the heterosexual world and then again in the closet of my first lesbian love affair. I could not go back. But there was no way I could see to go forward either. I knew I could never return to the ways in which I'd existed before that first relationship with a butch lover crystallized my lust. My own desires seemed to me too dangerous to live with. But I already knew what it would mean to live without them.

It was 1978. The Gay Pride March that year in San Francisco was a passionate testament against Anita Bryant and the loss of an important gay rights initiative in Dade County, Florida. It was a reply to the frightening wave of antigay politics sweeping the country. People were at that march in defiance, protest, mobilization. It galvanized gay resistance. I was proud to be part of it that year, angry and defiant about all the homophobia surrounding us. I was also full of inarticulate grief. The fundamental importance of gay liberation was unequivocally clear to me. But my desires, the ways I felt and expressed my own queer femme sexuality, now positioned me outside the rights I was marching to defend. My internal erotic identity made me an alien to the politics of my own movement—a movement I had helped start, a movement whose survival and growth I was committed to.

It was obvious to me that butch/femme sexuality, and my own particular high femme variation, had no place in the sexual politics of the time (as it barely has today). Then, the old-gay lesbian images and historical narratives, sepia-toned photographs from the past depicting femmes alone or with their partners, depicting butch dandies and their female lovers, were presented as larger-than-life icons representing a long-ago era that the lesbian movement was hesitantly willing to acknowledge and affirm. But, to the upper-middle-class voices of the movement, butch and femme now, in the present, current universe of lesbian and gay liberation descended from the Stonewall rebellions, was not seen as a vigorous living system, a powerful way of being, existing, and desiring. The movement in which I found myself viewed butch/femme desire and methods of social interaction as dangerous, odd, ridiculous, shameful, a ruinous erotic system which was considered antithetical to the goals and ambitions of that movement. Femme and butch eloquence was reduced, in the movement's eyes, to stereotypical masculine/feminine "roles". The lesbian and gay liberation movement of those days thought of itself as representing fluidity, androgyny, freedom. The battleground was established. There was no apparent way out.

I marched all that day, then left the march late in the afternoon and rented a motel room just outside the Castro. There I cried for hours, pacing between the bathroom and the bed. Finally, I took every pill I had managed to buy, steal, or collect, snorted large quantities of coke, drank a quart of something that was eighty proof, ran hot water in the sink, and held my wrists under it one by one until I had finished cutting them with a razor. I passed out.

To this day, I don't know why it didn't kill me.

When a cleaning woman found me the next morning, I was taken to the hospital by ambulance, questioned, treated, and released that afternoon. I returned to my commune; there was nowhere else for me to go. Though much of it is a blur, I remember swearing that day that, if I could somehow find a way to live through this sexual terror and come out the other side, I would never let anyone go to that place alone again. No movement, no community that I was a part of would ever again create a politics of sexual exclusion and rigid sexual judgment without me protesting loudly, publicly, insistently, until things changed. Then I started the hard work of unraveling my own sexual skeletons and investigating what moved them around inside me.

I know that, for some people, gay rights and gay liberation do not hinge on the particulars of sexual desire. I have heard for the last twenty-five years that we aren't *just* our erotic identities; the current movement is thick with it. But, for many of us, it *does* begin there, does revolve around the ways we organize our erotic choices. And erotic identities are not just behaviors or individual sexual actions; they reflect a much broader fabric that is the weave and crux of our very personhood, a way of mediating and measuring all that we experience, all that we can interpret through the language of our bodies, our histories, our eyes, our hips, our intelligence, our willful, desiring selves. However we've gotten there, erotic identity is not simply a specific activity or "lifestyle," a set of heels or ties that dress up the quirk. It is as deep and rich, as dangerous, explosive, and unique as each of us dares to be or become.

What I believe now, after all these years, is that it doesn't really matter what the erotic violation is. For some people, the forbidden may be any feelings of homosexual attraction at all; for others, it may be s/m—whether queer or straight—or it may be the specifics of butch/femme, top/bottom, dominance and submission, etc., etc. But, when individual desire rides that fiercely through a person's intrinsic, intimate set of principles, there can be no resolution of the crisis without an extraordinary self-confrontation, a coming to terms.

Because of that, this story is important to tell and remember.

By the time I tried to kill myself I had already survived incest at the hands of my father and violence—and silence—at the hands of my mother. I had worked for years as a hooker and a stripper. I had left my husband for a woman, then lived five years with her in the closet. I had found and joined and helped build the exploding gay liberation struggle in its first years. I had navigated all that sexual terrain while also participating openly in the effort to build the Left. I had every reason to believe I was skillful in handling issues of sexual conflict and identity, difference, politics. I had always traveled in a world of sexual appetites and sexual needs, a world charted by its passions, its hungers, and its sexual opposition, a world sketched by expression and resistance. I had the experience of choosing sex and setting its terms; I had experienced having no say in the face of violence and violation. I knew of all the reasons people turned to sex: for release, revenge, tenderness, aggression, to satisfy their own hunger or their need for power. I thought all this had given me the skills and seasoning necessary to survive the challenge that butch desire and femme identity had created for me. I thought I could ride out that storm and invent a bridge for it into the new movement I had helped establish. I was wrong.

It was insidious, really, how I had become worn down by the fear and shame, the ceaseless scrutiny and interrogation that flowed poisonously through the lesbian wing of the early gay liberation movement. Sometimes when I was with my lover we were treated like a joke: a frozen, fixed, antiquated, irrational vestige of comic buffoonery. We were deluded, they said; we were foolish, absurd. Sometimes it was more brittle, more hostile, more derogatory. At meetings I attended, marches I participated in, dances my lover and I showed up to attend, I was asked why we had bothered to come or told we were not welcome: "No femmie women with he/she men." How I looked, how I acted with a lover, how I acted by myself, how I walked, spoke, dressed, expressed my passion, all were constantly called into question. I was told I should find myself a "real" man if that's what I was into. I often had to escort and then remain with my butch lovers so they could use the women's bathroom at movement institutions. That was in 1973. In 1995, I and my stone butch lover of the time were refused entrance to a lesbian feminist women's dance at the New York City Lesbian and Gay Community Center during Gay Pride Week. We were told the same things I'd been told twenty-five years before: It—butch/femme—was a dangerous heterosexist trap. I was parroting heterosexuality because I was "into traditional male and female roles."

The hostility and ridicule we faced inside the lesbian movement paralleled and overlapped our lives in the broader straight world— where we were often treated as criminals. My first butch lover and I began to fear coming home after we found our cat murdered in front of our apartment, with a note pinned to the door saying we'd be next. We regularly fought with men who waited outside the bar for the most obvious bull daggers and their "faggot girlfriends," or we turned away and hated ourselves for giving in. We lived constantly with the rude looks and loud, bitterly spoken comments—in the restaurants where we ate, the stores where we bought our clothes and groceries. Insults could be flung at us as we walked along any street, at any time. Strolling together as a butch/femme couple, we were an erotic, magnetic, moving target for all the sexual fear, envy, and ignorance of this culture. Our movements and our decisions were fraught with potential danger: unexpected visits to the emergency room, how to rent a motel room when we traveled, crossing a border between the United States and Canada or Mexico, being busted at bars when the cops came for their weekly payoffs, getting an apartment. None of these acts were simple or could ever be taken for granted. I have always had to laugh whenever I hear that femmes are not as tough, capable, or rugged as our butch lovers. We fought together, we carried ourselves with our heads high, we protected the women we loved when we could—as they tried to protect us—we held each other when we didn't win, and we held each other when we did. We tried to make the world normal and predictable. Mostly, that meant being alone together, creating a little home somewhere that might provide a haven from the omnipresent hostility and ridicule. We also tried to create a smaller world that included others like ourselves, a world we could relax and function in. We were scared all the time about who we loved. We were often afraid about who we were. We lived each day in a hostile and volatile universe.

It is terrifying to live out your desire in a haunted system of ridicule and attack. The interior world of identity and desire becomes a place of fear and doubt, even as you actively give it expression. Whatever is difficult about being queer becomes a hundred times more provocative and full of menace when you struggle to understand a way of wanting and being which you know is held in contempt, even by other queers, which balances your selfhood and your erotic identity on the edge of continual humiliation. When my lover looks both male and female, wants a cock and wears one, thinks of herself as a faggot or a guy, is she a man? If I want a woman who looks like a man who is a woman who has a cock, what kind of hybrid gender does that make of me? Since my sexual landscape of desire always moves between variants on the butch spectrum and my own shades of femme self-construction, there is no escaping the issue. All these categories and states of being are full of strife.

In this internal struggle, you become "different" not just in terms of the gender you are or of the person you desire but in your own imagination as well — inside the treasured illusion and sexual invention of your own erotic self—although you struggle, you resist becoming paralyzed. To this day, the question of something apparently so simple as what to wear is fraught with political and sexual decision making; it is weighted down with considerations about who I will see and who I will be and of how to modify, soften, exaggerate, or edge out the worst of what might happen or of how to survive if I just go as I am. If I am with a lover who passes and refuses to hide, my partnering will be taken as a flamboyant challenge, a defiant statement of difference. If I am with a woman who is a softer butch, the challenge will be less confrontational—but it will remain. If, as a femme or a high femme, I am open about the centrality of that system to my world, I am always quickly reduceable to erotic trash in the eye of the beholder.

I had already entered butch/femme life with a preexisting set of sexual scars that permanently marked me. I wasn't a fool. I knew the cost of my own sexual history. But much of that sexual story had been shaped by my own internal anger and resistance—and by my ability to differentiate sex as desire from sex as a job, a violation, a paying event. My history was a part of me, but it was also me with a defiant face, a spit-at-you-if-you-don't-like-it persona. And, though sexual histories may prepare us for some things, they also serve to make us cautious, wary of being questioned. The doubts that people around me had about femme/butch life were most often not my own, were not at all where my own fear and worry centered. But, regardless of whether the questions being asked were my own or not, I was afraid to respond. And I knew that I nevertheless intended to go ahead with what I was doing—whatever the answers.

When I found butch/femme, it was like rediscovering my heart through my cunt. It signified myself, my most naked feelings and desires; it defined and reflected the spirit living at the center of me. Here, in this place, I was vulnerable. I had no armor at first to battle the assumptions of movement feminists that femme/butch was a gag, a perversion. I was in isolation as I faced all the accusations and silences made by those very people I trusted and valued inside my own gay political world, people I still needed in order to survive. And I knew where these interrogations could lead, even though I didn't have a clue, then, about how to respond.

I also knew deep down in my femme bones that the uncertainties and fears raised by an erotic identity can be answered only by living it, experiencing and learning about your own personal intersections with passionate singularity. And your own understanding of love and desire is traced and changed by the women you love, by the women you want and need. You will also discover who you are alone and to yourself, regardless of who you are partnering or sleeping with. You will begin to understand who you are in your own imagination. To see, through time, what really does or doesn't work. To determine what is absolutely necessary and what is changeable, what depends on you alone, what depends on a partner. It takes years. It takes a lifetime. And sometimes there is nothing as simple as one single answer. There is only the rich, multilayered understanding that the living of desire gleans.

In myself, over the years, I continued to face questions for which I had no immediate answers. What kind of woman did my desires make me? What in God's name was a femme lesbian—a high femme lesbian? Why did I continue to dream my dream? I needed to begin to comprehend my own strategy of desire in order to defend it. I have struggled to understand what fuels my own desires, what propels my feelings for the women I desire, for the last twenty-five years. This struggle has led me to study the larger worlds of sexual cravings and currencies as they swirl around me, around us all. I still have few things as simple as an answer.

So I have gone back to how it was for me in the beginning: first when I discovered women, later when I found butch women, and again when I fell in love with my first passing woman. Since I've loved women, it has always been those specific types of women I've wanted. Women the world refuses to acknowledge as female, women who turn people's heads toward us and then away in a single continuous motion. I have wanted these particular women whom the world often sees as men, and I have been seduced by women who are faggots with the eyes and the hopes of boys. Tricksters and she-guys and diesel dykes and bull daggers and softer butches. I have been given a gift of wonder by living alongside these other gay women's self-constructed truths.

Before there is thought, there is sensation and desire. Always the miracle appears when there are no expectations left for its arrival. Sex has always been that way for me. Explosive sex I mean—sex that is momentous enough or relentless enough to suck me totally into its savage, beautiful whirlpool. Sex that is so compelling, so necessary, so absolutely fundamental that it cannot be denied. That kind of sex—and my craving for it—has configured and reconfigured my life. It has branded me, punished me, and given me gifts unlike any others I've received or been able to create. Finally, it has proved to be, for me, a precarious and a life-transforming gift. Sex is the method I've used to search for wonder and awe. It is ecstasy I've craved and sought, nothing less. Sex is one of the few realms where my need for ecstasy was realizable, conceivable, resting on no resource save my own body and imagination. But miracles are usually double-edged swords. They open up worlds and catalyze unimaginable dreams, but they also fashion particular requirements and extract specific bounties, shaping and necessitating engagement with another. This is as it was for me: my longing for a woman's mouth or cock, the hunger, the search, and the completion I found through a butch lover's body thrusting forward.

I have also looked to other femmes for a powerful reflection and confirmation of myself and my own longings. I've tried to walk across the defenses that often separate women who desire similar partners and create friendships there. Sometimes I succeeded. It is here, late at night, on phones held in rage or tears or fiercely felt pleasure, leaning toward each other over restaurant tables, where I have finally talked with other femme women (and men) about our self-created femme identities, our search for erotic capability and fulfillment. Across generations and genders, through differences in color and class, I have listened with ongoing fascination and respect to other femmes' stories and survival strategies. I've been honored by the gift of those tales, and I've been challenged by these women in ways that no one else has ever managed to do.

The others I've most looked to, in order to understand and construct my own identity, have been drag queens. Drag queens are familiar to me in the way I feel about my own sense of femininity, and drag queens often have a physical affect very similar to mine when they enter a room. Being femme, for me, is a conscious way to be female—it does not mean merely accepting and existing within the preconstructed boundaries of "natural" womanhood. Daily I construct it and remove it, live it totally, betray it, reconstruct it from dust and fear, find it again. So do they. Like butches, drag queens make obvious what is usually masked, unquestioned, and assumed about gender. Gender is mutable and vibrant and not dependent on the biological body for its breath or its truth. Drag queens build women over their masculine bodies. I understand this. I am a woman whose femininity rests on a parental foundation far more like my father's than my mother's. I am my father's drag queen daughter.

I consider myself a feminist. I don't believe in "natural" womanhood or "normal" genders—of any category. Not for men, and not for women. No gender system is natural, no system of desire organic or removed from the way culture creates human experience. We are raised to become "masculine" or "feminine," and any rebellion against that still takes place within a constructed system of gender and erotic binaries—at least in white America. The expression and meanings of desire ride through our cultural body, leaving us intertwined with the roots of thousands of years of indoctrination that have sought to cement sexual identity, to point all erotic choice toward procreation, within the context of a purely male/female set of oppositions.

Our religions, our languages, our political theories, our family trees, our wars, our sciences, our work, and our categories of study have been bent to the task of creating and sustaining a gendered world of biologically specific people who we agree to call women or men. Sexual orientation is one of the pillars of that gender system, one of its most useful and necessary limbs. Heterosexuality is the core. To begin to question this complex set of systems is to begin a journey away from all the concepts used to structure the universe of common human existence we have developed as a nation. This is one of the reasons why the early women's liberation and gay liberation movements were seen as such a profound challenge to "normal" life and to the existence of family in this country. And it is why, to this day, the question of who is "normal"—and who determines it—is so fundamentally a political issue.

As our struggle developed over the years and those fundamental systems were challenged, something else happened. Some gay people began to represent normalcy, while some of us were left to stand at the outer edge of the homosexual circle. An internal hierarchy of deviance was instituted, by gay people, about each other. In the beginning, whether dressed as conservatively as possible or wearing drag, any gay person was queer in a collectively queer movement. But, through the years, the radical sexual politics of that early movement became more and more tempered, and the kinds of gay people considered important or central to the movement began to shift. Nowadays, all gay people are not seen as the same, and we are not all considered equal threats to the body politic of the nation. Some gay people are perceived to be "normal homosexuals," while some of us continue to represent a dangerous *otherness,* an ongoing threat of queer menace and deviance.

In the last twenty-five years of struggle, we have moved from gay liberation as a freedom struggle—a struggle for sexual, economic, and social justice—to a movement for gay legal rights. This struggle now parodies and duplicates a heterosexual middle-class/upper-class agenda based on re-creating the rights of heterosexuals for gay people, with all the implicit and explicit pieces of class and race prejudice that go with it. The freedom struggle of our movement, once committed to sexual liberation, has become, instead, a movement for gay nuclear family rights and for serial monogamy. It represents the entire movement as a sort of tame civil rights challenge: one of judicial battles in the courts and referenda in the towns, cities, and states. The gains have been significant. But, looking at the bigger picture, we have gone from a movement that was full of sensibility and humor, powerful difference and sexual contrast, a world of camp and butch and femme, of leather communities, drag queens and kings, flamboyant girls and effeminate gay boys, a movement full of our sexual cultures and creative, erotic dreams, to a movement that chooses only those representatives who may sit politely in the president's office, gender-appropriate gay representatives who work for gay inclusion and try very hard to show everyone else that "we are just like them."

This has also led to the creation of a group of assimilationist, power-hungry lesbian and gay male power brokers, negotiating their way back into class privilege—a privilege they feared they had once lost by being queer or coming out. For lesbians, the overwhelming sexual androgyny of this group of women deflects fear that they might appear to be too butch or too femme, too working class, too erotic. I have been asked to stand around in so many rooms, through the years, in some vain attempt to reassure straight people that I wasn't "too" gay— while knowing all along that I was. I believe that gay people are different, uniquely gifted with the insights and brilliance that stepping outside the heterosexual norm has given us. *That is exactly the source of our power.*

These last twenty years we have also had to fight an incurable, fatal epidemic. We have had to comfort and sustain each other in the terrible grief and loss which became our daily experience, to struggle, adapt, and change our sexuality because of that crisis. We have needed to find a way to give voice to new and challenging definitions of gayness—which is the birthright of each new gay generation. And in these twenty years of work we have become a movement even more divided by sexual politics, even more stratified by gender, class, and race. In that stratification and the struggle to articulate a common agenda, it has become necessary to vilify and marginalize many sexual and erotic communities and all the "differences" they have come to represent.

Sex is difficult to want, intricate to defend. To have our lives and our rights reduced to who we slept with was infuriating. But, in trying to respond, we gave up the fight for desire and sexual difference— as we gave up a more radical vision of the world we want to create. Homosexuality has always stood in for desire in this country—while heterosexuality has always been allowed to represent everything else. No matter where we speak and on what topic, sex, our sex, is always a current running through or below the discussion. Our civil rights struggle has had to give away desire in order to seem reasonable and legitimate. Only by not fucking, not sweating and feeling and wanting and possessing each other, will we be allowed to enter the Big House. Like Clinton's "don't ask, don't tell" military policy, so it goes with sex—now even we are expected "not to see" and "not to tell." Those of us who embody and expose the queerness of our still-existing and explicit sexual desires are kept at a distance or given no voice in a continually more straight-appearing gay movement. Because of that, though, the movement itself has also become a struggle full of dirty little secrets.

And it is the secrets we keep within our own communities that are killing us. We keep those secrets about sex and desire and the erotic as we have kept other secrets like class and color and addiction—because they seem too dangerous or too explosive, or we are too powerless, to have them acknowledged inside our communities or in the larger heterosexual world. And it is here that the tragedy of not being able to claim or struggle with our desires becomes obvious. Gay men cannot admit that they long for the taste of their male partners' semen or want anal sex without a condom, and they cannot say openly that they do not want to be monogamous. Lesbians and gay men of color are asked to choose between their communities of birth and their desires for other men or women. Gay women are not considered "real lesbians" if they fuck men, love dildos, believe their HIV infection came as a result of unprotected sex with an HIV-positive female partner, love a butch or a femme, or shoot drugs or are alcoholics. The warnings to not tell, not talk, not reveal, are like huge flashing neon signs that go off when any of these things are mentioned. For transsexual and transgender people, and for bisexual women and men caught between these very different communities, behaviors, and identities, the "secrets" which they are forced to carry in order to survive socially are brutal—and sometimes physically fatal.

I have always believed that it is secrets which propel homophobia and the fear of sex through every community, in every setting. What cannot be named, admitted to, or claimed delineates the geography of our risks, becomes the slippery slope of our needs and desires. The end result of keeping these secrets—and maintaining all the lies it takes to support them—will be the crisis this movement needs to break through. Silence and denial—such popular feminist, lesbian, and AIDS community code words—are what have to be dismantled here if we are to truly understand our own stake in those silences, our own stake in denial itself.

I do not say these things without being aware of the political context of erotiphobia, homophobia, racism, sexism, and class oppression or to let the government or our society off the hook. So many communities continue to struggle, in relative isolation, with the crisis of homophobia and HIV, with sexism and racism. But I fervently believe that the tragedy of our secrets and our lies is what we will have to confront and change, regardless of who is in power—this year or next. We are the leaders and activists in our own communities, and it is we who must challenge ourselves to speak—haltingly at first, perhaps, or with great fear—of a deeper set of truths in order for all of us to survive.

I believe that, as lesbians, gay men, bisexuals, and transgendered people, we share many collective bonds as well as some bitter commonalities, and it is around those commonalities that our struggle to affirm and demand sexual liberation must be built. We must, as a community, affirm desire. But we cannot take on sexual and erotic desire without also addressing the violence that happens internally in our communities and the daily violence, mandated by fear and hatred, that is visited on us from the outside. We cannot affirm butch and femme identities without seeing and valuing the contexts where it is most alive: in working-class communities, often in working-class communities of color. We cannot fight for sex shops staying open without addressing capitalism's relentless consumption of our cities, without addressing issues such as the workfare programs that serve to underwrite Wall Street's unbelievable profits. Unions, too, are seen as representing "somebody else," and the sexual scapegoating of women on our nation's welfare rolls is something we cannot continue to ignore. But our queerness, our desire, our otherness, cannot be removed from place and context. We are queer at the tables we eat at and at the tables we serve. Queer: femme, butch, trans, bisexual, wanting. Needed. Necessary.

There is one thing I've seen clearly from my earliest life: people will risk their most precious possessions to fulfill desire, no matter how dangerous the end result. No matter how awkward, damaging, or ill advised, sexual desire may spur people to leap off the cliff and go for broke. The key to organizing around sexual issues, its incredible power, lies precisely here: erotic desire, whether couched as romantic or ferocious, is what will make most people risk everything. This is precisely because sexual fulfillment is where most people hope to find true ecstasy. And there is no human hope without the promise of ecstasy. Organizers are confounded by this phenomenon, left dazed in the face of all the workplace affairs, wrecked marriages, unexpected pregnancies, queer liaisons, and sexual cover-ups that constitute the underbelly and folk fables of modern culture. But, instead of being confounded, organizers for true social and political change must learn how to use it—must learn how to incorporate the human yearning for ecstasy into the structure of struggle itself. Because this yearning, this search, is also the source of tremendous human energy, power, life.

I live in a world that makes wanting sex, actualizing and realizing desire, a thing of danger. But this is what I want: To be my own idiom and my own voice. To call the shots—even when what I most want is a lover who calls the shots. To love butch women without apology or fear. To be acclaimed in my own flagrant femme-girl body and high femme attitude. To be a warrior against shame of the erotic and for the right to taste and smell passion's will. To finally be at peace in my own body, my own desires, my experiences and most secret dreams. To give my children the right to their own sexual beauty, as they discover it. To fight for a world which values human sexual possibility without extracting a terrible human price. To battle human greed and human fear in any of its forms. To create a movement willing to live the politics of sexual danger in order to create a culture of human hope.

This is my dream today. These are my most dangerous desires.

In gratitude to Paula

Publication Notes

"Sexuality and the State: The Defeat of the Briggs Initiative and Beyond" originally was published in *Socialist Review,* May/June 1979.

"What We're Rollin' around in Bed With" originally was published in *Heresies,*
the Sex Issue, no. 12, 1981, and reprinted in *Powers of Desire: The Politics of
Sexuality,* edited by Ann Snitow, Christine Stansell, and Sharon Thompson
(New York: Monthly Review Press, 1983), and also in *The Persistent Desire:
A Femme-Butch Reader,* edited by Joan Nestle (Boston: Alyson Publications,
1992).

"Desire for the Future: Radical Hope in Passion and Danger" originally was
published in *Pleasure and Danger: Exploring Female Sexuality,* edited by
Carol Vance (Boston: Routledge, 1984). A version of this essay also appeared as "The Erotophobic Voice of Women," in the *New York Native,* no. 7,
September 25, 1983.

"The Right to Rebel," based on an interview by Philip Derbyshire, was first
published in *Gay Left Journal,* no. 9, 1979.

"Talking Sex: A Conversation on Sexuality and Feminism" originally was published in *Socialist Review,* July/August 1981.

"Another Place to Breathe" originally was published in *Opposite Sex: Gay Men
on Lesbians, Lesbians on Gay Men,* edited by Sara Miles and Eric Rofes (New
York: New York University Press, 1998).

"Femme Fables" originally were published in the *New York Native,* 1983/1984.

"Sympathy of the Blood" originally was published in the *Village Voice,* vol. 29,
no. 26 (June 26, 1984).

"Strategies for Freedom" originally was published in *The Nation,* May 1993.

"Transmission, Transmission, Where's the Transmission?" originally was
published in *Sojourner* newspaper, June 1994.

"Lesbian Denial and Lesbian Leadership in the AIDS Epidemic: Bravery and
Fear in the Construction of a Lesbian Geography of Risk" originally was
published in *Women Resisting AIDS: Feminist Strategies of Empowerment,*
edited by Beth E. Schneider and Nancy E. Stoller (Philadelphia: Temple
University Press, 1999).

"Sexuality, Labor, and the New Trade Unionism" originally was published in

Social Text 17, no. 4 (winter 1999), and in *Out at Work: Building a Gay-Labor Alliance,* edited by Kitty Krupat and Patrick McCreery (Minneapolis: University of Minnesota Press, 2000).

"Gender Warriors" originally was published in *Femme: Feminists, Lesbians, and Bad Girls,* edited by Laura Harris and Elizabeth Crocker (New York: Routledge, 1997).

Index

Amber L. Hollibaugh is a lesbian writer and
activist living in New York City.

Library of Congress Cataloging-in-Publication Data

Hollibaugh, Amber L.
My dangerous desires: A Queer Girl Dreaming Her
Way Home / Amber L. Hollibaugh ; foreword by
Dorothy Allison.
p.   cm. — (Series Q)
Includes bibliographical references and index.
ISBN 0-8223-2625-6 (cloth : alk. paper) — ISBN
0-8223-2619-1 (pbk. : alk. paper)
1. Lesbians—United States—Social conditions.
2. Lesbians—United States—Interviews.   3. Lesbian
feminism—United States.   I. Title.   II. Series.
HQ75.6.U5 H65   2000
305.48'9664'0973—dc21   00-030307